W9-ASK-173

Red Carpet Ready

Harmony Books / New York

Red Carpet Ready

Secrets for

Making the Most

of Any Moment

You're in

the Spotlight

Melissa Rivers

with Tim Vandehey

BOCA RATON PUBLIC LIBRARY
BOCA RATON, FLORIDA

Copyright © 2010 by Melissa Rivers

All rights reserved.

Published in the United States by Harmony Books, an
imprint of the Crown Publishing Group, a division of
Random House, Inc., New York.
www.crownpublishing.com

Harmony Books is a registered trademark and the
Harmony Books colophon is a trademark of Random
House, Inc.

Library of Congress Cataloging-in-Publication Data
Rivers, Melissa.
Red carpet ready: secrets for making the most of any
moment you're in the spotlight / Melissa Rivers with Tim
Vandehey.—1st ed.
1. Self-confidence.   2. Success.   3. Celebrities—Case
studies.   I. Vandehey, Tim.   II. Title.
BF575.S39R58 2010
158—dc22   2009021817

ISBN 978-0-307-39532-0

Printed in the United States of America

10 9 8 7 6 5 4 3 2 1

First Edition

BOCA RATON PUBLIC LIBRARY
BOCA RATON, FLORIDA

To Sabrina Lott Miller for keeping all the balls
in the air with grace and elegance.

To Cooper, who I love.

To my mother, because she expects it.

AND

To all of the staff and crews who have been in the trenches
with me. You are the true stars of the red carpet.

CONTENTS

INTRODUCTION

3 A.M., Dead Body, No Questions Asked   1

LESSON 1

Be Comfortable in Your Own Skin   13

LESSON 2

Get Some Perspective   38

LESSON 3

Trust Your Gut   66

LESSON 4

Show Grace Under Pressure   90

LESSON 5

Be Prepared   118

LESSON 6

Be Nice on the Way Up   144

LESSON 7
Find the Balance 172

LESSON 8
Fall Forward 195

LESSON 9
Take a Risk 216

ARE YOU RED CARPET READY?
Take the Red Carpet Quiz 237

AFTERWORD
The Best Worst Thing That
Ever Happened 257

ACKNOWLEDGMENTS 267

INDEX 269

Red Carpet Ready

3 A.M., Dead Body,
No Questions Asked

*My theory is that if you look confident you can pull off
anything, even if you have no clue what you're doing.*

—JESSICA ALBA

*I*t was Oscar night, 1996. *Braveheart* was the favorite for Best
Picture. Sharon Stone set fashionistas around the globe buzzing
when she emerged from her limo wearing a Valentino skirt, vel-
vet jacket, and a Gap T-shirt that, according to urban legend,
she had "thrown on" when she didn't like the look of her Vera
Wang dress. Later on, host Whoopi Goldberg would quip, "Elisabeth Shue played a hooker. Sharon Stone played a hooker. Mira
Sorvino played a hooker. How many times did Charlie Sheen get
to vote?"

But I wasn't thinking about gowns, statuettes, or posh
après-Oscar parties. I was trying to prevent my clammy palms
from losing their grip on my microphone. When I wasn't doing
that, I was harassing my poor sound guy about the irritating

thump-thump in my earpiece—which turned out to be the hammering of my heart. I was, to put it mildly, a nervous wreck. Why not? My mother and I were about to step onto the storied red carpet and directly into the sights of millions—no, let's be honest, billions—of TV viewers to create a new genre of live television for the E! Network: the real-time red carpet interview broadcast and fashion extravaganza. No one had ever done such an audacious thing. We would be accosting the likes of Tom Cruise and Susan Sarandon as they sashayed past throngs of adoring fans, smiling and waving and probably thinking, "God, I hope I don't have something in my teeth!"

An executive at E! came up with the idea for a live red carpet show a few years earlier, after realizing that the Oscars were like the parents of the bride at a society wedding: too uptight and serious for their own good. The thinking was that the fans would really embrace something off-the-cuff, fresh, and, most of all, funny. Mom did one show and then somebody at E! said, "Hey, what if you and Melissa worked together?" I had just finished a stint at CBS News and MTV, so they knew I could handle myself in front of and behind the camera, and everyone figured that our natural mother-daughter tension might create some memorable chemistry. I loved the idea. Who better to celebrate and add some sizzle to the Academy Awards scene than Joan Rivers and her intrepid daughter, by walking up to the likes of Juliette Binoche and asking, "Juliette, honey, my God, was that dress inspired by the title of one of your films, *Damage*?" It was a can't-miss proposition. Mom and I were ready to stroll down that carpet, poured into our designer frocks and sparkling with borrowed jewelry, and make television history.

The trouble was that we were the only ones who thought the whole crazy scheme would work. Hardly anyone else believed we could pull it off—not our agents, colleagues, managers, or friends. Daring, original thinking is scary, especially in Hollywood, where people are more interested in sequels than originality. I began to hear "Melissa, I don't think that's such a good idea" in my sleep. In fact, that's the defining phrase of my career. Every time I encounter it, it's like waving a red flag in front of a bull. I become obsessed with bringing my idea to fruition; my nostrils have even been known to flare. So when I get involved in a venture that gets others shaking their heads, I know I'm on to something good. Like the song says, they all laughed at Christopher Columbus.

But as the weeks passed and the first Oscar telecast drew closer, Mom and I began to feel less like pioneers and more like sitting ducks. We started to think that maybe it would be best if E! listened to the naysayers and pulled the plug on our little misadventure. Remember, these were the days when celebrities could still protect part of their lives from public view, the Internet was still mostly about chat rooms, and Britney Spears was a cute teenager with one hit record and no entourage of paparazzi. Back then, celebrities still enjoyed a smidgen of privacy and expected the press to respect their personal space. What would happen when Mom and I yanked them off the red carpet, stuck a microphone in their faces, asked terribly personal questions, and then criticized what they were wearing? My God, we'd get slapped. We'd be led away by security. Worst of all, we'd be ignored.

Red Carpet Moments

Of course, none of those things happened. Mom and I were under more pressure than the clasps on some of the gravity-defying dresses we saw that evening. After all, we were either going to make Oscar history or make our careers history. But in spite of all our trepidation, the night went great. It was terrifying and exhilarating and frantic and marvelous, all at the same time.

There were some minor disasters, of course. The heel fell off my Jimmy Choo strappy sandals. My gorgeous Vera Wang dress practically disintegrated as I was about to go on camera. Only the quick intervention of my tech crew (with gaffer's tape, electrical clips, and safety pins) kept me from making my red carpet debut showing as much skin as Kristin Scott Thomas in her bathtub scene with Ralph Fiennes in *The English Patient*. If you were there I looked like a fourth-grade craft project gone terribly wrong, but on camera I still looked great.

But as awkward as the scene sometimes was, as much as we were making it all up as we went along, we really pulled it off. The stars walking up the red carpet were gracious and endearingly surprised at the two nervy women pulling them aside to ask how they were feeling or who designed their outfits. Our first red carpet interview was with John Travolta, who, as always, was simply wonderful. I repeated the words "Back to you, Mom!" about a thousand times. Now and again, when the cameras were elsewhere, our eyes would meet and we'd exchange an amazed look that said, "We're really doing this!" At the end of the evening, while the crews rolled cable and took down lights, we sat down, exhausted and still pumped with adrenaline, dying to get into some flat shoes. We had no idea at the time if viewers had loved us or hated us, but I didn't really care. I'd never had so much fun. Maybe they'd let us do this for one more year.

Fast-forward twelve years and our semi-improvised mad dash down the red carpet became *Joan & Melissa: Live at the Academy Awards*. It was an annual ratings smash. Four times a year, from that first Academy Awards to the 2007 Emmys, we brought enough scaffolds, klieg lights, cameras, and helicopters to the Oscars, Golden Globes, Emmys, and Grammys to invade a small Central American country. I called it Operation Entertainment Storm. What started off being about stars and the honor of one's peers became a fashion show: who's wearing what, who's going to wish she hadn't worn that in the morning, the behind-the-scenes deals to convince one nominee to wear Dior instead of Randolph Duke, rumored payola to get the hot actress of the moment to drop her Harry Winston bling for Chopard, and so on.

It turned out that people loved what Mom and I were doing. Okay, some of them loved to hate us because we said what everyone else was thinking. But love or loathe us, people watched year after year. As Eric Olsen wrote in *Blogcritics* magazine,

> whether one admits it or not, the Rivers' foul-mouthed, off-color, live pre-show, where every star is fair game for their acid-tongued reviews, has become the guilty viewing pleasure of millions, setting ratings records year after year.

I like to think our intolerance for sartorial mediocrity also convinced the stars to pull out all the stops to look extra-gorgeous, sparing America some ghastly fashion crimes and creating more work for an army of grateful stylists and designers.

But it's the individual special moments that stand out for me: Doing our one-thousandth interview at the fifty-eighth Emmys in 2006 and awarding our interviewee, the lovely Debra Messing, a commemorative sash. Major movie stars like Catherine Zeta-Jones coming down the carpet actually excited to talk with us. George Clooney offering me his jacket (a swooning moment if there ever was one) when he saw I was freezing. Being the belles of the ball at the A-list *Vanity Fair* post-Oscar party. Warren Beatty flirting with me. Jack Nicholson ignoring us and getting away with it because he's Jack. Matt Damon and Ben Affleck taking pictures like a couple of buddies on spring break. Jokes that killed and jokes that flopped. Things we said that, looking back, we can't believe we got away with. Those are the times I cherish. I call them Red Carpet Moments.

You're in the Spotlight

What I've come to realize is that Red Carpet Moments aren't limited to the red carpet, and it's not just the stars who have them. All of us have Red Carpet Moments throughout our lives. They're weddings, bat mitzvahs, and interviews for dream jobs. They're also breakups and painful apologies. A Red Carpet Moment is any time when the spotlight is on you, for better or worse. They're times when the pressure is on to look your best, to say the right thing, or to deliver the goods. Some Red Carpet Moments are once-in-a-lifetime affairs, while others come along time and again. But what I've learned in watching thousands of celebrities have their Red Carpet Moments is that nobody turns in a star performance in the spotlight by accident.

I've become an expert on Red Carpet Moments, not just because I've had plenty of my own, both triumphant (the birth of my son, Cooper) and harrowing (the end of my marriage), but because I've watched so many entertainment professionals stroll past over the years. I've started to see a pattern: The ones who know how to make the most of their Red Carpet Moments are the ones you see year after year. Meryl Streep. Tom Hanks. Julia Roberts. Michael Douglas. They're superstars with decades-long careers because they get it. They're grateful for their success. They prepare themselves for every eventuality. They look after their bodies and minds. They're respectful. They work their butts off. They take care of the people who take care of them. They've mastered what I call the Red Carpet Life Lessons:

Be comfortable in your own skin.
Get some perspective.
Trust your gut.
Show grace under pressure.
Be prepared.
Be nice on the way up.
Find the balance.
Fall forward.
Take a risk.

People who learn the Lessons have the ability to get the most from their Red Carpet Moments when they come along, to make the most of the great times and to weather the storms with dignity and a sense of hope. For example, when Jennifer Aniston showed up at the 2005 Oscars as a presenter, just months after her marriage to Brad Pitt had broken up, she was dying inside. She could have stayed home in her sweats and watched the awards on TV with a bowl of Ben & Jerry's. But instead, she sucked it up, got her stylist to make her look fantastic, and walked the carpet. That's showing grace under pressure. She never let anyone know that the night was torture, and all of Hollywood respected and loved her for it.

Shallow and Deep

I'm going to share with you the nine Red Carpet Life Lessons
I've learned over the years, along with some of my most helpful
tips and suggestions for being successful in your own Red Carpet Moments. Some of my advice comes from what I call the
"shallow end," the stuff most women obsess about: dresses and
makeup and getting gorgeous hair and taking a great photo and
making sure you don't have a "nipple slip" on a first date. But
that's not all the Lessons are about. I'm also going to share my
insights from the "deep end" about living with gratitude and
awareness and honesty, seeing that failure isn't the end of the
world, being true to yourself, and knowing that if you feel beautiful in your dress, you're going to *be* beautiful. The deep end is
about realizing that nothing lasts forever and you are not entitled
to anything, so you should relish every second of that joyful
sweep down the red carpet . . . because it might not come again.

I've also added some fun, fascinating little extras, like nuts
in a chocolate chip cookie. "Know-It-All" features some of the
smartest people in Hollywood—stylists and personal trainers
and publicists—sharing their takes on the Lessons. "The Gospel
According to Joan" showcases my mom's brutally honest and
always-original opinions on life, the universe, and couture.
"Mel's Belles" turns the spotlight on some of the women in Hollywood I admire most, ladies who embody what the Lessons are
all about and always exude class, confidence, and inner beauty.
"Red Carpet Rules" gives you quick, practical tips for specific
Red Carpet Moments (like how not to fall on your face in slip-
pery new shoes at your reunion). Finally, "Swept Under the Carpet" reveals some of the behind-the-scenes secrets Mom and

I have witnessed for years but that almost nobody else knows about, like the fact that Sharon Stone's "spur-of-the-moment" Gap T-shirt had actually been professionally fitted for her.

Now, it's been said that Hollywood is just like high school only with a lot more money. So is this book. After the lessons, there's going to be a test: the Red Carpet Quiz. Don't groan! It's going to be fun. You're going to test how ready you are for the Red Carpet Moments of your own life, and see the areas where you might need a little work to be completely fabulous.

My goal with all of this is simple: I want to help you learn how to become a superstar in your life, to face life's spotlight moments with poise and élan and come out smelling like a rose. Because nobody—not even Jack—is exempt from the Lessons. But who am I to be telling you all this? I'd better introduce myself, because if you think you already know me, you might be in for a surprise.

Who Everyone Thinks I Am

I'm a spoiled rich kid. A Hollywood brat who fell into my job thanks to her famous mother. A raging party girl. A no-talent who, if not for a few family connections, would be flipping burgers. A neurotic who had the poor taste to take her turbulent relationship with her mom public in a 1994 TV movie. A snarky fashionista. Did I miss anything?

Actually, the fashionista one is true. I'm unapologetic. Spend a decade trashing or honoring some of the best and worst apparel decisions ever made and you're going to make some good friends and plenty of enemies, not just among worshipful fans but among the Oscar de la Rentas and Donna Karans of the world. I called 'em as I saw 'em, and I still do. You can't make a Happy Meal without burning a few fries.

But the rest? Let's set the record straight.

Who I Really Am

I went to an Ivy League university. I held down internships and logged tapes at shows like *Entertainment Tonight*. Out of college I began building my résumé by starting as a research assistant and working my way up on a show called *Rescue 911*, by screen-testing and becoming a host on MTV, and by working insane hours at the Clinton Inaugural to be able to present features live on the *CBS Morning News* (I came home from that with strep throat and seven pounds lighter from staying up all night to cover parties and have stories ready for a 7 A.M. airtime). I know what every gaffer and grip does on a set, how the lights are set, and how the camera works. Nobody has given me a thing. I never wanted to give anyone the opportunity to claim that I rode my mother's coattails.

I'm also the daughter of Edgar Rosenberg, who committed suicide in 1987, shattering my relationship with my mother for a time. In the twenty-three years since, life has been about healing, growing, and discovering how to be Dad's daughter even after his death. A great deal of that happened on the red carpet, in front of millions of strangers. You try going through your "awkward phase" with people from 160 countries watching.

Working with my mother on the red carpet pre-shows meant nonstop work, since she is one of the hardest-working women in the business. There have been no free rides for this chick. As for the partying, that makes me laugh. I'm a divorced single mom, and an ideal Saturday night is spent at home with my seven-year-old son, who is the love of my life and the best thing that ever happened to me. When Cooper's with his dad, I'd rather be hanging at the beach with my girlfriends than at the hot club of the moment with the cast of *Lost*.

I'm also the go-to girl for a wacky group of misfits I'm lucky enough to call my friends. That means I'm the friend you call when it's three in the morning, you have a dead body in the back of your car, and you need somebody to help you bury it, no questions asked. I'm the one who'll show up with a shovel and a flashlight and remember to bring two pairs of gloves, one for each of us. A saying I love goes, "Be a well, not a fountain." It means being the person other people can draw on to get what they need, but never gushing out your own needs to anyone who happens to be within crying distance. I am incredibly blessed with wonderful people in my life who trust me to be their well, with whom I can allow myself to be vulnerable, and who love me for myself . . . and sometimes in spite of myself.

What Doesn't Kill You . . .

Most of all, I'm fortunate to be doing what I'm doing, with the opportunities I have and the life I'm leading. I don't know why, but for me what seem like tragedies at first end up becoming victories. For example, when Mom and I were replaced on the red carpet and I lost the job I had adored for a dozen years, I thought it was the worst thing that could ever happen to me. But instead, the end of that commitment has freed me to do things I might never have considered otherwise: writing a book, creating a number of new TV shows, even taking the red carpet fashion commentary to a huge and grateful audience on AOL.

I'm busier and happier than I've ever been, all because of some-thing that, when it happened, felt like Armageddon.

I've had my Red Carpet Moments, too. I've failed publicly. I've had a fairy-tale wedding. I've stood on camera in front of one-sixth of the world's population and told *Brokeback Mountain* jokes. I've lived the Lessons, and they've helped me come away from every one of my Red Carpet Moments still standing and looking for something better to come. That's what I'm offering you—the knowledge to put the Lessons to work behind the scenes, so that when your Red Carpet Moments come, you're not only ready but have what it takes to make the most of each one.

So, as they say when counting me in on a live show, "and in five, four, three, two . . ."

Be Comfortable in Your Own Skin

*I think I've evolved into someone pretty
confident—myself and in my skin.* —HALLE BERRY

*H*ow many actresses would star in a one-woman show called *Wake Up, I'm Fat!*? In Hollywood, where the accessory to a great pair of jeans is a rib cage, not many. That's what makes Camryn Manheim so amazing to me. Camryn won an Emmy in 1998 for her work on *The Practice* and is roundly recognized as a terrific artist. But she wasn't always. She's a plus-size woman in a business of waifs, and for most of her life, her passion for acting ran headlong into the perception that she was too fat to make it. This led to crippling self-esteem problems, yo-yo weight loss and weight gain, and drug problems that nearly killed her.

But one day Camryn had a revelation: *She didn't need to be anyone other than who she was.* That seems elementary, but you'd be shocked at how the entertainment business can make even the most secure person feel inadequate. Armed with new self-awareness, Camryn created her own opportunity. She wrote and starred in a one-woman show that turned out to be a smash hit. This led to her now-famous meeting with David E. Kelley, the brilliant creator of *Ally McBeal,* where she challenged him to a game of cribbage (David is a great player) for the right to read for a part in his new series, *The Practice.* They didn't play, but he was so impressed with Camryn's chutzpah that not only did she get the audition, but they rewrote the part for her. When she won her Emmy, she held the statuette high and announced, "This is for all the fat girls!"

Love Who You Are and Who You're Becoming

That's what I call being comfortable in your own skin. It's a fantastic way to be, but it's not easy to get there. Camryn almost died getting there. But that was just because she was overweight in an industry that treats heavy folks like they don't exist, right? Wrong. Look at the quote that begins this chapter. Halle Berry has had to *evolve* into someone who's comfortable in her skin. She's one of the most beautiful women in the world and an Oscar-winning actress to boot. Are you kidding me? How could she possibly feel anything but radiant in that flawless mocha skin of hers?

Here's how: She's human. Like I said, Hollywood is like being permanently in high school; everybody wants to sit at the lunch table with the cool kids and be popular. Kate Walsh wants to look stunning in her dress. Anne Hathaway wants to say the right thing on camera and make her fans happy. There's not a single fabulous superstar who's walked the red carpet in an incredible gown or tux who doesn't have demons or insecurities. They've all had their hearts broken or failed at something that meant the world to them. Most of all, they've all heard that nasty little voice welling up from the gut, whispering, "You're not good enough." The great ones use that voice to push them to become better actors, smarter businesspeople, or more caring human beings. But nobody stops hearing it. When you're comfortable in your skin, you use the voice as motivation to build yourself up rather than break you down.

Being comfortable in your own skin means loving how you look, who you are today, and the woman you're becoming. We're all evolving and changing every moment, discovering new truths about ourselves, flexing our muscles in new areas of life, and hopefully becoming better people who bring a little more light to the world. When you love the person you are today and tomorrow, you approach everything that happens in your life—every Red Carpet Moment—with pride and self-assurance. You know you can handle anything and that you're the best person you can be. You root for others and wish them well because you have nothing to prove to anybody, least of all yourself. You have faith in the path you're walking, and if other people don't understand it, that's okay.

Two women who personify this Lesson are Kate Winslet and Demi Moore. I remember Kate being bubbly and wide-eyed back when she was nominated for *Titanic*, but that was also a time when she got a lot of flak for being too curvaceous for Hollywood standards. But over the years, she has become a true beauty inside and out, shining with confidence. She's a serene soul with a fabulous sense of humor. She's married to the director Sam Mendes, and she glows brighter every time I see her. When she's on the red carpet, I see a sleek, sophisticated woman who's not only changed her body and her clothes, but her outlook and her approach to life. Now that she's finally won her Oscar, that's even truer.

Demi has had more barbs tossed at her than a Pacific salmon, in part because she's never been afraid to stick out her tongue at conventional wisdom. There was the time she wore a strange bicycle-shorts-and-bustier outfit to the Oscars back in 1989, an ensemble that made *People*'s "Worst-Ever Oscars Fashions" list. She posed nude and pregnant on the cover of *Vanity Fair* in 1991, and did it again in 1992 in her famous body paint suit. And today, at forty-seven, she's turned Tinseltown's older guy–younger woman tradition upside down by unabashedly dating and marrying thirty-two-year-old hunk Ashton Kutcher. There's never been a hint of apology in Demi, never a whiff of backing down from who she is and how she wants to live. You've got to love a woman like that.

MEL'S BELLES

I can't say enough about Susan Sarandon. She's gorgeous and sexy at an age when most women treat sex appeal like an antique in the attic. She's outspoken and stands up for the causes she cares about. She's classy and elegant. I will never forget the year that her partner, Tim Robbins, was nominated for *Mystic River* and they walked up the carpet together. But when it came time for Tim to do his big interview, Susan subtly stepped a few feet away so she wouldn't be on camera. She let Tim have his Oscar moment all to himself. Talk about self-aware and generous! She had no need to bask in a reflected spotlight. That was pure class and confidence. She's an amazing lady.

Comfortable on Your Own Carpet

But wait, you're not a celebrity. Tabloid photographers aren't chasing you while you're driving around Los Angeles at 5 A.M. wearing a pink wig (at least, I hope they aren't). What does being comfortable in your own skin mean to you? Everything. All happiness in life starts with having the self-esteem to look at the reflection you see in the mirror when you get up in the morning and say, "You deserve the best!" It's okay if you're brushing your teeth when you say it; just try not to get foam on the glass.

If there's one thing I've learned from my own experience it's that most of life's Red Carpet Moments don't come about by accident. With the possible exception of running into your ex when he's with his underwear-model girlfriend at the cineplex or suddenly getting dumped on a Friday night, you're going to be able to prepare for your time in the spotlight. You'll even have a hand in creating some of your Red Carpet Moments from the beginning, such as your wedding or the birth of your child (I certainly *hope* you were involved in that). But if you're not comfortable in your skin, you're going to doubt yourself. You're going to second-guess your judgment. You're going to settle for less than you really want because you're afraid to speak up. You're going to look less than your best at critical times because you're going to *feel* less than your best.

But when you're happy with who and what you are, you're confident when meeting your fiancé's parents. You ace the big presentation because you trust your ideas. You handle the uncomfortable apology fairly and straightforwardly, because admitting you're wrong doesn't make you feel threatened. And you look gorgeous at your birthday bash not because you have the most expensive dress in the room but because you feel splendid in what you're wearing.

Being comfortable in your own skin is like being Camryn Manheim, Margaret Cho, or even my own mother, starring in your own one-woman show. You're unafraid to stroll into the spotlight, look out at the audience, lift your arms in the air, and say, "Here I am! Aren't I marvelous?" You don't mind being the only one out there on the stage with all those people looking at you, because you know you're a show worth seeing.

How You Know You're Comfortable in Your Own Skin

I live for Hollywood gossip. I spend a tidy portion of my rare downtime surfing Web sites like TMZ.com and PerezHilton.com, looking for dirt, rumors, and snarky comments about the rich and famous. I'm not proud of it, but at least my addiction isn't fattening, right? Anyway, every so often the whole picture gets depressing; LiLo this, Jon and Kate that. That's when someone like Hayden Panettiere is such a breath of fresh air. Not long ago, the star of *Heroes* told *Cosmopolitan,* "I don't have a model's body. But I'm not one of those crazy girls who thinks that they're fat. I'm okay with what I have. I can rock this body, you know."

The girl is all of twenty years old and she's already got it figured out. I hope that attitude spreads throughout Hollywood because feeling that way about yourself is one way you know you're comfortable in your skin. You're normal and healthy. You're not telling everyone how hard it is to be you, using everyone as your personal therapist, or sucking other people into your petty dramas.

Matt Damon is a great example of being normal in the face of fame. Matt's a good-looking guy and with the three *Bourne* movies he's become a legit action star. You'd think he would be hard to eclipse in the constellation Hollywood. But three of his best friends are George Clooney, Ben Affleck, and Brad Pitt. That's like being a backup infielder in the big leagues of sexy. George and Brad have twice been named *People* magazine's "Sexiest Man Alive," and a few years back they started a campaign to get Matt named sexiest. It was a joke, of course, but at some point the whole thing had to be bringing back bad high-school memories for Matt. Despite it all, he's still a normal, down-to-earth guy with a great sense of humor—real, nice, and funny. He knows how incredibly lucky he is to be doing what he's doing. And in 2007 Matt finally received *People*'s coveted "sexiest" label, so I guess all the campaigning paid off.

What other ways do you know you're comfortable in your own skin? Here are a few:

• *You don't kowtow to other people's opinions.* You know that you don't have to live up to anyone else's expectations or stereotypes. I've known artists who grew goatees that they hated because they thought that was how an artist was *supposed* to look. I've known young actresses who hit all the hot night-clubs every weekend—when they would've rather hung out at home with a couple of close friends watching *American Idol* and eating pizza—because they thought clubbing was expected of them. That's ridiculous. The only expectations you should worry about are your own. Set them, and then live up to them.

Not caring doesn't give you carte blanche to be a bitch, but it does free you to speak your mind about things you don't like without worrying, or to simply let something go when it's not right. You stick up for yourself when things aren't working instead of keeping your mouth shut so as not to rock the boat.

THE GOSPEL ACCORDING TO JOAN

To be comfortable in your own skin in Hollywood, you've got to know who you are and not follow the crowd. Everyone has had something done cosmetically. No one is thin enough. The joke used to be that the women stopped at the jewelers' and the vomitorium on the way to the Academy Awards. People coming out of Auschwitz have been told by producers to slim down.

I have never once felt comfortable in this town. I have never once walked on the red carpet when I didn't feel lumpy, ungainly, and uncomfortable. But you have to put yourself out there. You have to feel comfortable in what you're wearing. If there's an old dress that I love, I'll wear it with new jewelry. I invented the word *vintage,* and that takes the onus off an old dress. To me, vintage starts when you cut off the price tag.

Anytime you're really going someplace, you are your billboard, like it or not. If you want to feel comfortable, you damn well better have a good-looking billboard. That's not the time to experiment with your hair.

My secret for feeling comfortable is that when I go to a dinner party alone, that afternoon I will make a list of five things—a play and movie I've seen, the latest book I've read, something unusual in the newspaper that day, a witty anecdote—and keep it tucked in my purse. That way, I know I'm not going to just sit there and not contribute to the conversation. The only rule: The topics shouldn't be about you.

You know that at the end of the day, you have to look at yourself and ask, "Was I true to myself today?" The answer should be yes as often as possible. That happens when you become the only critic that matters.

Also, not caring about the wider world's expectations doesn't mean you should stop caring about people, especially the ones you love most. From my mother to my assistant to my stylist to my wild and woolly friends, there will always be people I care about as much as they care about me, maybe more. That's a love affair that's not going anywhere.

• *You can better handle life's elevator ride.* Like the song says, you can be riding high in April only to be shot down in May. Remember, for every award category there are five nominees, which means at the end of the night there are four losers. Eddie Murphy came to the Oscars in 2006 as the favorite to win Best Supporting Actor for his role in *Dreamgirls,* but had to do the forced-smile-and-applaud routine when Alan Arkin shocked everyone by taking the statuette for his foulmouthed grandfather in *Little Miss Sunshine.* For the actors who lose in the first thirty minutes of the show, there are still two more *long* hours to sit through, looking gracious and relaxed when they're dying inside. To their credit, they do it.

Being comfortable in your skin equips you to handle life's inevitable ups and downs with grace and optimism. I think actress Virginia Madsen is a great example of this quality. When she came on the scene in the mid-1980s she was seen as a rising star. Then she disappeared for nearly twenty years, doing B movies like *Candyman,* only to reemerge with an Oscar nomination for her role in *Sideways* in 2004. But when I asked her about her choices and her long time in the shadows, she said that she took full responsibility for the career choices she'd made. "No one made me make them," she told me. She could have blamed her agent, bad luck, or a Gypsy curse. She had the self-esteem not to.

I've had plenty of ups and down, personal and professional. But one of the things I'm most proud of is that after all of them I've bounced back stronger than ever. Leaving the red carpet in early 2007 just forced me to explore a lot of other areas of life that I'd been thinking about but not pursued. When life throws you a curve, you put on your big-girl panties and deal with it.

• *You're generous of spirit.* I learned the importance of this when my live run on the red carpet ended. At first, I found myself wishing lightning bolts and horrible ratings on subsequent red carpet pre-shows and nitpicking every decision the new hosts and the network made. Then I realized how much negative energy I was bringing into my life and said to myself, "Honey, you're better than this!" It dawned on me that any successes the new red carpet regime might have didn't taint what I had accomplished. I had helped pioneer something great, and I will always be proud of that. (Our ratings were still better, though.)

People who are comfortable in their skin always wish others the best. They're gracious and generous with their intentions and their praise. They're genuinely happy when someone they know gets a promotion or marries the perfect guy. It's those without an ounce of self-esteem who hide in their cubicles sticking pins in a voodoo doll or who leave teeth marks in their own tongues when the best man makes his toast.

Being happy for other people's Red Carpet Moments is one of the most important parts of being comfortable in your skin. It elevates your spirit. When you're giving enough to applaud even your rivals, you're demonstrating class and confidence. You don't need to beat up someone else to feel special. I'm glad to say that I can truly celebrate when a woman looks stunning in a dress that I would have loved to wear.

SWEPT UNDER THE CARPET

You thought the rumors of stylists getting kickbacks from designers to get their actresses in certain brands of jewelry was an urban myth? Think again. Word was that an Oscar-winning actress (who shall remain nameless) got paid an obscene amount of money to wear a particular company's jewelry, with the stylist brokering the deal. Now, it's one thing to be a paid spokesperson for a jeweler, but this was something else entirely. As you might imagine, A-list actresses carry incredible cachet in the fashion world, and an Oscar winner wearing your baubles could make you a small fortune. So what we had was a few stylists working for A-listers for free while charging B-list actors outrageous fees. Fortunately for the credibility of the whole awards culture, this appears to be a thing of the past.

How You Know You're Not Comfortable in Your Own Skin

For years, I tried to please everyone. I had no idea how to say no to anybody about anything. I didn't think enough of myself to turn down any job, opportunity, or personal appearance. I was like a woman who stays in a relationship with a guy who cheats on her because deep down she believes that if she breaks up with him, she'll never find anyone else who will want her. Keep in mind, I don't think there's anything wrong with grabbing every opportunity you can find as long as you plan to do your best with it, but when you're whoring yourself out or spreading yourself perilously thin because you're afraid to say no, you're not comfortable with who you are.

I'm smarter these days. I've finally learned to be selective about what I say yes to. I probably qualify for a graduate degree in analyzing the risk-versus-reward equation. But learning to say no wasn't easy. My first big no came as recently as 2006, when I turned down—and I am not making this up—the chance to judge a *dog breath contest* for a radio station. No, that wasn't a misprint. Can't you just picture me walking soberly down a line of pert puppies, my arms clasped behind my back, pausing to let each one exhale its butt-and-Alpo vapors in my face? No, I couldn't, either. I declined.

But when you don't hold yourself in high regard, you're going to be reluctant to say no to anybody. You're going to find yourself doing ridiculous things to make other people happy because you crave their approval. There's a word for that: *desperation*. Ever wonder why you can walk into a party with your man on your arm and the guys will still swarm like bees to honey, but you can't buy a date after a bad breakup? Desperation has an odor that repels.

Here are a few other telltale warning signs that you're not comfortable in your skin:

• **The "Look at me!" attitude.** You see this all the time in "pop tarts" who seem to spend their time "accidentally" flashing their private parts while getting out of limos. Accidentally? Right. Honey, even if you were dumb enough to forget that you "forgot" to put on underwear, it's obvious that disembarking from the back of a car with your legs open equals a free show.

(Want to help me make scientific history? I'm going to name the shortest span of time yet known to man: the Paris.

One Paris is the interval between a paparazzo snapping a portrait of a celebutante's exposed crotch and the photo appearing on the Internet. I'll be expecting my letter from the Nobel committee any day now.)

But I digress. I'm sure you know people like this. They're the ones who are always "on," doing or saying something that screams, "Look at me!" They're miserable in their skin, so they crave the attention of others to give them validation. They're tough to be around because it's painful to watch someone make a fool of himself or herself. To be fair, we all have our insecure moments, when we need someone else to tell us that we look good, that we're right for the job, that we have talent. Hollywood runs on personal insecurity and double-shot lattes. There's nothing wrong with needing validation as long as it's the exception, not the rule. If you're healthy, you thrive on praise and attention that you've *earned*. Nobody really wants "She was famous for being famous" on her gravestone.

• *You're viciously self-critical.* There are some people who never give themselves a break. I'm guilty of that from time to time, though I hear from reliable authorities that I'm getting better. But if you can't accept a compliment without qualifying it, if you can't present your work to your boss without apologizing for it, if you trash yourself mercilessly for even the smallest screwup and assume any choice you make is doomed before you even see how things turn out . . . you have a skin problem.

Of course, some level of self-criticism is fine; like I said earlier, the biggest stars use it to drive themselves to improve constantly at their craft. There's a great story about the band U2 being in the studio trying to record their hit song "Vertigo." They had been working for days on the tune and what they finally laid down on tape was good . . . but good wasn't enough

KNOW-IT-ALL

Cary Fetman, Celebrity Stylist

When I began in this business, I was good friends with Oprah, but I didn't know anything about design. She was trying on clothes and I said, "How do you know what will work?" She said to me the most important thing I've ever heard: "If I don't feel pretty in front of that mirror, I won't feel pretty in front of that camera."

I try to see what each person is seeing in the mirror, because everyone sees something different from what I see. There's no celebrity I've ever worked with who didn't have something they wanted to change. But when you look at yourself, you have to know that there's a way you can be pretty. That's what stylists do: We don't change you, we cover the things that bother you and bring out the things about you that you find beautiful.

I think the ordinary person thinks that famous women have it all because they're so beautiful. They just throw on a piece of clothing and look great, because they have a perfect figure. But that's not true. These people have insecurities like anybody else, but they don't have the luxury of letting their insecurities affect them. They have to work through them.

As a stylist, I have to be able to look in the mirror and see what my client sees and say, "You're crazy, your hips don't look big, your butt's not sagging." A good stylist reinforces what's best about you and polishes your look.

for Bono, The Edge, and the guys. It would have been a hit for certain, but that wasn't the point. As artists, they held themselves to higher standards. So they trashed what they'd recorded, went back into the studio, wrote a new melody and arrangement, and recorded new vocals. The result: a classic.

That kind of self-criticism is laudable because it's positive. The other kind is just savaging yourself for no good reason. Worse, people who do this are also fishing for someone to say, "Oh, no, honey, you look wonderful," like the helpless heroine dropping her hankie so the dashing gentleman will pick it up and return it to her. It's manipulative and profoundly unhealthy.

• *You settle.* This is when you marry the man who always tells you what you want to hear instead of holding out for the Casanova with whom you can fall passionately in love. This is when you wear an outdated dress to your high-school reunion rather than splurge on the gown you adore. It's when you spend years being underpaid and underappreciated at your job instead of sucking it up, walking into your boss's office, and demanding the promotion you deserve. Settling is one of the most insidious symptoms of not being comfortable in your own skin, but it's the one that can do the most damage over the long term. When you don't love yourself enough to insist on the best, you die a slow death. Suddenly you look up, twenty years have gone by, and you're living what Thoreau called a "life of quiet desperation."

You won't find many people in Hollywood who settle, at least not professionally. The competition is cutthroat, and not just for roles. There's also a ferocious competition among actresses to see who can be the thinnest. That was the subject of a 2007 feature in the *Los Angeles Times:*

> Us *editor-in-chief Janice Min, another close observer of Hollywood's mores, agrees that extreme thinness "has definitely become an issue." Min says for many actresses, it has come to seem like a question of survival. "Obviously, being a female celebrity, you're in constant competition whether you want to believe it or not. You're competing for roles, parts, male attention, and it's a competition primarily involving looks. It's a system of rewards, and you are rewarded for being the most beautiful, the sexiest, and the competition has almost extended to being the thinnest."*

But in their personal lives, Hollywood is brimming over with people who settle. It makes sense: Unless you're Denzel Washington or Nicole Kidman, you spend a lot of your time being told how inadequate you are. So if career survival forces you to dive into the competitive fray anyway, you let that insecurity loose in your romantic life. That's why so many marriages between the bold and the beautiful seem doomed to fail. Instead of taking time to find Mr. Right, Hollywood's finest are stopping at Mr. Right Now, the first guy who gives their fragile egos some soothing approval, often in the charged atmosphere of a movie set. Small wonder those pairings usually end in divorce.

Are you constantly saying things like "It's good enough" and "I don't want to make waves"? Then you're probably a settler. Ask yourself why. Why can't you say three of the most important words anyone can say, "I deserve better"? What's stopping you from demanding more from your life? What are you afraid of? Because I can guarantee you that speaking up is a lot less scary than letting life pass you by.

RED CARPET RULES
Weddings

- Go classic with your look. Remember, pictures last forever. Choose another life event to experiment with your hair or clothing.

- Everyone has to capitulate a little. You don't have to turn into a Bridezilla who must have everything her way. Identify what's most important to you and go to the mat for it. But remember it's not just about you. If your husband-to-be cares a lot about the food and you don't, let him make final decisions about the food. If your parents are concerned about the seating arrangements, ask them to oversee them. Be generous.

- As soon as you set your date, start working on yourself. Go on a healthy diet. Grow out your hair. Start working out if you don't; if you already do, hire a trainer.

- Give your vendors as much lead time as you can, because stuff happens.

- If you're having the wedding at a place where you'll be staying overnight, pack in advance. Don't wait until you're stressed and buzzing with adrenaline or you'll forget important things.

- Rest the night before. No bachelorette parties. You don't want bags under your eyes in your wedding photos.

- Don't feel compelled to entertain everyone, or you'll be run ragged. You're the bride, not a magician at a children's party. Greet every guest, thank them for coming, and move on.

- If you're having a nighttime wedding, don't bring children or let anyone else bring them. Tired children have meltdowns, and no one enjoys those. It's your wedding; it's okay to say, "Get a babysitter."

Report from the Shallow End

I think shallowness gets a bad rap, and before we move on, I'd like to address it. It's very politically correct to claim that we care only about character and the inner self, to work on personal growth without worrying about how our eyebrows look. Nonsense. Every woman cares about looking great when she's having a Red Carpet Moment. Appearance matters.

In fact, it's not shallow to care about what's on the surface. You could be the most beautiful woman on earth on the inside, but that beauty isn't just going to shine through on its own. People can't sense telepathically what a loving, giving, and creative person you are. You've got to advertise. You let your inner beauty shine through your outer beauty. Like it or not, people are going to judge you by how you put yourself together. You might be incredibly qualified for a job, but if you show up for the interview wearing shorts and flip-flops while every other woman is wearing Ralph Lauren, you're going to be collecting unemployment for a while.

I was at a party not long ago and I met a woman whose family is worth billions. But she attended the extremely dressy event wearing shoes that were beat-up and unkempt. All I could think was, "She's too successful to be doing that!" It made me question her attitude and her respect for the other people at the party. She may not have deserved that, but it was natural to look for clues to who she was in what she wore. So give yourself permission to be shallow. Shallow, to paraphrase Gordon Gekko, is good. Some wisdom from the shallow end:

- *Don't let the dress wear you.* No matter how great a dress looks on the rack, no matter how much you love the designer, no matter how many other people tell you that you look smashing in it, if you don't feel beautiful in something, don't wear it. I've seen so many gorgeous women walk down the red carpet looking tragic because they were in dresses they knew they didn't belong in. Even if the dress and the woman are stunning separately, the combination can be just the opposite. When you know an outfit isn't right for you, it's impossible to carry yourself with the confidence that makes you truly gorgeous. You look self-conscious, and everybody knows it.

I am a shameless label whore. When I see a Dolce & Gabbana or Gucci gown on my rack, I automatically want it. I'm drawn to dresses that are bad for me in the same way some women are drawn to tattooed bikers on parole. My stylists, God bless them, have to hide them from me like you hide booze from someone going to AA meetings.

One year, I fell head over heels in love with the wrong dress. My eyes met the dress's stitches from across a crowded showroom and I was smitten. It flirted with me from its hanger. I sidled up to it and we talked about long walks on the runway together. I tried it on and it fit like it had been made for me.

On Oscar day I slid my beloved on my body . . . and began to itch. Not right away, when I could have done something about it, but when I was ready to go on camera and it was too late to change. Turns out that the dress was beaded but hadn't been lined. The edges of the beads were scratching my skin, and by the end of the night the area where my arms rubbed against the dress looked like a combination of road rash and rare hamburger. If you saw the Oscar pre-show that year, you might have wondered why I was moving so stiffly. I was trying to minimize the excruciating friction between the dress and my skin. Talk about uncomfortable in my own skin!

By 2003, I had learned my lesson. I put on my dress on Golden Globes morning and it still didn't fit, even after alterations. In a panic, I pulled out an old Pamela Dennis long satin skirt and a Dolce & Gabbana top I had gotten from a photo shoot three years before, and voilà. That year, everyone commented on how great I looked. Why? Because I looked like me. I really liked what I was wearing and knew it made me look good. People felt my confidence.

• *Weep once; buy quality.* There's a pair of suede boots I've had for seven years and absolutely love. Each winter I take them to a shoe-repair shop and have the soles and heels repaired. They cost a small fortune, but I've gotten more wear out of them than any footwear I've ever owned. If you can, spend money on quality where quality is essential: a classic black cocktail dress, your shoes, cosmetics. My uncle always said, "Buy quality and weep once." That means the price might be a shock to your credit card, but you won't suffer the extra pain of having to replace what you bought in a year because you went cheap. There's nothing wrong with saving money, and it's not a bad idea to bargain-hunt for something you're going to wear only a few times, but you'll never go wrong spending on quality for the go-to items in your wardrobe.

• *Know your critical detail and attend to it.* God is in the details. I have to do my fingernails and toenails before I go out or I feel slovenly. Everyone has her critical detail that simply has to get done before she'll feel like she's put together. Know what your detail is and take it up a notch for big events. As my mother likes to say, "Go in with all your flags flying."

• *Take care of your shoes.* Nothing ruins your put-together look like shoes that are battered, scuffed, or just old-looking. It's so easy to clean and polish any decent pair of shoes that I'm amazed more women don't take the time. If you seriously don't have the time, find a shoe-repair shop that can give your footwear a quick once-over before you go out.

• **_Test-drive your haircut._** Why wait until the day of a Red Carpet Moment to see if your hairstyle is going to be a hit or a miss? A date or a job interview is no different from a trip down the red carpet on awards night: Leave nothing to chance. If you're going to try a daring new cut, test it out a few weeks beforehand. That way, if what looked so good in the salon turns out in daylight to look like a dead cat sitting on your head, you have some time to make changes.

• **_Make important changes_** before **_panic time._** Don't wait until two weeks before your red carpet event to try to lose those last five pounds. They're not going to come off, and you're going to stress yourself out so badly trying to diet and sweat them off that you'll add another pound in new acne. Instead, prepare for the spotlight months in advance with a healthy lifestyle: good diet, exercise routine, skin care, and so on. That way, you can approach your Red Carpet Moment knowing that you look healthy and radiant, and you'll have the confidence that comes with knowing you're as prepared as you can be.

• **_Flaunt what you've got._** There are some women who look good in just about anything: Nicole Kidman, Charlize Theron, Hilary Swank, Jennifer Garner, Cate Blanchett, Catherine Zeta-Jones. I've interviewed them and their energy is as sparkling as their fashion. They know exactly how to dress to complement what God gave them—and God gave them quite a lot.

Most of us aren't so lucky. We have to dance with the body that brung us. Everybody has something about them that's exceptional. Figure out what that is for you and *work it*. If you have a great chest, show some skin. If you're too shy to let your décolletage come out to play, show off your arms or back. If you have great legs, flash them. If you want to wear a higher neck, wear a shorter skirt.

RED CARPET RULES
Job Interviews

- Grooming, grooming, grooming. Make sure your nose hair is trimmed, your nails are clean and filed, and your hair is attractive but not Saturday-night daring.
- Know who you're meeting with. Do your research and know names and titles ahead of time.
- Be organized. Don't end up having to riffle through your bag looking for your résumé while everyone stares in uncomfortable silence.
- When describing your past achievements, give credit to others where credit is due, but don't downplay your own role.
- Don't be cookie-cutter. It's okay to have a unique bag or piece of jewelry, as long as it's in good taste.
- Be confident, but not arrogant.
- There's nothing wrong with being early. If you arrive at your destination too early, take a walk around the block, but don't walk in until your appointment.
- You're not the only one who gets stuck in traffic. If you're going to be late, call. You don't have to be perfect. But if you're going to be really late, you *do* have to offer to reschedule.
- Remember that the interviewers want you to do well. It makes their job easier to hire someone quickly, and it makes them look smarter to hire someone who's perfect for the job. So relax and don't treat them like the enemy.

Of course, this goes far beyond clothes. Maybe you're a terrific conversationalist, have a knack with a joke, have musical talent, or you just make other people feel good about themselves. Bring what's extraordinary about you out for others to appreciate it. As they do, you'll be able to appreciate it more, too.

Dispatches from the Deep End

When you have strong self-esteem and you're happy with the person you've become, Red Carpet Moments come along all the time. They don't have to be when you get that perfect job, buy the house you've been dreaming about, or walk down the aisle. They can be any moment when you step back, look around, and say, "Damn, life is good and I'm lucky to be here."

This is the best advice I can give you from the deep end, where celebrity meets philosophy:

• *Don't apologize for who you are.* Don't mistake this for don't apologize, period. If you poach a friend's guy or inadvertently insult her outfit, you damn well better offer up a convincing "Sorry." But when it comes to the choices you've made in your life—your career path or your significant other—never apologize for anything. You don't owe anyone an explanation about why you're on your journey; it's *yours,* and you have your reasons. They don't need to make sense for anyone else. Instead of comparing yourself with people who might have achieved more, take pride in what you've achieved so far. Everyone has their time; yours might still be coming. There are many ways to measure success, and the most meaningful have nothing to do with how much you make, where you live, or what you drive.

- **Follow your passion.** Your lifestyle is not anybody else's. Why should it be? We live in a world where we're encouraged to conform, and then we celebrate people who don't conform. Be yourself. When you find something that sings to you, make it your own and to hell with what anybody else thinks.

I've witnessed this phenomenon many times on the red carpet, and you know what? Every actress who defied convention to wear what she loved was radiant to me, and not necessarily because I thought their outfits were beautiful. But each woman loved what her clothes said about her. For an evening, she was completely unique. Think Diane Keaton in her tuxedo, bowler hat, and black lace gloves or Björk in her swan outfit. They wouldn't work for most people, but they worked for them.

I want to see you do the same in your life. Forget conventional wisdom—it's usually wrong. Find something you're passionate about and make it happen. If no one else gets it, to heck with them. If you find someone else who shares your passion, marry him. Or at least date him.

- **Be fearless.** When awards season rolls around, the stars are flooded with offers for Botox, dermal fillers, eyebrow arches, teeth whitening, expensive jewelry, you name it. The implied message is "Don't let anyone see what you're really like." Nonsense. There's nothing wrong with how you look or who you are. We all have flaws, but so many of our troubles would be behind us if we could all just snap our fingers and say, "This is who I am and I like it, so stand back!"

For inspiration, look to the red carpet. Look who's walking it these days: It's not just the girls who look like they're on their way to an anorexia twelve-step program. It's the full-figured ladies who are turning heads. Jennifer Hudson not only strutted down the carpet in 2006 but she won the Oscar for *Dreamgirls*. Queen Latifah knows how to work it, especially now that she's reinvented herself as a jazz chanteuse. Vanessa Williams and Salma Hayek revel in their gorgeous curves. They feel fit and proud and show the world what they've got. Fear is the last thing on their minds.

• *Have fun.* Most of us leave play behind when we're children, and I've never understood why. Some of my greatest days are when I do nothing more than play silly kid games with Cooper. When you're in the middle of a Red Carpet Moment or just going through your daily life, remember to play a little. Do something silly. Find a friend and do it together. Enjoy what's happening. Start a conga line on the dance floor at your anniversary party. When I see red carpet events now, I can tell right away who's having fun with the experience and who's treating the night like one more obligation on his or her calendar. Funny thing is, the brightest stars never lose that sense of fun or wonder. Goldie Hawn always looks thrilled to be there. George Clooney is always glad to see everyone else. That's the spirit I'm talking about.

I'm inspired by everyone I know, famous and not-so-famous, who manages to be comfortable in his or her own skin. It's not always easy to do. Maybe someday, when I get it right, I can strut my stuff with their brand of confidence. When I do, I think I'll dedicate my performance to Camryn Manheim and all the other "fat girls."

Get Some Perspective

I guess I just prefer to see the dark side of things.
The glass is always half empty. And cracked.
And I just cut my lip on it. And chipped a tooth.

—JANEANE GAROFALO

*M*y mother has a gorgeous home in Connecticut, and I love to take Cooper there to escape from time to time. While I was working on this book, the kind of life event that spurs thoughts of escape came about: My ex-husband, John, and his second wife announced they were divorcing. Cooper was only nine months old when John and I ended our marriage, so he remembers nothing of that time. This breakup between his father and the woman he had come to love as his second mother would come when he was seven years old, smart, highly impressionable, and more than capable of picking up ugly vibes. So a few weeks after that bombshell dropped on me (but Coop still didn't know), it was time to run away to Mom's place for some R & R.

While we were there, I had a moment of blinding perspective that still haunts me. My mother's backyard has a black stone terrace in back with two steps down to a lawn, with a pool and pond at the end. We were sitting outside in the gorgeous spring sunshine and Cooper was running around with Mom, wearing a blue-and-white-striped rugby shirt and looking very handsome. It was like a photo from a coffee-table book. That was when the epiphany hit me like an ice pick in the forehead: The next day, John was going to tell Cooper about the divorce. Our son was going to find out that he was going to be separated from his half sister and that the living arrangement he had known for fifty percent of his life was going to be blown apart forever. I realized with an intensity that nauseated me that I was watching my son's last true moment of innocence. In twenty-four hours his world would never be the same again.

The knowledge was both poignantly beautiful and utterly devastating. It destroyed me for a moment. If you have children, you understand the overwhelming intensity of holding your child for the first time—how everything in your world lurches in a new direction. Suddenly, there's nothing you would not do to protect this little person from any pain or unhappiness. It was that kind of moment, but inverted: I knew my child was about to suffer due to someone else's problems and his refusal to deal with them, and there was *nothing* I could do to prevent it. The sense of impending loss was worse than finding out someone has died. Death isn't personal; this was.

Savor the Moment but See the Big Picture

What did I do? I did what grown-ups do, sucked it up and put on a brave face for my boy. I also text-messaged several of my closest friends for support and fought back a massive panic attack later that evening. But as sickening as my revelation was, it helped me with the most important task of all: making sure I was ready to help Cooper deal with his fear, anger, and uncertainty. I wasn't sitting back deluding myself that things were going to be hunky-dory; there was going to be pain. But thanks to my flash of brutal perspective, I was able to circle the wagons around my son and keep him as safe as I could. There were tears and lots of questions and a new guardedness that breaks my heart, but he's going to be all right. So am I.

Perspective is the ability to step back and see an aspect of your life—career, relationships, health, family, money, faith—clearly, without self-delusion, and understand what it *means* as part of the bigger picture. You see the significance of things. Instead of just going to a job day after day, you're able to step back and see whether or not that job fits your greater goals. Rather than send a longtime friend a perfunctory card on her birthday, you have the insight to realize how often she's been there for you over the years and how important it is that you express your true gratitude to her. Perspective is the key to recognizing your Red Carpet Moments when they're happening . . . and to making more of them.

For a book that's all about making the most of moments, having the perspective to appreciate those luminous little spans of time may be the most important lesson. Often, the most exquisite moments in life are the ones that don't announce themselves or take up space on your calendar for a year: the first time you read your child a bedtime story, a fist-pumping moment in the elevator after the end of a great first date, a mind-blowing sunset, or stopping in the middle of a bridge over the Seine and realizing, after years of dreaming about Paris, that "I'm here." Living a rich, grateful life means being self-aware enough to savor those rare moments—especially the ones that would otherwise fade into the background of an ordinary day.

Perspective is also a bittersweet gift, kind of like getting a treadmill from your significant other on your birthday. It can sting to get a clear view of yourself and your choices and realize that you've treated some of the people in your life badly, or that you've let yourself go. But as wrenching as they can be (especially when you're young, successful, and think you can do no wrong), perspective and self-knowledge are gifts because of what they give you the power to do: *make wiser decisions*. That's where maturity and experience matter. Only when you've survived dark times can you truly appreciate having what it takes to break destructive habits, heal old wounds, get off the career treadmill, or enjoy your Red Carpet Moments while they last. Because if there's one thing perspective teaches you, it's that nothing is forever.

MEL'S BELLES

Julia Roberts might be the most down-to-earth superstar I've ever seen. Every year on the red carpet, she would practically run up to me and my mother and say, "Okay, tell me what you think."

Julia is also disarmingly normal. One year, she twirled for Mom to show off her new gown. She was looking a little thinner than usual, so Mom asked if she was dieting. Julia got a worried look and said, "Why, should I be?" This gorgeous star was actually insecure about her weight, which I find so charming. Plus, if she can be so marvelous without being perfect, maybe there's hope for me yet.

Thanks, Julia, for being as real as you are beautiful.

Dropping the Illusion of Control

I'm lucky in that I've always had the ability to step out of the stream of crazy that most of us live in, look around, and say, "Wow, check it out." That's why, even in the grip of the chaos that defined the early red carpet telecasts, I was always able to step back and appreciate the wonder of what Mom and I were doing. It's also why, in the later years when our pre-shows became a huge Hollywood event in their own right, I never stopped being grateful and slightly amazed at the whole affair. In the first few years of *Joan & Melissa: Live at the Academy Awards*, the celebrities didn't realize that we were actually doing a live broadcast; they just thought we were part of the press line and accosting them in a typically ballsy Rivers style. Early on we learned to be appreciative when they took the time to talk with us. I'm proud to say that through the years I never lost that stunned gratitude that our insane little production became such a big deal to so many.

One reason I was able to keep my view of the big picture during those frantic hours was that I surrendered my illusions of being in control. Those red carpet telecasts ran on a blend of sweat, caffeine, electricity, and adrenaline (though we missed out on Gary Busey going all creepy, kissy-faced stalker on Jennifer Garner and Laura Linney at the 2008 Academy Awards; I always leave before the best parts). It would have been easy to get caught up in the rush to the next cue or joke, then look up at the end of the night and say, "Is it over already?" But I never did that, because instead of trying to get control of the commotion, I accepted that it was beyond my control. The craziness was part of the red carpet experience, so why fight it? I treated each show as a gift, an adventure, and a chance to discover something new.

I knew that at the end of the night I would be completely spent . . . and happy I had been part of the scene in the first place.

A wedding is a Red Carpet Moment most of us are likely to face, and it's one where giving up on the idea that you can control things is the path not only to happiness, but to sanity. The only difference between a wedding and the bedlam of a red carpet telecast is that at a wedding, you get cake. If you obsess about controlling every detail of your wedding, you'll pull an Ira Gershwin and scream, "Let's call the whole thing off." One of the best pieces of advice I've ever received was from my godmother about my wedding: "Melissa," she said, "if you really want to enjoy your wedding, walk to the back of the room by yourself and just watch." So I did. I saw people dancing, getting acquainted, toasting, laughing, and having a ball. Not everything was going according to plan and that was okay. I saw the joy I had created and felt honored and blessed. I did the same thing on the red carpet many times: stopped for a second, looked around at what I had helped create, and thought, "Pinch me." Quarterbacks in the Super Bowl and astronauts in orbit do the same thing, if they're smart.

Celebrity, Just Add Internet

Way back in the olden days (thirty years ago), before the Internet and cable TV ruled the news cycle, that sense of appreciation was much more common in Hollywood. It took hard work and sacrifice for actors or musicians to become superstars. As Monty Hall said, "I'm an overnight success. But it took twenty years." Actors like Robert Redford and Meg Ryan paid their dues for years before they became famous, and you can see the result in the longevity of their careers. They've been doing great work for decades in part because they've continued to grow. Their egos never got so out of control that they assumed they could coast on their fame alone. No one does.

Today's landscape, however, is drastically different. We live in the age of "microcelebrity" that comes in twenty-four hours with a hot YouTube video and disappears just as quickly. With hundreds of cable and satellite TV channels, production companies are creating new programming at a dizzying pace, and each new show is a chance for some dimpled teenage girl to become the next Miley Cyrus. Insta-fame can come as easily as Susan Boyle wowing Simon Cowell on *Britain's Got Talent* or someone being an ironclad bitch on *The Apprentice*. These days, we're manufacturing pseudo-celebrities like soap bubbles, but a lot of them don't understand that this kind of notoriety pops as fast as it appears. And nobody—especially the youngsters— wants to hear that. They want to believe the ride is going to last forever.

But the good times don't last—whether you're twenty-three and starring in a top-rated TV series or working in an office— unless there's substance behind what you're doing. I draw a distinction here between *fame* and *notoriety*. Fame is the side effect of dedication, craft, and years of hard work. It's ironic that if you want to become famous, the last thing you should do is care too much about being famous. Fame is about doing great work and growing professionally, not riding the roller coaster. That's why the Oscars will always be bigger than the Golden Globes and the People's Choice Awards: They're about the respect of your peers. The other actors, directors, and writers in the Academy don't give a damn who your publicist is or what parties you go to. They've been to Oz and they know who's behind the curtain. The work is everything. When you win an Oscar, it matters because the people who've given it to you know how you've slaved and sacrificed because they've done the same.

Notoriety, on the other hand, is empty and fleeting. One day, you're strutting down the red carpet as a young hottie with a number-one movie; the next, you're grateful to appear in *The Surreal Life*. The trouble with being young and having fame and big money come too easily is that you think you *deserve* it. The thought process goes something like this:

A. *I'm only twenty and I've been on the cover of* People, *make $6 million a film, and Timbaland produced my first CD even though I couldn't carry a tune if it came with handles.*

B. *I got into the business only five years ago. What's all this "paying your dues" stuff that people talk about?*

C. *Ergo, I must have an inborn right to all this fame, adulation, and wealth.*

I call this attitude the Divine Right of Bling. Trouble is when you have that attitude, you lose all perspective on your career. You don't take steps to ensure that when your star fades you can keep having a career—steps like honing your acting chops, cutting an R & B record, or starting a company. Even when Mom and I were riding the red carpet juggernaut, I never assumed anything. I stockpiled ideas for new shows, businesses, and projects, and when the red carpet ride ended I was ready to move on.

A great example of this frame of mind is Shoshanna Lonstein Gruss, who discovered how toxic notoriety could be when she dated Jerry Seinfeld at age seventeen. When that affair ended, did she cling desperately to the fleeting fame? No, she started her own successful clothing company, became a contributing editor for *Cosmopolitan*, got married, and had a daughter. That's a lesson anyone can love: Don't get so enamored of where you are that you forget to plan on where you'll go next.

THE GOSPEL ACCORDING TO JOAN

It's hard to keep your perspective in this industry. I just mind my business and wear blinders like a racehorse. I'm very careful and I absolutely divide my time between the projects I'm working on. If I have seven projects, I go from one to the next to the next and give total concentration to what I'm doing at any time. That way, I'm always in the moment and always able to give my best.

Live with the Masses, Eat with the Classes

My mother has a favorite saying: "If you live with the masses you'll eat with the classes, and if you live with the classes you'll eat with the masses." Come again? This means that if you want to "eat with the classes," meaning have the money and status to dine at the best places and be invited to the best parties, then do work that connects with the masses, the average people on the street. On the other hand, if you live with the classes—if you have such a high opinion of yourself that you do work that appeals only to a small elite—you're probably going to end up brown-bagging it and begging for work. You become Dennis Miller, so intent on showing off your knowledge of Etruscan history and quantum mechanics on *Monday Night Football* that you alienate ninety percent of your audience and have to re-invent yourself as a Fox News talking head.

One of the hallmarks of perspective is that you have empathy for the masses—you're able to comprehend that not everyone lives the same life you do. That's especially important if you're experiencing hard times. If you have perspective on life and understand that any situation can change, you don't give up hope. You keep working to make things better, and if you keep at it you usually succeed. If you're working at a lousy job it's vital to step back and realize that it's not forever, so you can develop your skills, build your network, gain experience, and move on to brighter things. If you're an actor scuffling in lame roles, you keep learning your craft and going to auditions and bam—you're Rodney Dangerfield, who quit comedy to become a salesman and didn't hit it big until he was forty-two.

The opposite—not realizing how good you have it—is all too common among the Hollywood crowd. Even the really good people lose perspective from time to time. I have a beach house and a few years ago I was throwing a twenty-fourth-birthday party there for Jessica Simpson. Jessica is a sweet girl who's managed to keep her life on an even keel in spite of our culture's tendency to inhale nubile young starlets and spit them out looking like they've been through a cement mixer. Jessica was in tears because paparazzi were hanging out on the beach photographing every move she made. I cracked my knuckles, took her aside, and went to work.

"Jessica, do you think anyone cared when I turned twenty-four?" I said. "The reason they care is because of all you've accomplished at your age. Be happy that enough people love you that they want to take your picture in the first place." This dose of reality made her stop crying. She smiled and I think she understood what I was getting at. She moved the party to another location, and clearly she has survived.

· The trouble comes when nothing and no one can knock someone rich or famous out of their rarefied state of delusion. I've known celebs like this; their sense of entitlement is gruesome and their presumption that reality bends for them is staggering. A couple of years ago, a friend of mine happened to be in a Las Vegas hotel's VIP lounge when Britney Spears and her entourage rolled in. Apparently, the assembled peons were instructed by Ms. Spears's bodyguards "not to make eye contact with her." The masses had become an intrusion, an inconvenience . . . and we know how sadly that story played out for a while. Lose touch with the people around you and you lose touch with yourself.

How You Know You Have Perspective

Perspective is a bit like bad breath: It's hard to detect it in yourself. You're just too close to your own life to see it clearly. But there are some telltale signs:

• *You're normal.* A few years back, I was attending an elegant dinner party at a friend's house where I didn't know anyone else. I was chatting with Walter Coblenz, the producer of *The Onion Field,* and he said, "Our friend Al is coming, we have to save a seat for him." My friend the host is a collector of people and I figured "Al" would be pretty interesting, so I saved the seat next to me and I turned back to talk with the other guests. This was during the second season of *Dancing with the Stars,* the reality show that has become a monster hit and to which I was and am hopelessly addicted. When someone suggested that some people didn't watch the show or reality TV at all, I would have none of it.

"Come on, everybody watches reality television!" I said. Out of the corner of my eye I could see that my seatmate had arrived, so I turned with a flourish and said, "You watch it, don't you?" Staring back at me was Al Pacino.

He is one of the most respected actors of his generation; what would he say to my goofy cheerleading? Well, Al couldn't have been nicer. He was also a big fan of the show, and we had a great time talking about all the dancers and the judges' decisions. Now, whenever I see him, we talk about *Dancing*, his daughter's college softball games, and whatever else comes up. He's "my pal Al." The point is, he's a normal person. He doesn't act like a guy who's won an Oscar, been nominated seven other times, and acted with Brando in *The Godfather*. When you have perspective, you don't think your shit smells sweeter than anybody else's because of your job, your income, where you live, or what you drive. You don't think everyone else should be obsessed with what you're obsessed with. You care about what other people have to say and share the mundane details of your own life. You admit to bad days like anybody else, you apologize when it's appropriate, and you don't always have to be the center of attention.

When you're planning your bridal shower and, despite the fact that everyone is telling you you're a princess and no one else should matter, you find the time to hug and lend a shoulder to a friend who's just been dumped by the guy she was going to bring to your wedding, you're normal.

• *You can see through other people's eyes.* I've always struggled with snap responses to things. I'm known for getting an e-mail that pushes my outrage button, dashing off a furious reply, hitting SEND, and then regretting it. It's classic Melissa. But as the years pass, I'm learning to restrain my trigger finger with a dose of perspective: understanding that another person's view is just as valid as mine.

You know the saying "The villain is never the villain in his own mind"? Well, if someone says or e-mails something that I think is a load of garbage, chances are that he or she did it for a reason. Even Los Angeles Lakers coach Phil Jackson, the Zen master, loses his temper and rips his players in the locker room from time to time. The players may not like it, but they take it. Why? Because they know the tirade has a purpose. It's a sign of wisdom to see other people's viewpoints. Even if you think they're out of line, it's worth walking around the opinion like you would walk around a used car, looking at every aspect, before you jump in with guns blazing and pass judgment. I still don't have that skill mastered, but I'm working on it.

SWEPT UNDER THE CARPET

People don't realize how tricky the weather in L.A. can be. It's not uncommon at the Golden Globes and Oscars (which happen in February and March) for it to be raining and freezing. At the Emmys, which are held in September, it's not unheard of to have hundred-degree heat. That's Armageddon. There, the people are sweating through their clothes. Hug the men and their tux jackets are soaked. Meanwhile, at the Oscars, women are blue and shaking in their gowns, but nobody wants to cover up and miss the photo op. Then there's the rain, which can be torrential. One year at the Golden Globes, the dye from the red carpet soaked into the bottom of everyone's dresses and shoes—everyone was stained red. You can feel like Ramses in *The Ten Commandments:* wind, cold, and $500 hairdos thrashed.

- *You're generous.* When you're a star it's very easy to be a person who takes, because everyone is always trying to give you things, especially at Oscar time. For example, until the fun-meisters at the IRS ruled that everyone who received one would have to pay income tax on its value, every Oscar nominee received a jaw-dropping bag of swag. For the 2006 Oscars, the gift bag included four-star vacation tickets to Hawaii, California, or Whistler, British Columbia; a diamond and pearl necklace; an iPod; and a cashmere blanket, just for starters. You get enough of those thrown your way and you start believing that everyone owes you something.

Let me tell you something: No one owes anyone anything. We earn what we get, and when we do, it's important to remember that not everyone has had the same good fortune. The world is full of dedicated, passionate, hardworking men and women whose stars didn't align. So when you have something worth sharing, whether it's a business opportunity or some hard-earned wisdom, share it.

One time, a friend of mine asked me to go to dinner with her, and we walked into a restaurant and sat down at a table. Sharing the table with us were Sean Penn, Gabriel Byrne, and Harry Dean Stanton. Intimidating? You bet your Prada handbag. But by the end of the evening, I was sitting there with Sean laughing my ass off, and he was giving me divorce advice. It was so completely endearing I still smile about it. Gabriel Byrne gave me excellent advice on custody issues. Sure, they're big stars, but they are also wonderful men who have accumulated life experience that they knew I could learn from, and they were kind enough to take the time to share it with me.

They didn't have to do it to make me feel good; they could have mouthed meaningless pleasantries and I still would have been floating on air just sitting with them. They did it because they *wanted* to give what they had. Hollywood is full of people like that when you get past the so-called glamour and the autograph seekers. So is the rest of life. When you realize that giving of yourself doesn't cost you anything—and take pleasure and pride in the glow it gives to someone else—you're truly evolved.

• *You count your blessings.* Ever know one of those people whose troubles are always the worst thing in the world? A friend might have just been diagnosed with cancer, while Ms. X's biggest problem is not being able to find pumps the same shade of black as her dress, but guess who's doing all the kvetching at lunch? I know a few people like that, and it's all I can do not to shake them when they start in with a litany of their petty tribulations.

There's an old Jewish proverb about standing with other people in a circle and each person throwing his or her problems into the middle. Each person then gets to take the set of problems out of the circle they think they are best equipped to handle. After everyone's had their turn, each person has his or her own set of original problems back. There are two morals. First, your problems are no worse than anybody else's. Second, you've got what it takes to handle the obstacles in your life.

When you have perspective you're grateful for the things you have and the troubles you don't have. You don't look at someone with cancer and say, "That sucks, but did I tell you about my living room rug?" You thank God for your health and the health of the people you love, and then you figure out what you can do to make the other person's burden a little lighter. You have a sense of how lucky you are and how easily you could be the one staring at chemotherapy, going to divorce court, or collecting unemployment. Stars who understand how blessed they are tend to be the ones who stick around. Will Smith comes to mind. He's gorgeous and unspeakably talented, but he always comes across like he's thinking, "Wow, they still let me do this, how cool!" That's why he'll have a long, long career.

KNOW-IT-ALL

David Scott May, M.D., Adolescent and Adult Psychiatrist

There are certain issues I feel are important to explore in helping my patients develop perspective on a situation. Why are they making a choice between one thing or another, and do they have to choose? I also think that people live too much in the future or the past, so they miss the moment. The challenge is to have a future and a past but to stay in the moment, because that's where the joy is. And finally, so many people are having a wild ride, but I ask them, "If you had only three months to live, what would you change?"

How You Know You Lack Perspective

This is a tough one, because if you don't have any perspective on yourself, you by definition have no idea what I'm talking about and probably wish I would get into some juicy gossip about Lindsay Lohan. Sorry, no can do. However, I'm going to give you the benefit of the doubt and assume you can spot some of the warning signs of the "perspective challenged":

• *You're cynical.* One of the most common diseases of age is cynicism, that seen-it-all attitude that some people have. They're sure they know more and have seen more than everyone else, and there's nothing you can do to surprise or delight them. Everyone has an ulterior motive and everybody wants something. So when something really surprising comes along, they've got so much invested in that world-weary facade that they don't dare shed it. Instead they look down their noses at things that fill others with joy.

Joaquin Phoenix was this way at the 2006 Country Music Awards, where he had been nominated for his work in *Walk the Line*. He stood out as the one guy who didn't want to be there. Johnny Cash's memory deserved better. I feel sorry for the cynics, because they miss out on so much. I'm proud that even as I approach forty, I have not become cynical. Neither has my mother, which I find admirable.

Cynicism is basically fear of being vulnerable. When you let yourself be astonished or surprised by something, you can also be wounded. Cynics put on a suit of armor to protect themselves from slings and arrows that, ninety-nine percent of the time, exist only in their imaginations. The wonderful Molly Ivins wrote, "It's hard to argue against cynics—they always sound smarter than optimists because they have so much evidence on their side." But the evidence is almost always false, and by the time the cynics figure that out, everyone in their lives has left the building. If you find yourself underwhelmed by things that move others to tears and rolling your eyes at real kindnesses, you're at risk.

• **It's got to be about you.** On the opposite end of the spectrum from the folks like Sean Penn, you will find the "takers," the people who can't stand the spotlight being on someone else. Now, it's true that Red Carpet Moments are when the spotlight is on you, but part of having the perspective to appreciate those moments is being generous and wise enough to share the stage when it's appropriate. When you're being honored by your alma mater, call your favorite professor up to the podium and thank him. When you get a promotion, give a standing ovation to the team who helped you get there. Perspective is about being made larger, not diminished, by giving.

Sadly, there are plenty of people for whom every headline has to be all about them. They make my skin crawl because they're so transparently self-obsessed, and also because there's a lie inherent in their egotism. For instance, in Hollywood, unless you also ran the camera, laid the cable, did your own makeup, and handled about a thousand other jobs that made your blockbuster movie possible, it's not all about you. If you have the perfect fairy-tale wedding, you didn't make it happen with a wave of your wand. An army of well-intentioned people made you the belle of the ball. Not sharing the love and gratitude doesn't make you look cool; it just reveals your poverty of spirit.

Case in point: One year at the Emmys, actress Lucy Liu had been kind enough to bring her mother with her. All was well and good until, when mother and daughter were posing for the camera, Lucy reached up and flicked her mom's hand off her shoulder just before the shutter clicked—so she could be alone in the shot. Mom and I literally stopped breathing. We could hardly believe what we'd just seen. That gesture spoke volumes.

• *You're never in the moment.* "What? Did you say something? What was your name again? I'm just terrible with names." Sorry, I'm not buying it. Almost everyone knows someone who never seems to be listening to what anyone says, or who always seems to be thinking about being somewhere else or being with someone else. It's maddening to feel like you're not worthy of someone's full attention, yet that's precisely what a person who refuses to ground himself in the moment is telling you: You're not important enough for my full attention. People

---

RED CARPET RULES: BREAKUPS

- It's going to suck. We've all been there and there's nothing fun about it, whether you're doing the breaking up or being broken up with. Don't try to deny it or smile through it. Accept it.

- It's going to pass. This won't be the end of the world, although as the old line goes, you'll be able to see it from there. Life will get better.

- Have your major breakup well before swimsuit season, because you're probably going to lose a lot of weight thanks to depression. Don't hide your slim new body under a lot of layers. The best time to end the affair is late March or early April, because by June you'll look hot and by July you'll be prancing along the beach meeting new people.

- Use the breakup as a life milestone and an excuse to start healthy new habits. Start eating better, exercising, meditating, reading, reflecting on what you could do better, and so on.

Continued . . .

---

with a sense of perspective have the empathy to know that if the situation was reversed—if the person they were talking to nodded politely without hearing a word they said and forgot their name three seconds after they said it—they would be furious and humiliated.

Are you in the moment with the people in your life, or are you always looking to the next scene, the next person, the next opportunity? That's the kind of person I call best-offer Barbie. If you're not paying attention, you're missing everything that matters.

- Give yourself time to detox. Someone told me it takes half the time that you were together with the other person to get over it completely. So if you were together for eighteen months, figure you've got nine months of blues, anger, and fear to deal with. Plan for that if you're thinking about jumping into a new relationship.
- For God's sake, resist the temptation to get back together after a few weeks when you get lonely. You'll both forget about what was bad and be all hot for a booty call. Don't do it! Unless both people truly change (which rarely happens without a crisis), the relationship will get poisonous again quickly, and the next breakup will be uglier. Move on to someone new.
- Don't break up via e-mail.
- Remember the good and take that with you. Your relationship may have failed but *you* are not a failure. Learn the lessons you can learn from this experience and move ahead.

The Shallow Perspective

Listening and enjoying the moment are the most obvious aspects of perspective, but that's because there's nothing about them that's necessarily deep and philosophical. Sure, you can go all Buddhist and talk about living in each infinite moment as a way of achieving immortality, but I give you my personal guarantee that you don't need a Bodhi tree to appreciate how exquisite the individual moments of any day can be, or to discover something marvelous in really listening to what someone else is saying. Being present is its own reward, as you know if you've ever stood and watched kids play in sprinklers or bitten into a garden-fresh tomato, stopped, and said to yourself, "You know, it's good to be alive."

But since we're swimming in shallow waters here, let's be honest: It's fun to wallow in the Red Carpet Moments that let you wear haute couture, draw every eye as you enter a room, and bask in your accomplishments just for a few minutes. Graduation, a milestone wedding anniversary, receiving an award—these are your chances to rock the moment and shine. And it's much easier to relish those times when you've taken care of some basic personal housekeeping—and you're not taking a header in your new Manolo Blahnik heels. So, to paraphrase the song, let's direct our feet to the shallow side of the street and talk about some tips that make great moments even more memorable:

• *Take time to spoil yourself.* When I do something like QVC, I always get my nails done beforehand, because no matter what happens, I know my nails will look good on air, and that makes me feel more confident. It's also a pleasure to have a professional manicurist giving me a little pampering before a long session under the hot lights. I recommend doing the same thing prior to any Red Carpet Moment. Give your self-esteem and confidence a boost by spoiling yourself rotten in some way that also makes you look and feel fabulous. Get a pedicure. Have your hair colored by a professional (it horrifies me to see how many women still make the mistake of doing it themselves at home and frying their hair). Get a massage, and if you're too busy to go to a day spa, hire one of those services that sends a masseuse with a portable massage table to your home. My attitude is, the more relaxed and gorgeous you feel before a Red Carpet Moment, the more you'll make the most of it.

• *Enjoy the preparation.* The moment isn't just the camera flash when they hand you the award; it's all the steps leading up to that split second. Savor each one of them. I know when I was getting ready for red carpet pre-shows, I loved the ritual of my stylist coming over to my house with racks of stunning new dresses for me to try on. It was the sartorial equivalent of being turned loose in a Godiva store after-hours. I also enjoyed going to stores to check out the latest dresses; I felt a little like Carrie and Samantha from *Sex and the City,* parading from boutique to boutique with a hip soundtrack playing in my head. And if my hard work and time led to the perfect dress that made me look fantastic, the evening was that much sweeter.

Whatever prep you're doing for your big moment, whether it's a night out or dinner with your boss, make it fun. If you're going to get your hair done, invite some friends and have lunch. I know a couple of ladies who actually work shopping and lunch along Rodeo Drive into their annual mammogram, for God's sake. That's what I call joie de vivre.

• *Step back.* Remember my godmother's wedding advice to step back and take in the whole scene? You can't go wrong with that at any red carpet event. Stop for a second and take your mind out of the stream of time. Quit being a participant in your unfolding drama and take a moment to observe. On the way back from the bathroom while you're on a first date that's going really well, stop before you head back to the table at a place where your date can't see you. Look around. Feel who you are and where you are, right now. Is this someone with potential? Is he or she worthy of you? You don't even need a Red Carpet Moment to do this. Just stop in your tracks anytime, anywhere, and find the beauty in what's happening. Enjoy the fact that this unique tick of the clock will never come again. It's a great perspective builder.

• *Use sandpaper on your shoes.* There was a reason your mom and dad sandpapered the soles of your new shoes

RED CARPET RULES
Having a Baby

- Be prepared. You don't want to be caught with your pants down (literally). Have your nails done, your hair blown out, and the works waxed. Yes, especially down there. You're going to be in pictures afterward, even though you'll be sweaty and gross, and pictures last forever. Look as good as you can.

- Pack everything you think you might need—a robe, soap, a magazine, whatever.

- You don't have to pack as much if you have a person on call who will serve as your gofer and bring you the things you need on demand. Hey, you're queen for a few hours. Milk it.

- Bring two pairs of socks. You'll want them.

- Don't eat a heavy meal beforehand. I don't need to go into detail on this one, do I?

- Know what works for *you*. Until that baby pops out, you are the center of attention—not your husband, not your mother-in-law. You decide who's in the room, who's taking pictures, and so on. That is until . . .

Continued . . .

before you wore them: They didn't want you falling on your butt and missing school. Please, before you go out to a big event where you're planning on wearing new shoes, scuff the soles with some medium-grain sandpaper. Just a couple of swipes to roughen the surface is all it takes to make sure you don't do a Naomi Campbell at the Vivienne Westwood fashion show. It may seem oh-so-gauche to go all Bob Vila on your Cole Haans, but

- The baby comes out, and then you're forgotten. When I had Cooper, they took him to the nursery to weigh him and the nurse brought in a wheelchair to take me to the recovery room. When I got there, the room was full of people, including my baby, celebrating. No one seemed to notice that I was missing. Prepare to become an instant afterthought.

- Throw everyone else out of the room when you can't take any more. Be polite but firm about it. You've just pushed something the size of a softball out of an opening the size of a golf ball. You don't need an excuse.

- No cell phones during the birth. My ex's cell phone rang during my delivery and he answered it out of habit. Your child is being born! Texting can wait. Turn the damn things off.

- Make sure there's a phone tree set up so you can call six people with the happy news, then they will take care of calling the other three thousand who surely want to know. This frees you to sleep.

- No one wants to watch the video of the birth. Trust me.

trust me, no shoe looks hot when it's on the broken leg you just got tumbling ass over teakettle down a flight of stairs.

- ***Accept the pain.*** Beautiful shoes and beautiful dresses are not designed for comfort. They are designed to push the female body into contortions never imagined by God or Nature in order to make you look great. There's a couture formula that everyone should memorize: *beauty* = *pain*. I'm always slightly amazed when women who have never gone out to a truly elegant event show up in Dior or Vera Wang and complain all night long about how uncomfortable they are.

Know that there's a direct correlation between how hot your dress and shoes make you look and how uncomfortable they are. The pain won't be crippling, but you're not going to be as comfortable as you would be in jeans. So to keep things from getting too bad, test-drive your dress before you choose it as *the one*. Check the pressure points and make sure nothing's going to rub you raw after six hours. Make sure you can go to the bathroom in it (without having to remove the entire dress in the stall, as I once had to). Make sure you can sit (or perch) without being too uncomfortable or showing too much skin.

Deep Perspective

Going deep in the perspective pool isn't just about handling individual moments, but about your whole frame of mind with regard to the events and people in your life. It's about nurturing in yourself what I see as the three most important aspects of lifelong healthy perspective: *appreciation, awareness, and joy*.

• ***Cultivate wonder.*** I work in a business where we create fantasy, wear princess dresses, have people screaming our names, and fly on private jets. Is there anything cooler? If you can't let your eyes bug out once in a while and approach things with a sense of pure wonder, something's wrong with you.

When Abigail Breslin was nominated for an Oscar in 2006 for her role in *Little Miss Sunshine,* she was ten years old. When I asked her if she was enjoying herself, she looked at me like I was nuts. "It's all so exciting," she said. "I can't believe how long the red carpet is and how many people are here. My mom and my friend Ashley went to a store in Brentwood with me, and it was there that I fell in love with this dress. I love seeing all the beautiful gowns and I feel so glamorous." The way she ended just about put me on the floor: "My secret to the red carpet is to wear comfortable shoes." She'll definitely be back.

You don't have to be a child to have that spirit. One of my favorite red carpet memories is of Mark Wahlberg making his walk down the red carpet in 2006 after being nominated for Martin Scorsese's *The Departed*. Here was a guy who had come of age in a rough neighborhood in Boston and had every reason to be jaded. But he wasn't. "I was invited to the parties and the big show," he said to me. "I am happy to be here. People warned me about the red carpet. They said, 'You'll be pushed and shoved and pulled.' But I'm having a great time, I really am."

• *Imagine looking back.* Nothing lasts forever except the credits from a Pixar movie. Stop yourself and imagine looking back on your Red Carpet Moment years from now, after it's all over. What will you remember? What do you want to take away? This is important because so many of today's younger celebrities who rise and fall quickly don't appreciate that there comes a point in the wild ride when you have to get off. You stop being the hottest girl at the party, someone else comes out with a groundbreaking record, or the "tween" girls simply start shrieking for some other young hunk. Take a mental snapshot of the times that you want to look back on with pride and delight.

It's so important to appreciate that moment when you get your diploma, when your dad walks you down the aisle, when you finish writing your first short story. When I see nominees walking up the red carpet I want to remind them, "Smile. Please smile and soak up every second of this." Drink it in while you can, folks. Every one of us has a limited supply of wonderful moments coming to us in our lives, and that's what makes them precious. But it also makes them unrecoverable. Don't miss out because you get complacent. Remember that for all the talk about being honored to be nominated, at the end of the night there's still one winner and four losers, and while the losers might smile and clap, many of them are in their limos sobbing the minute they leave the auditorium.

• *Be happy for others.* So many people have told me that they miss me and Mom on the red carpet, that the shows aren't as fun. And to be truthful, in the beginning it sucked to watch Ryan Seacrest and Lisa Rinna work the carpet instead of us. I found myself jumping out of my chair at home like a football fan after a tipped pass, screaming, "No, you can't ask Jessica Alba about her breast-feeding!" But if you have perspective and you're a grown-up, you find it in your heart to be happy for people who have achieved something good for themselves. It doesn't diminish you or make you feel envious. I'm like a retired pro athlete who misses the locker room and the camaraderie, except in my case I miss asking Angelina Jolie, "Who are you wearing?" The excitement is gone, but I still take great pride in what we accomplished and that it's going to go on.

I think it's vital to move forward but be able to look back without bitterness. If your friend marries the guy of her dreams but you're still looking, be genuinely thrilled for her. If a pal's career is taking off while yours seems to be in neutral, cheer for him and hope that the "rising tide lifts all boats" theory actually works. Good wishes elevate your spirit; envy and spite drag you down.

• *Show respect.* A Red Carpet Moment—especially someone else's—is not the time to make an angry personal point like you're Vanessa Redgrave getting up and ranting about Zionism. Red Carpet Moments are for appreciation and for acknowledging the work of all the other people who made it possible for you to be where you are. Don't be sarcastically detached. Don't wear a backward baseball cap to the prom. Take occasions seriously and show respect.

Janeane Garofalo ran afoul of this principle in my book. Janeane arrived at the Emmys one year wearing a T-shirt and jeans. She tends to dress down most of the time, and I respect her outspoken, antiestablishment passion, but come on. At least look like you care, because you know what, Janeane? You're not just there representing yourself, you're also representing all the people who work their butts off to get you on the air—grips, gaffers, makeup and lighting people, you name it. You're there for them, and when you thumb your nose at the event you may as well be flipping a different finger at all those dedicated professionals.

• *Keep a record.* Finally, don't trust your memory. Time and a few too many cosmopolitans will blur what really happened at your twenty-fifth high-school reunion. Carry a small digital camera and take pictures. Keep a journal of the event and write everything you can remember when you get home. Write in your blog, collect souvenirs and make a scrapbook, do whatever you can to memorialize your Red Carpet Moment so years later, when things have changed, you can look back with accurate memories and say, "Yeah, I was there, I danced with him, we looked good, and life was grand."

Life is grand. It was yesterday, it is today, and it will be tomorrow. Having perspective lets you appreciate the big and small moments that make up the whole wacky tapestry.

Trust Your Gut

You have to leave the city of your comfort and go into the
wilderness of your intuition. What you'll discover will be
wonderful. What you'll discover is yourself.

—ALAN ALDA

*A*t the 2002 Golden Globes, the gorgeous actress Sela
Ward was wearing an awful red gown. Now, I understand that
some people didn't care for Mom and me and our red carpet
antics because they thought all we did was beat people up. We
weren't being mean; we just tried to make viewers laugh and
keep them entertained, and for millions of viewers who tuned
in, entertainment was watching us sink our claws into the badly
dressed. Everybody who gets in the limo to attend a red carpet
awards night knows the ground rules: When you sashay down
that carpet, you're fair game.

Well, my mother took one look at Sela's dress and asked her,
with withering Joan Rivers sarcasm, who had dressed her.
Embarrassed, Sela mumbled, "Valentino." Mom and I both

cringed. This gorgeous woman had been the victim of a fashion drive-by courtesy of one of the world's top designers, proof that even the gods make mistakes. That year, Sela won our Worst Dressed Award—and everyone else's. Okay, awkward moment, but it's in the past, right? Not quite.

Fast-forward four months and I was at Cannes, pregnant and feeling terrible from morning sickness (Coop, you were worth every heave). Who do you think I find myself seated next to? Give yourself a gold star if you answered, "Sela Ward." I groaned. I squirmed. I prayed she wouldn't know I was one of the people who had said such mean things about her dress. So I had to pick my jaw up off the floor when Sela opened our conversation by leaning over and saying, "Thank you."

"You're welcome," I stammered, "but for what?"

"For making me trust my instincts." She told me that she had known her dress wasn't right for her, but her stylist and hair and makeup people had worked so hard to create her look that she didn't want to let them down. Mom and I had reminded her not to let the dress wear her. For Cannes she looked marvelous in Dior, and we had a delightful time together.

Your Instincts Are (Almost) Always Right

If Sela had followed her gut before the Golden Globes, she wouldn't have looked like puff pastry. When she listened to her instincts and wore what she loved, not what her stylist pushed on her, she was radiant. That's one of the essential lessons I've picked up on the red carpet: Trust your gut. That means having confidence in your instincts and what they tell you—good or bad—about a person, a situation, or a choice that's before you.

When you trust your gut, you're listening to that inner voice that says, "I don't think that's such a good idea," rather than rationalizing that everything is okay.

I'm no neurologist or psychologist, but I have a theory on how this all works. After twelve years watching the good, the bad, and the unspeakably ugly walk past me on the red carpet, I've earned a Ph.D. in instinct. It goes like this: Each of us lives with constant tension between our passion and our intuition. The wisest people I know maintain a sense of balance between the part of the mind that wants to act out of lust or desire or fear—the part that tells us there's nothing wrong with the hot guy we just started dating having duct tape, a blindfold, and a chain saw in the backseat of his car when he picks us up for dinner—and the commonsense part that screams from our solar plexus to lock ourselves in the house and dial 911. The trick is knowing when to obey your passion and when to listen to that nagging voice in your gut. I don't think most of us obey our intuition nearly often enough.

The trouble is that passion has an accomplice. It's bad enough that our emotional, greedy side gets us all revved up over a house we can't afford or a bikini that our best friend told us makes our butt look fat. But then passion pulls the intellect into the dressing room and they gang up on us, the bastards. The intellect constructs neat rationalizations that make us think we're making our decision based on logic when in fact we're making it based on the self-delusion that we can lose forty pounds by summer. Before we know it, we've blown $200 on a bathing suit that will never see the light of day—or worse, $750,000 on a house that will belong to the bank once the interest rate resets.

Your gut instinct is always sitting back absorbing the lessons of life, collecting experiences and impressions about people and circumstances. Even when you've buried the memory of how a past lover cheated on you, or how you lost out on a job because you didn't go for it aggressively enough, your instinct has it archived under "lessons learned." When something comes along in life that sets off those alarms from yesterday, the hairs on the back of your neck come to attention and a voice from your gut purrs, "Are you sure you want to do that?" or "You know, I don't think I'd pass up that chance." Passion is all about fantasy; your gut is the voice of harsh reality. The trouble is that we don't want to pay attention. Some part of us understands that we're choosing a guy for the same dysfunctional, codependent reasons we stuck with our last jerk boyfriend for three years, but we hear ourselves saying those fateful words: "This time it will be different." Well, boys and girls, it's almost never different. The most infuriating thing about gut instinct is that it's usually right. It's like a cosmic traffic cone designed to stop us from making terrible mistakes.

MEL'S BELLES

Some people think Nicole Kidman is distant and aloof. But nothing could be further from the truth. I think it's because she's just so ethereally gorgeous, with her flawless pale skin and that mane of crimson hair, that she seems untouchable. But underneath the glamour is the sweet Australian girl who first made a splash in *Dead Calm*. Nicole is always kind and generous with her time on the red carpet and always classy, confident, and looking wonderful. She understands that for her fans, her appearance on the carpet is important, and she makes you believe there is no place she would rather be. She is really an extraordinary lady, and I think more people would be aware of it if she weren't so damn beautiful.

Where's Dustin Hoffman When You Need Him?

So why don't we do what our gut says more often? In part, because following your gut is damn hard. We live in a relentlessly rational world that teaches us to trust Nielsen ratings and NAS-DAQ prices, not our inner voices. So we feel foolish listening to them, and when intuition fights with what you think you're supposed to be doing, the pressure to deny it can be a terrible strain.

Sadly, I have personal experience with what it's like to ignore intuitive red flags the size of Yankee Stadium: my wedding and marriage. My ex-husband, John, and I met in 1992 and dated for five and a half years. We were engaged for another year and a half before we finally tied the knot in 1999. During our entire engagement, I was a wreck. Some part of me knew that getting married was not the right decision—that we were not going to be good for each other. But inertia takes over, doesn't it? If you've ever been engaged and had serious second thoughts, you know. Once the invitations are sent and the hall is reserved and the showers are thrown, the whole thing takes on a life of its own. I lost a lot of weight in the months leading up to my wedding, but I didn't have the sense to call it off.

On the day of the event, I woke up with laryngitis. Hint number one. I think it came from not saying something that I needed to say. I got the dry heaves when I put on my dress. Hint number two. And when I was walking down the aisle, my inner voice was screaming, "Turn and run!" I saw myself sprinting away from the altar like Katharine Ross at the end of *The Graduate*. But I didn't listen. I rationalized my feelings and said those vows anyway. Less than two years later John and I were separated. All in all things worked out well, because I would never have had my beautiful Cooper, who's the greatest thing in my life. But he came at a steep price.

Sometimes your instincts are smarter than you are, and it's your job to know when. I've learned the hard way to listen to my inner nag; in fact, my entire career has been built on finding projects that I had a passion for and trusting my gut when it said, "Yeah, this will be great. Go for it." In fact, I've been told so often that this venture or that was a terrible idea that I've developed my own law about gut instinct called the "You're Out of Your %$#@& Mind" Law. It goes like this:

> The likelihood of your instinct being right is in direct proportion to the number of times people tell you that you're insane when they learn what you have in mind.

Most folks don't like it when someone defies the normal way of doing things. It makes them uncomfortable. That's why they react so vehemently, but I take that as a positive sign. Only truly daring ideas really piss people off. For instance, a few years ago I came up with the idea for an Internet-based world along the lines of Second Life, except that players could navigate through a virtual Hollywood and wind up on the red carpet being interviewed by Mom and me. After our stint on the real red carpet came to an end, I built a team of wickedly smart people and started looking for funding to create this virtual world. You would have thought I had announced I was applying for sex reassignment surgery. My advisors started calling the project Melissa's Folly. Well, Melissa's Folly secured funding and actually launched before we decided to put the project on hold because of the tough economy.

My best red carpet example of the "You're Out of Your %$#@& Mind" Law in action involves Cybill Shepherd. Cybill has gone from being the starlet in *The Last Picture Show* who slept with Elvis to a poised forty-year showbiz veteran and Emmy winner. At the 1985 Emmys, she created one of the most audacious red carpet moments ever.

Cybill has short toes and an irregular heel, so for her, most pumps are torture instruments worthy of Torquemada. As she was in her limo on the way to the awards that year, nominated for *Moonlighting*, she was wearing Day-Glo orange high-top sneakers for comfort. Her plan was to put the pumps on for the red carpet walk and grit her teeth. But when the time came to get out of the limo, she hesitated. These were the days when you had to be at the auditorium all five hours of the show—her feet would be screaming. Should she just wear the high-tops? Everyone else in the limo was yelling, "No, you can't!"

She could and did. Cybill walked up the carpet in her orange sneakers. The press went nuts. "I felt as if half the women there wished they had worn their sneakers," she says. "I felt like the other half hated me. In some ways it was the most important

THE GOSPEL ACCORDING TO JOAN

I think you trust your gut instincts and then you also do your research. Gut instincts can also be very wrong. There have been people who I have liked in the beginning who I found in the end were not what I thought they were, and vice versa. Usually your gut is right, but in this kind of a business, you can never go purely by gut instinct. However, if you don't like somebody at the start, you're probably right. There are very few surprises in this world.

thing I have ever done." Make no mistake, the shoes looked awful, but that didn't matter. Some people applauded, some booed, but the sky didn't fall. Today Cybill says, "The most outrageous thing you can do on the red carpet is tell the truth. It took me ten years to be myself on the red carpet or a talk show."

Great Moments in Trusting One's Gut

So many aspects of human endeavor—art, business, inventing—are practically defined by the maverick genius going against conventional wisdom and trusting his or her intuition to bring about some incredible new idea. It's a stereotype for a reason: Nails that stick out get hammered down, so you've got to be inhumanly persistent to bring a new idea to fruition, especially when you're surrounded by people insisting it will never work. As Malcolm Gladwell writes in his bestseller *Blink,* the gut is always a powerful voice, and listening to it usually pays dividends. Some of my favorite examples:

- From the time he started his animation company, Walt Disney had been doing things like mortgaging his home to keep it running. When in 1937 he told his staff he was going to make the first feature-length animated film, *Snow White and the Seven Dwarfs,* his associates were aghast, warning him that it would bankrupt Disney Studios. The film was a smash that took home an Oscar. But in 1948, with the studio again deep in debt, Disney went public with his plans to build a utopian theme park, Disneyland, in a field in Anaheim, California. His brother and partner, Roy, among others, thought he'd lost his mind, but Walt mortgaged everything he owned, including his animation company, to build his park—and, of course, it remains a resounding success. "If you can dream it, you can do it," Disney was known to say.

- Donald Trump, who has made, lost, and remade more fortunes than you or I will ever see, says that relying on his gut is one of his keys to making profitable decisions that also have the advantage of surprising the competition. "I'm a great believer in asking everyone for an opinion before I make a decision," he says. "I ask I ask I ask, until I begin to get a gut feeling about something. And that's when I make a decision. I have learned much more from conducting my own random surveys than I could ever have learned from the greatest of consulting firms." Of course, you've got to have the nerve to follow your gut when billions of dollars are on the line.

- Producer Jerry Bruckheimer says that his main criterion for choosing which films to make is his gut feeling about the project, not the script, the actors, or whether it fits in with a popular trend. His string of box-office hits includes *Beverly Hills Cop, Top Gun, Armageddon, National Treasure,* and *Pirates of the Caribbean,* to name a few. That's . . . pretty good.

- Jeff Bezos started his online store in 1995 and rode the first wave of Internet craziness to a big net worth and a lot of publicity, but naysayers everywhere insisted that his only prayer was to sell the business to Microsoft or some other major player. You couldn't make money selling books and other merchandise on the Internet, the experts insisted; the margins were too low and there was too much competition. Somehow, Bezos kept things afloat, fended off his critics, and never lost faith in his "customer obsessed" company. Today, it's the undisputed king of Internet retailers and one of the strongest brands in the world. Its name? Amazon.com.

One of the better Hollywood examples of trusting the gut and riding it to wild success is the story of how, when they were planning to make a live-action movie about a mermaid who washes up on shore and falls in love with a New York business owner, Brian Grazer and Ron Howard rejected hundreds of better-known actors their financial partners wanted. Their choice for the role in *Splash* was an actor whose main exposure to that point had been the sitcom *Bosom Buddies:* Tom Hanks. Twenty years later Hanks is a superstar and Imagine Entertainment is a hit-making machine.

But forget Hollywood and Wall Street. No matter what circles you run in, life is full of times—some of them full-fledged Red Carpet Moments—when you have to know whether you should trust your gut. That inner guide speaks up when you meet a potential date for the first time and size him up based on subtle cues that your conscious mind might not even be aware of. It flashes when you're looking at your newly minted bachelor's degree and pondering a question as old as mankind itself: "Do I go for the safe, fallback career or drive my parents nuts and chase my dream as a performance artist?" Bells go off when you're shopping for clothing and wondering if you should follow the latest trend or go for what you know makes you look great. (Hint: Go for what works regardless of what's on the magazine covers.) In the midst of high-pressure Red Carpet Moments, your gut usually knows the right thing to say or the right gesture to make. When you can't think, but only react, you've got to have honed instincts you can depend on.

If you've made a habit of suppressing your instincts up to now, this might be a good time to start paying attention to them and seeing if that helps you make more successful decisions about people, jobs, fashion, or what have you. At the same time, you've got to know when *not* to trust your gut. Here's why: When it's not serving as an early warning system, your gut can hold you in a comfort zone that's preventing you from growing out and growing up. Instinct can reinforce habits that lock us in a box, afraid to break out and try a new career or take a risk that might end up enhancing our lives. Let's say you encounter a job opportunity that's outside your professional training but that you find fascinating. It would require you to move to a different city and jump into something unknown, but your passionate side is utterly smitten by the idea. Then your gut speaks up and says, "Wait, play it safe, stick to what you know." You retreat into that cloistered place and ignore your passion . . . and you usually regret it.

Basically, it's important to know when you should and shouldn't listen to your instincts. If they're based on a healthy history, then you can probably trust them. However, if you were royally screwed by a past lover and now your gut tells you that you should distrust all men, you may want to consider collecting more evidence before you react on instinct alone.

SWEPT UNDER THE CARPET

One of the first years I was at the Oscars, I was up in my tower near the limo drop-off, so I could see who was coming on the carpet. Up pulled this limo a short distance from the end of the red carpet. Someone tried to open the door from within, and I saw a lovely gloved arm reach out the window and pull the door shut. The car inched forward and the same thing happened again. And again. And again. By this time I was itching to know what was going on. Finally, the limo was precisely at the end of the red carpet. This time the door swung open and out came the beautiful arm followed by the rest of Sharon Stone, looking resplendent. She had engineered her drop-off down to the millimeter. That's called making an entrance.

The Wreck of the Juan Valdez

What can happen when your rational mind and your instinct aren't in sync? Bad, bad decisions that can haunt you for years. For instance, in 1962, the head of Decca Records told Beatles manager Brian Epstein, "Guitar groups are on their way out, Mr. Epstein." There's no record of what purgatory that gent was banished to, but I bet it wasn't distant enough to avoid hearing the eight years of mega-hits that followed as the greatest rock band in history signed with the label then known as Parlophone.

When your instincts are off, you turn down the lead in *Pretty Woman,* as Molly Ringwald did. While I can't see the star of *The Breakfast Club* slutting around with Richard Gere, the role did launch Julia Roberts's career while Molly has been pretty invisible for the past fifteen years. Something was clearly off-kilter when Mel Gibson said no to *Gladiator,* the role that made Russell Crowe a superstar. Instead, Mel has gone down a rather . . . odd . . . path in the last few years. Hollywood lore is filled with stories of actors rejecting roles that would have sent their careers into the stratosphere.

Even after my marital fiasco, I'm still learning to listen to my intuition. Just when you think you've got a crystal-clear signal going between your gut and your conscious mind, the call gets dropped and you make a decision you know you will regret. It's humbling. In September 2007 I was asked to make a personal appearance for the Colombian Coffee Federation, the people with Juan Valdez as their symbol. They wanted me to walk the red carpet at the *Us Weekly* "Hot Hollywood" Party. This set off warning alarms that would have drowned out a 747. The Hot Hollywood Party was pretty much reserved for sexy young things like Vanessa Anne Hudgens and Zac Efron. I felt uncomfortable with the whole thing. I wasn't part of the under-twenty-five club-hopping crowd anymore; I knew I didn't belong there.

My instinct was screaming, "Turn it down!" But my agent soothed my nerves, saying that all I had to do was walk the red carpet and pose for a few pictures. Piece of cake, right? Maybe you're worrying about nothing, my intellect rationalized. My desire center kicked in: The money was good. I agreed to take the job, but I would deeply regret not paying attention to my gut.

A few nights later I arrived at the party. Fans and paparazzi lined the red carpet and flashes were going off everywhere. I stepped out of my limo to shouts of "Melissa! Melissa!" I smiled; maybe this wouldn't be so bad. God, was I mistaken. Hitting the carpet right before me had been Amanda Bynes wearing an outrageously small "bandage dress" that left nothing to the imagination. She was working the red carpet and wouldn't leave, so I was stuck standing there, waiting. Behind me, another limo pulled up and Kanye West stepped out, looking sleek and gorgeous. Everybody went crazy for him, and suddenly I realized that I was standing between these two young stars and no one was taking my picture. The fans and photographers couldn't have cared less about me.

The truth I'd tried to deny hit home like a spike between the eyes: To youth-obsessed Hollywood, I was over the hill and irrelevant. I felt the blood rush to my face, turned around, got back in my limo, and told my agent, "Get me the hell out of here." Then I sobbed all the way home. Worse yet, I had to go in the next day and face the client, which I did, because that's what you do when you're a professional . . . and when the check has cleared.

KNOW-IT-ALL

Samantha Daniels, Matchmaker, Founder of
Samantha's Table and author of
Matchbook: The Diary of a Modern-Day Matchmaker

My business is very instinctual. One of the reasons I'm a good matchmaker is that I have good instincts about people.

Your instincts will give you a broad picture of someone—is he good or bad for you? But at the same time, you have to trust your own instincts. Look at yourself and understand why you react at a gut level in certain ways to certain people. If you don't trust anyone, or you're basing your instincts on past experiences that don't apply to the present, then you probably can't trust your gut to guide you.

Chemistry is a tangible thing. When you meet someone, if you feel instinctively that this person might be good for you, it's probably best to give them a chance. Instinct is great for knowing if you're interested, but over the long term you have to be more strategic. I wouldn't depend on instinct for choosing someone to marry, for instance.

What I find is that many of the people I work with have a laundry list of what they're looking for in a partner, but that chemistry trumps everything. You might want a certain height, a certain income, or an Ivy League education, but it's better to trust your instincts and "go for" someone who intrigues you rather than sit back and wait for the perfect person to drop into your lap.

How You Know You Can Trust Your Gut

If I had listened to my gut about that appearance instead of allowing my agent to talk me into doing it, I would have spared myself a lot of humiliation. Of course, that's a cop-out. The chief lesson about following your gut is that no one can talk you into anything. You talk yourself into it and blame your friends or associates for "making you" go on the date or take the job. I've learned this the hard way, which is why I keep my own counsel now. You have only yourself to blame when you ignore your gut and go down the wrong road—but at the same time, you get to bask in the glow when you follow your gut despite what everyone else is saying and you're proven right. That's fun.

How do you know if you can trust your instincts to lead you in the right direction? A few telltale signs:

• *You're not impulsive.* There's a difference between instinct and irresponsible impulse that you *blame* on instinct. If you're in a store and you covet something, think about if you'll really use it. If you have to think about it, put it on hold. If you're still unsure a couple of days later, then forget it. You didn't really want it. This is a great check on impulsive behavior. If you can manage this sort of control, then you can probably trust your instincts not to lead you into debt or romantic disaster.

• *You're not defensive about your "gut decisions."* Once you've chosen your path, you don't get your back up when people tell you that you're crazy or question your judgment. That's a sign of confidence in your inner voice; you're secure that you've got good balance between your "I want" side and your "Be careful" side. It's only people who don't really trust their gut who get mad and start doubting themselves when people say, "Are you sure?" over and over again.

• *You learn from your mistakes.* A therapist friend once told me a great parable about how we learn from our screwups in love and life. You're walking down a street and suddenly you fall into a hole. Damn, you say, and you scramble out and keep walking. A while later, you fall into another hole, this one a little deeper. Wow, how did that happen? you ask, and climb out and keep walking along the same street. Time passes and you tumble into yet *another* hole. This one's even deeper, and now you're angry. It takes some time to climb out and you blithely continue walking. Eventually you tumble into a fourth hole, the deepest yet. Now you're really mad at yourself. You struggle and claw and finally escape. Then you walk down a different street.

If you keep falling into holes—dating the same jerks or sticking with a job you hate—you're not following your gut. When you're learning from your past, facing the hard truth about poor choices, and moving on to make better ones, that's called wisdom, and it's not cheap. You pay for it with all those bruises you got from falling.

• *You find opportunities no one else can.* One of the best stories in the publishing business is what Mark Victor Hansen and Jack Canfield had to do to get their first book published. They had this cool idea for a book of touching stories, but no publisher wanted to buy it. They spent years shopping it, agents quit on them, and finally, after pitching it to more than 130 publishers, they found one that was interested. That little book was *Chicken Soup for the Soul*. More than a hundred books in the series and countless licensed products later, they sold the franchise in 2008 for eight figures. Bravo.

When you defy conventional wisdom and really believe in something that no one else will pursue, it's amazing what kind of opportunities you can create seemingly out of thin air. I'm not just talking about business, either. Dating someone

RED CARPET RULES

Meeting the Parents

- Always err on the side of conservative the first time around. Keep the conversation light. I have a tendency to swear—a lot. My friends and their parents know I'm going to drop F-bombs. A date's parents don't.

- No miniskirts or stripper heels. If you think your blouse is cut too low, it is.

- Be respectful. If you don't like them, remember it's just a few hours. Anybody can keep her shit together for brunch.

- Give the first meeting a predetermined beginning and ending time. This gives you an escape hatch if things are miserable, but allows you some flexibility if you're having fun. A friend made the mistake of keeping the first meeting open-ended, and her mother proved to be a nightmare. Kiss that relationship good-bye.

- Be honest with your date about your parents—their views, their habits, if they pass gas liberally, whatever. "Dad's going to smoke his cigar throughout the meal, just so you know" is fine.

- At the same time, don't be hypercritical. I have a girlfriend who moved cross-country to be with a man and she was taken aback when he trashed his parents before their first get-together. She got to know his folks and really liked them, but his criticism made her wonder about their son.

- Clarify the ground rules going in, like "Don't talk politics" or "Don't criticize my mom to me." Be clear so that everybody knows what's kosher and what's not.

- Keep in mind that everyone has an off day.

everyone tells you is wrong for you but who your gut tells you is right can turn into a lifelong relationship. Pursuing the career that you're driven to go for instead of the one that keeps Mom and Dad from worrying about you can give you a lifestyle that other people only dream about. When your instincts lead you to walk ground that few others will tread, don't be surprised when you end up somewhere new and unexpected.

Also, don't be surprised when people follow you in droves saying, "I always knew this was a good idea!"

How You Know You Can't Trust Your Gut

Some people just shouldn't be trusted with life decisions. A few young pop singers and actresses come to mind, but this isn't limited to them. There are just some people who overintellectualize everything and who need an empirical justification for every decision. If they're forced to act on instinct, they're like a deer in the headlights of a Greyhound bus. There's nothing inherently wrong with being that way . . . as long as you know you shouldn't trust your intuition and don't act based on it. Because living by poor instincts can be ugly.

Are you gut-challenged? Here are some signs:

• *You've made repeated bad calls.* If you keep making the same mistakes over and over after following your gut, your gut may not be so smart. Remember Cuba Gooding Jr.? Well, since winning the Oscar for *Jerry Maguire,* he's shown an incredible nose for bad scripts. *Harold*? *Daddy Day Camp*? Cuba, I've got nothing but love for you, man, but what up? If you're in a hole, stop digging. If you keep getting your heart broken, ask yourself why you keep choosing the same kind of person.

- *Paralysis by analysis.* You're presented with a decision that might involve trusting your instincts—say, leaving a so-so job for one that offers vastly greater opportunity but also might disappear in a year. You spend weeks obsessively researching everything you can find on the new company, asking everyone you know for advice, and Googling the phrase "difficult career decisions." You're petrified to make a move without feeling that you have all the data you need, but you can never have enough data because data's not your trouble. You don't trust your gut and you're paralyzed. Eventually, the company offers the gig to somebody else.

- *You give up too easily.* I gave up on calling off my wedding in the face of all the implied pressure that came with invitations being ordered, a dress being designed, and all the rest. If you make a call from your gut and then, as soon as someone gives you that inevitable "Are you out of your mind?" look, you back down and change course, then you're way out of touch with your instincts. Either learn to trust them by taking baby steps, quit telling other people about your decisions so you don't encounter the peer pressure, or quit listening to your gut.

Go Shallow

Remember, I'm a charter member of the Shallowness Fan Club. You should be developing your instincts by making decisions about things that aren't life-altering: clothing, accessories, makeup, and so on (though I know some stylists who will insist that every one of those is of world-shaking importance). When you know you can trust your inner voice to give you sound advice—and that you can balance passion, reason, and instinct before you take out your credit card—you're ready to move on to guys, careers, kids, and life. Consider the boutiques, malls, parties, and clubs of the world your boot camp. It's hell, I know, but life's lessons can be grueling.

Some advice on prospering as you wade instinct-first into the shallow end of the pool:

• *When your friends tell you it doesn't fit, take it off.* I've fallen in love with so many gowns over the years that I call myself a dress whore. But that's dangerous, because you can easily fall in love with something and not realize that on you, it looks hideous. That's why you should always go shopping with a friend you trust. Ask her to rate you "Hot or Not" in anything you're considering buying, especially if it's expensive. Your gut can lie to you. A good friend won't.

• *Go to affairs where you don't know anybody.* Instinctively, we tend to go to parties and events where we already know people, because then we're not faced with the awkwardness of making small talk and meeting new people. But then how do you make fascinating new friends? Just once, RSVP "no thanks" to the party where you know everyone and attend an occasion where you're likely to know nobody. Then trust your gut to tell you who to chat up. You might start a wonderful new relationship . . . or at least get some great new gossip.

• *Know when you're too old for a pierced tongue.* Sometimes, following your gut can make you appear like a rebel. That's fine, but know if your brand of rebellion is age-appropriate. If you're in your late thirties and work in a law office, and your gut is telling you that the best way to feel youthful is to dye your hair purple, you might want to think again. You don't want your instinct to lead you in a direction that's going to make you feel foolish. Wearing jungle print underwear and getting your tongue pierced so you can wear a stud in it after-hours? Sure, go for it.

• **_If you hate your hairstyle, go to a new stylist._** I can't believe how many women I know who complain about

RED CARPET RULES
Apologizing

- Don't apologize via e-mail or text message. That's cowardly. The phone is okay if you can't get face time or just know you'll fall apart in person.

- Don't attack. Take responsibility for what you did and try to see it from the other person's perspective.

- Trust your gut about the need to apologize. If you think you need to say, "I'm sorry," then you do.

- Don't qualify what you did. Saying, "But I never would have done it if you hadn't . . ." is a great way to turn a misunder-standing into a war.

- Keep it clear, short, and sincere, and then move on. Know when to shut up.

- Flowers or a small gift never hurt, as long as they're not seen as a bribe in place of a real apology.

- Plan what you're going to say ahead of time—at least the major points—but leave room for spontaneity.

- Once you're done, give the other person a chance to respond. If you've got a tongue-lashing coming, take it like a grown-up.

their haircuts then keep going back to the same stylist again and again! Ladies, if you're sick of the same cut, ask around and try somebody new. Speak up and tell the stylist what you want to look like—what you would look like in your perfect magazine cover photo shoot. If it's not right, try someone new the next time. The great thing about hair is that it grows back.

• *Leave before the date goes bad.* How often have you heard this? "Well, we went to the trouble and he's paying, so I figured I'd just finish the date." News flash: If you're on a date and you're not having a good time, chances are the other person isn't, either. Cut your losses, be honest, thank him, call a cab, and go home before things get unpleasant. Don't consume precious hours of your life on a date that's going nowhere.

Deep in Your Gut

Then we come to the big life decisions—whom to love, where to live, what do to. Once you've mastered the shallow aspect of trusting your gut, you're ready to turn your finely honed instincts into a tool to aid you in making the choices that will shape your future, guide your health and safety, and affect your relationships. No pressure, right? Hey, you're not in this alone. I'm proud to say that I've become an advanced practitioner of the art of trusting my gut and letting it guide me into—and out of—some of my life's most rewarding situations. And there are several tricks I've learned over the years that have helped me turn my inner voice into an ally and use it to make better decisions:

• *Don't second-guess yourself.* Remember when you took the SAT? Your instinctive first answer was usually right, and it still is. If you find a guy creepy for no apparent reason, don't go out with him. If you're not comfortable walking across an empty parking lot at night, don't. Don't be embarrassed to tell someone who asks, "Why did you change your mind?" that something just didn't "feel right." That's a legitimate reason. Don't apologize for trusting yourself.

• *Be adaptable.* Rushing headlong after something your gut tells you is right may seem romantic, but it's not always practical. Be flexible and, when it's appropriate, try to find a middle ground between chasing after what you want and being able to pay the bills, especially if other people depend on you. Don't back down but don't be inflexible, either. There's a difference between being courageously driven by your inner voice and being obstinate. You might want to be Joan of Arc, but remember that she was burned at the stake.

• *Learn to assess how intensely your gut is speaking to you.* Sometimes our instincts just whisper to us; other times they shriek like Sarah Michelle Gellar in a *Scream* movie. It's not only important to learn to recognize where your gut is leading you, but also how strongly it's communicating. If you're about to confide in someone you know with very private and potentially damaging personal information and your inner voice is waving its arms and hollering, "Don't tell her! She's going to spill your secret before lunchtime and make you sound like a tramp!" then pay attention.

• *If more than three people give you the same advice independently, take it.* This is a big one. Independent corroboration, as journalists say, is the hallmark of truth. If three people whose judgment you respect, but who don't know one another, take you to lunch and tell you you're wasting your life in your job, you'd better take that seriously. Once is chance, twice is a trend, three times is a consensus. Plus, not only do you get great advice but three free lunches.

• **_If you have to ask the question, you know the answer._** I know a woman who for eighteen years constantly asked, "Should I divorce my husband?" Eighteen years! Talk about wasting your life away. The obvious answer was "Yes!" If you harbor doubts or fears strong enough to raise traumatic questions about your life, then you've already decided what you should do. You just need the courage to do it, and that can take some time. Please don't let it take eighteen years. By the way, the lady finally divorced her husband, but how much better off would she have been if she'd been able to pull the trigger about fifteen years earlier?

Trusting your gut is a matter of trial and error. Nobody is born wise. People who "have great instincts" have usually been knocked into the dirt so many times following their instincts that they had to become better at it or they would never have gotten up. The key is, don't be afraid to trust yourself, whether the issue is clothes and cars or marriage and kids. You're going to make some bad calls, but you're going to learn. And your gut can lead you to some incredible places you never thought you'd go. That's what makes life cool.

Show Grace Under Pressure

Courage is grace under pressure.

—ERNEST HEMINGWAY

*I*n November 2006, Ellen Barkin and some friends were having a nice night out at the Waverly Inn in New York. At least, it was nice until Ellen saw her recent and much-loathed ex-husband, jewelry billionaire Ron Perelman, advancing toward her table. The divorce had been anything but amicable, with Perelman having Ellen removed from his lavish Sixty-third Street mansion a month before, and it was about to get uglier.

The accounts vary, as they always do when there are many eyewitnesses and many rooting interests. But one thing remains clear: As Perelman approached Ellen's table, she warned him to stay away, and when he got too close, she flung a full glass of ice water in his face. Some say he was moving in for an unwanted kiss; others say he was headed for the little boy's room and her table was in the path. Either way, New York gossip history was made, and as she hurried from the restaurant, Ellen stopped by Perelman's table and hit his psychotherapist date with this parting line: "I feel sorry for you that you have to f—k him tonight."

That is *not* necessarily what I would call acting with grace under pressure. Did Ms. Barkin enjoy the hell out of it? Of course she did. Did her ex deserve a dousing? Maybe, maybe not. But in the red carpet world, doing what feels righteous in the moment doesn't count. What does count is showing grace in situations where the pressure is on and all eyes are glued to you. As good as delivering that ice water bath must have felt to Ellen at the time, I'll bet she woke up the next morning hating herself for it. But it was a moment that almost every one of us has dreamed of living, and Ellen Barkin was just about the only woman who could get away with it and get a standing ovation from the masses. We were all living vicariously through her.

When Your Nipple Shows, Smile

If Ellen Barkin had shown the red carpet version of grace under pressure, she would have ignored her ex as he walked by. She would have killed him with class. The lesson of showing grace under pressure is just this: You never win when you freak out, lose your cool, break down when adversity comes, or turn into a raving lunatic over a minor inconvenience. I agree with the statement that "adversity doesn't build character, it reveals it." When you fail or things don't go your way, how you handle the situation—both in the moment and after you've had time to think things over—says more about your character than almost anything else. The choices you make when the shit hits the fan can leave a deep impression. For instance, do you think more people will remember Russell Crowe for his Oscar or for the phone he threw at a hotel clerk in a fit of childish rage? My point exactly.

In Hollywood and in life, stuff happens. Most of the time it's minor and embarrassing, like a stray breast falling out of the top of your dress. Other times, it's major—a lawsuit or a divorce or a project you've invested years in falling apart overnight. Failure is normal: The best baseball players get a hit only one out of three times, and four out of the five Oscar nominees are going home with an empty space in their guts where that gold statue should have been. All you can do is show grace under pressure. And here's an important fact to remember: *Most people won't know about your humiliation or failure unless you clue them in by acting like the world is ending.* The exception would be the public nipple slip, which will be YouTube masturbation material before you can say "cease and desist order." The only thing you can do is tuck that stray mammary back where it belongs, smile, and keep your chin up.

Grace under pressure means that when you're embarrassed, grieving, or get hit by a bolt of misfortune from the blue, you don't act as if you were the one person who was supposed to be exempt, like you had some sort of Get Out of Humiliation Free card. I'm sure you've seen people like this: They're so certain of their own brilliance and superiority (like some coddled entertainers and athletes, maybe they've had people in their lives making sure they never had to deal with consequences) that when an inevitable reversal hits, they're stunned. Frozen. Then they're enraged. How dare the universe do this to me? Don't the gods know who I am? When you react to failure or misfortune this way, three things are virtually guaranteed:

a. You're going to make a fool of yourself.
b. You're going to overreact and make the problem worse.
c. You're going to alienate people who could otherwise help you.

Here's how it should be done. In 1997, Minnie Driver arrived at the Oscars alone and everyone knew what was going on. She had, of course, starred in *Good Will Hunting* and had been dating Matt Damon at the time, and she was a nominee as well. Well, a few weeks before the Academy Awards, Matt had broken up with her. It happens. But now she had to show up with billions of people watching, sit right behind her ex-boyfriend, and smile and clap as he and Ben Affleck won the award for Original Screenplay. Poor Minnie must have been shrieking inside, but you would never have known it. She looked sleek and fabulous and was as nice as she could be. Did she fall apart as soon as she got in her limo where no one could see her? Probably. But not in public.

We all want to lose it. We all want to scream at God. You really, really want to throw a drink in your ex-boyfriend's face after he cheated on you with your best friend. But you can't. Acting with dignity and poise is the best revenge. After the Oscars, everybody was Minnie's best friend. They all commented on how classy and cool she was, and Matt Damon was tarred and feathered a little, though he really is a decent guy. The point is, Minnie didn't let them see her sweat and she was lauded for it. You've got to be a gracious winner and a gracious loser. Only one person in a thousand has the genius-level talent to get away with being a vase-throwing, high-maintenance prima donna.

Put On Your Big-Girl Panties and Deal

Grace under pressure also means doing what you need to do when you'd rather crawl into a hole and hide. Remember the Juan Valdez story? I had to suck it up and meet with the client the day after my humiliation in front of the Hot Hollywood

Party, so I did. Why didn't I just have my agent tell the client I was sick? Because when you're a grown-up and a professional you step up to the plate, even if the bases are loaded and your knees are shaking. You do what you've got to do, especially when people are depending on you, even when the whole world is looking.

In 1995, Jane Seymour was up for a Golden Globe for *Dr. Quinn, Medicine Woman*. Six weeks before the event, she had given birth to twins. The night of the awards show, she wore an original Pamela Barish red silk satin dress, a crazy decision after having two babies—especially when you're still nursing.

Well, she won, went up to the podium with her statuette, and thanked her babies for having given her a break from breast-feeding. "I looked at all these famous faces; the movie people were up front," she says. "I had just mentioned I had twins weeks ago, and I had on this slinky dress, and I had these enormous boobs. Then suddenly, my milk came in. I grabbed my award and held my head high until I was safely off camera." As someone who's done red carpet events while lactating like a Guernsey cow, I'm right there with you, sister.

Life is full of times when you have to suck it up and do what has to be done even though you're furious, embarrassed, or brokenhearted. You're in a meeting and someone throws you a curveball question that you have no idea how to answer. You have to walk into your workplace when everyone knows that you were just turned down for the big promotion, smile, sit down at your desk, and do your job. You run into your ex at a social event with his or her new significant other. Or, in a personal example, your TV show doesn't get picked up. When Mom and I were let go by TV Guide, everyone was asking me, "What are you going to do now?" I learned an important lesson after that experience:

Sometimes it's okay not to have a plan for what comes next. Just get through today with as much grace and composure as you can.

I had to deal with the shock of being not being renewed first. Then I could plot my magnificent comeback. There's no rule that says you have to land on your feet right away; just *look* as though you have.

MEL'S BELLES

I love Catherine Zeta-Jones: her style, her sense of knowing exactly who she is, her cool in the face of her own Oops! Moments, even her ability to bounce back after two pregnancies to be one of the most beautiful women in Hollywood . . . damn her. Not to mention her apparently crackling, joyful marriage to Michael Douglas. I adore Catherine because she always carries herself like a queen no matter where she is: on the red carpet, faced with paparazzi, even parading around the streets of Manhattan without makeup—something many top actresses would never dare to do. She has chutzpah, intelligence, and, as we saw in *Chicago*, a great deal of talent as a singer and dancer as well. She seems to have it all. I'd hate her guts if she wasn't so impossible to dislike.

Don't Snatch Defeat from the Jaws of Victory

Often, the hardest part about staying cool and collected during tough times is that it denies you instant gratification. It's one thing for me to say, "Take the high road, it will pay off in the long run," and another to find out that a coworker stole your idea and presented it to the CEO as her own. It's very tempting to say, "Screw restraint, Melissa, I'm throwing the chair through the window!" And yeah, that self-righteous adrenaline rush feels better than sex. You feel like Sigourney Weaver in *Aliens* when she tells the alien queen, "Get away from her, you bitch!" If only that high lasted. But it never does.

The truth is, being professional and soldiering on through your anger or grief can bring rewards that go far beyond just knowing you acted with class. But that means delaying the visceral buzz that comes with throwing something or screaming at somebody and instead looking at the long-term picture. Keep your cool and behave with maturity and you can snatch victory from what appeared to be the jaws of defeat.

Last year, I was asked to do a guest appearance for a new reality show. The catch: The show was about the search for the next great stylist, making it a carbon copy of a show I had created and produced for TV Guide as a special but that never aired. I was not happy about this. I went to work and I was grumbly. After the producers threw out the usual "We're so glad to have you here" platitudes, I calmly dropped the Big One: "You know, this is a direct copy of a show I created at TV Guide. If you were so glad to have me, you would have made me a regular panelist or host." All the oxygen suddenly left the room. You could have heard a career drop. Sabrina, my ever-marvelous right-hand woman, shot me a look that said, "What the hell are you doing, girl?"

What was I doing? I was letting them know I was not to be trifled with, but once I made my point, I moved on. The production team didn't know what to say, so I started talking about what they wanted me to do. Relieved, they got back into their groove. More important, when I taped the show, I hit the ball out of the park. When things ran late, I smiled and said, "No problem." The producer immediately asked me to come back for the season finale and tried to figure out other ways they could use me. Heck, I ended up brainstorming with the production team and coming up with five new ideas for the show! I could have stormed out, but I chose not to. I let them know there was an issue, then I chose to rise above it and be the ultimate team player. I traded a short-term feeling of self-righteousness for a long-term opportunity. FYI, they used my ideas and never had me back. Typical Hollywood.

Oops! Moments Versus 911 Moments

Ahh, awards season. The scent of spring is in the air. The limos are being polished. The waiting lists for dental veneers and Botox grow long. And, inevitably, a handful of men and women will experience soul-crushing loss under the brightest spotlight imaginable. If it were a sport, there would be lions and they would ban women and children. Let's be honest, part of the drama of red carpet season is watching how the people who don't walk away with statuettes keep it together. Remember, for every winner there are four losers wondering why they spent so much money on their stupid dresses. It hurts to be rejected or denied your chance, whether you didn't get asked to homecoming, didn't get the promotion, or you're Susan Lucci being passed over for a Daytime Emmy so many times that you become a

Hollywood cliché. Some of the better-known grace under pressure moments from past awards seasons:

• At the 2005 Emmys, Eva Longoria was the only lead actress in *Desperate Housewives* not to be nominated. The emcee poked fun at her, and to her credit Eva played right along even though she had to be dying inside. She just smiled and cheered when her castmates won. The Emmy voters paid her back for her class the following year, when she was nominated.

• The same thing happened with *Will and Grace* in two different years. One year the entire lead cast was nominated except for Eric McCormack. The next year, Debra Messing was the one on the outside looking in. No matter. You cheer for your team even if you were the guy who just dropped the ball. Eric and Debra had to and they did.

• And yes, after being nominated nineteen times without winning, Susan Lucci finally took home the Daytime Emmy for Outstanding Actress in 1999. In her acceptance speech, no one would have blamed her for indulging in a little indignation at the podium. But instead, she thanked everyone under the sun and concluded by saying, "I'm going to go back to that studio Monday and I'm going to play Erica Kane for all she's worth."

I don't know this for a fact, but I'd like to think one reason these and other celebrities who have handled themselves with such class is that they kept things in perspective. They knew that at the end of the day, nobody was dying. Homes weren't burning. That's vital. Is your Red Carpet Moment, the one when you've got to show grace under pressure, an Oops! Moment, when the worst thing that can happen is that you'll be red-faced? Or is it a 911 Moment, when someone's life, health, job, or marriage is at stake? If you don't know the difference, you're liable to spend all your rage and energy on the small things and have nothing left in the tank for dealing with the real-life disasters.

Just so we're clear, here's the difference between "Oh, damn," and "Call 911!"

Oops! Moments

• **Wardrobe malfunctions.** At those same 1997 Oscars where she showed such post-Damon poise, Minnie Driver was sashaying down the red carpet in a smashing red Randolph Duke dress, and I'll never forget the look on her face as her dress suddenly fell well below her bosom while she was in the photo line. She distracted the cameras with her smile and quickly got her "golden globes" back in order. It was a rough night for Minnie, but she handled it beautifully.

• **Losing things.** One year when Whoopi Goldberg was hosting the Oscars, she nearly had a heart attack because she thought she'd lost a multimillion-dollar necklace. But she kept it together onstage and found the necklace in her cleavage after a costume change. Now that's accessorizing.

• **Dumb mistakes.** One year at the Oscars, Jenny McCarthy wore a Valentino dress with an *extremely* revealing sheer front panel—so much so that even Hollywood was buzzing about how inappropriate the dress was. And a few days later Valentino himself issued a public statement saying that the dress was fine—Jenny had put it on *backward*. Ouch. She smiled as if to say, "What a dumb blonde I am!"

• **Screwups on the job.** My mother, God bless her, has committed her share of gaffes in fifty years in the business. One year on the red carpet, we were live on camera and things were chaotic. Mom screamed, "What the fuck is going on here?" I froze like a deer in the headlights while the phones lit up. But the worst was at the Oscars when she interviewed Sir Anthony

Hopkins, always the picture of style and elegance. Everything was going fine until Mom addressed the elderly looking woman standing next to Sir Anthony by saying, "How nice it is for you to share the night with your mother." Anthony calmly informed her that the woman was not his mother but his *wife*. I don't know how Mom did it, but she kept her composure and finished the interview. I would have crawled under the red carpet and begged the Teamsters to trample me into a paste.

• ***Breakups.*** It feels like the end of the world, but you can and will survive. In the wake of their bitter 2006 divorce, both Charlie Sheen and Denise Richards went a little nuts. Charlie was called on the carpet for an obscene 2005 voice-mail tirade that even seasoned Hollywood gossipers found over the top, while Denise tried to recapture some limelight with her own reality series, immediately alienating her neighbors and being accused of exploiting her kids.

911 Moments

These are the moments that change your life forever. You'll get over not winning the award or not getting the job you thought you had in the bag, but these leave scars:

• ***Infidelity.*** You'd think Hollywood would be blasé about marriages. After all, they come and go like the wind. But I guess we all believe in the fairy tale (which is kind of sweet), so we're all bummed when a great couple like Jimmy Kimmel and Sarah Silverman split, and we're all devastated when so-and-so is caught with so-and-so. This is a heart-stopper, and nobody faces the grace under pressure test like the cuckold. If you can keep your composure when everybody in the world finds out the one you trusted has been screwing someone else, you have my undying admiration.

Take Hillary Clinton. I don't know how she did it when the whole world knew her husband had been *schtupping* an intern in the White House. Same with Silda Wall Spitzer, wife of former New York governor Eliot Spitzer, who was caught with his hand in the prostitute jar, or Elizabeth Edwards, who found out about John's affair with a campaign aide—while she was fighting cancer. These women set their jaws and didn't miss a step during what has to be the most searing humiliation a person can endure. Incredible.

- **Divorce.** Been there, done that. My divorce from John was as public as our wedding, and it was exceedingly painful—not because I regretted the end of our marriage, but because I lamented my poor judgment and my inability to see what was going to happen, despite the signs. But I sucked it up and found two blessings. One was, of course, my Cooper. The second was some hard-earned personal insight. Because of that experience, I'm learning how to change the patterns that made my past relationships dysfunctional. As I reluctantly get older, I'm getting smarter. I hear the same thing from a lot of women and men around my age, which is one of the reasons I think everybody loves *Desperate Housewives:* They're just as clueless as the rest of us.

- **Disease.** Nothing prepares you for facing your mortality and finding out you're as vulnerable as anyone else—especially if you're rich, famous, and successful. However, some people don't let health catastrophe stop them. After his awful accident, Christopher Reeve acted, directed, and became a fierce advocate for spinal research. TV producer and NBC executive Brandon Tartikoff worked ceaselessly for twenty-five years after being diagnosed with Hodgkin's disease. Magic Johnson hasn't let HIV stop him from becoming a major entrepreneur who's trying to bring thriving businesses into inner-city neighborhoods. The list goes on.

• *Sudden death.* Sadly, I know about this one, too. When I graduated from Penn, I was still swimming against a rip current of grief over my father's suicide. It would have been a whole lot easier for me to hibernate for a while, sit on the beach and think, and tell everyone I was "finding myself." But instead, I went to work at shows like *Rescue 911,* and I did everything: logged tapes, ran errands, did research. I did every basement-level job you can do in the entertainment industry. Why? Because life goes on whether you want it to or not, and sometimes the best way to deal with the pain of someone dying is to remind yourself that you're still alive, and to honor his or her memory by really, really living. That's what I do for my father every single day.

• *Ruined career.* Trashed futures are thick on the ground in the entertainment world and every other industry. They fall to all kinds of axes: politics, grudges, downsizing, unfortunate words said in the heat of the moment, even proposed dates that somehow mutate into sexual harassment accusations. Suddenly, what you've been building is gone in a flash. Michael Jackson's career basically ended when he was accused of pedophilia. One minute he was the biggest star in the world, the next he was "Wacko Jacko." Even though he was found not guilty, the damage was done.

• *Betrayals.* The friend who tells lies about you behind your back, the colleague who spreads rumors about you so he can get the promotion—it's agony. Yeah, I know about this one, too. I was working on a big TV project a couple years back when one of my partners tried to get me kicked off the team. I rode out the storm, but it hurt like hell. A year later, the head of the network kicked my former friend out the door. As he was freaking out and venting to me, I said pointedly, "Yeah, I know how you feel." He got very quiet and I knew he knew exactly what I meant. I didn't lift a finger to prevent his ouster.

The point is, know which are the Oops! Moments and which are the 911 Moments, and harness your energies and resources appropriately.

THE GOSPEL ACCORDING TO JOAN

Grace under pressure means putting your head down and just doing what you have to do. There's a saying, "When you're in hell, walk faster." You shut up and do what you have to do to get out of the situation. When I'm onstage and I'm out to please people, if my routine isn't working, I go to a different routine. I'm out to please them; they are paying to see me, and it's not about me or my ego. That's grace under pressure.

You have to know where you are in the pecking order, what your final goal is, and never put yourself in a corner. Another thing is, when you're negotiating, never give someone the ability to say yes or no and end the negotiation. You should always give yourself and the other person a way to get out so everyone can save face.

Until You've Walked in Someone's Jimmy Choos . . .

After she appeared at the 2007 Golden Globes, Angelina Jolie was given a hard time for looking aloof and sullen. Oh, she's being a temperamental diva, people assumed. Only later did the public find out that her mother, Marcheline Bertrand, lay dying of cancer in an L.A. hospital. Brad Pitt was nominated that year, but instead of bringing up her mother's illness and pulling focus away from Brad, she kept her pain to herself and let him have his night. She took major heat for it. Takes some of the luster off the celebrity life, doesn't it? When was the last time you had to smile for the press when you had a parent on his or her deathbed, then get raked over the coals for it?

We've talked about knowing which disasters are worth screaming over and which aren't. It's also important to realize that you may never know when someone else is facing a moment that demands incredible grace under pressure. If a friend is having a rough day or seems under stress, think twice before you take it personally or criticize her. For all you know, she's keeping it together under circumstances that would make most people's knees buckle.

I learned this when I spoke with Dale Earnhardt Jr. After his father, racing legend Dale Earnhardt Sr., was killed in a crash during the last lap of the Daytona 500 in February 2001, Dale Jr. had to grieve privately while simultaneously taking over his dad's racing empire. I know Dale, and I know what it was like after my father died when I was eighteen, so I asked him how he managed to keep things going at a time when the racing world was looking to him to, in essence, step into his father's shoes.

"I would look around me and see people in pieces, and I'd say, 'Pull it together, you can't act like that,'" he says. "I would wonder if I was denying myself the remorse over my father. Was it going to hurt further on down the road? All kinds of strange things ran through my mind, but I would look around and see all kinds of people I knew, people who were close to him, just in pieces. Was I stronger, colder, and more defensive about it because of that? I don't know. People deal with death differently."

Until you've walked down a few red carpets in someone else's designer pumps, don't assume you know what they're dealing with. This works the other way, too: Don't expect everyone else to understand what you're going through or to react appropriately. Remember early on when I talked about the saying "Be a well, not a fountain"? This is what I'm talking about. Don't spill your guts to everyone you meet about how much life sucks at the moment. Everyone is carrying their own baggage, and they don't appreciate the weight of yours. Have some good people in your life upon whom you can lean, and be stoic and brave to the rest of the world. The time to break down is when you're behind closed doors and work is done, not when everyone is watching you. When you're in the spotlight, you suck it up and do whatever you have to do to keep your dignity. It's not much, but it's yours.

Work when you're sick. Take it when a boss is putting the screws to you. Refrain from strangling a superior when he or she takes credit for your great idea. Have the guts to call off your wedding even though the RSVPs have started coming in. Do what's right, not what's easy. Nobody gets a pass from the tedious, painful moments of life; even if you're a big star with personal assistants and people to buffer you from the gritty "real" world, you've got to pay your dues. Everybody has to do the hard jobs when they're hurting. No exceptions.

How You Know You're Showing Grace Under Pressure

I'm more a football than a basketball fan, but the story of Lakers guard Derek Fisher was impossible to miss. In 2007, when he was with the Utah Jazz, Fisher left the team before game one of the first round of the play-offs—as it turned out, to be with his eleven-month-old daughter when she had surgery for a rare form of eye cancer. Two days later, he flew his family back to Utah, went to the arena where his team was already playing game two, entered the game without any warm-up or preparation, and wound up hitting the game-clinching three-point shot in overtime.

It doesn't get more graceful than that. Here are some ways you know if you're acting with Fisherian poise during a tough period:

• *No one treats you differently.* That's because they don't know that your three-year lover just announced he was moving out. They don't know because you sucked it up and didn't let them know. You had your cry (and you'll have another one the next night), then blew out your hair, put on your best outfit, and went to work. You didn't gush your pain all over and expect everyone to slam the brakes on their day because you got your heart broken. You kept your trauma private and quiet.

• *Your emotions are under control.* You don't feel as if you're about to cry all the time. You're not one wrong look from flying off into a rage. You've got a strong hold on yourself. This is critical to maintaining the strong public facade you need when a Red Carpet Moment is brutal. Hollywood legend is filled with tales of divas and head cases; heck, getting cut off in traffic a few years back sparked Jack Nicholson to smash the other guy's windshield with a golf club and he ended up in court. But what does that accomplish, other than to make them look out of control and rather sad? It's much more satisfying when things feel like they're falling apart around you to know you'll be able to keep your cool when someone says something dumb or reminds you of your ex or your recently deceased loved one. You can take pride in that.

• *Your adversary is driven to distraction.* Okay, so you may not always have an adversary in tough times, like when dis-

ease or death comes to call. But when you're dealing with a relationship ending or being screwed by someone at work, the very
best thing you can do to get a touch of payback is to act as if the
whole thing has just rolled off your back. I've seen people make
themselves crazy wondering why the lover they just cheated on
and dumped wasn't more depressed. What did it mean? Did she
already have another guy? Did he make a mistake? This isn't to
say that it's fun watching someone else twist in the wind—and
possibly make a public fool of him- or herself—while you're
playing it cool as the other side of the pillow . . . but it really is,
just a little bit.

• *People's respect for you jumps a notch.* This is a big
one. We all want to be with and work with the person who keeps
his or her head when the walls of Jericho are coming down.
Everyone respects the people who tough it out and get the job
done without complaining when they just found out the tumor
was malignant or they didn't get the house. Those are the people
who earn our trust, who get asked to come back, who we call on
years later when the right opportunity comes up. We admire
people who suck it up and handle life's difficult Red Carpet
Moments with aplomb and self-possession. Even if you've
never made an impression on your coworkers, friends, or
church members in the past, you'll win allies and respect when
you persevere.

• *You create a diamond out of garbage.* This grows
directly from respect. Acting with grace under pressure is the
best way to turn bad situations into good. For example, quite a
few years back, the current wife of a good friend of mine was
shocked when her estranged husband shot himself. They had
been separated and the marriage had been rocky, but she was
half a country away from all her other family, dealing with grief
and anger and confusion. Her family told her, "Come home,

we'll find you a place to live and get you a job." But she said no. She had always been the baby and knew that if she ran back home, she would remain so. "I think I'll stay out here," she said, and she created her own life in California, one that now includes two gorgeous children. Rather than panic, she kept her cool and kept focused on what she wanted. As a result, she turned tragedy into a springboard for her own growth.

SWEPT UNDER THE CARPET

There's a select society of party crashers who live for awards season. Seriously, there are about fifty people in Los Angeles who consider themselves the party-crashing elite and share their secret strategies with nobody. Rex Reginald is the original, but there are quite a few who have the balls, smooth talk, and quick thinking to get past the airtight security at some of the after-bashes. One guy pretended to be a journalist to crash the 1994 *Vanity Fair* party. A creative woman brought an impostor pig with her and made it in the door the year that *Babe* was a huge hit.

One of the greats was a middle-aged white guy named Michael Minutoli who, in 2003, somehow persuaded security that he was part of the posse for hip-hop stars OutKast (who are otherwise all black and all young) and actually ended up spending the night at their post-Grammy party. That's chutzpah. One of the latest tricks I've heard about: crashing in a fire marshal's uniform with a tuxedo underneath. People are truly creative (and nuts) in their desire to be where the stars are.

How You Know You're Not Showing Grace Under Pressure

In 2007 Alec Baldwin, in the midst of the always-tumultuous relationship with his ex-wife, Kim Basinger, left an angry, abusive voice-mail message for their daughter, Ireland. I won't write it here; it makes me sick to think of anyone saying things that vile to his child. Of course, it turned out that the voice mail was leaked to the press by someone in Kim's camp; Alec actually handled the whole affair pretty well and Kim ended up looking like she was exploiting her daughter's issues with her father for her own gain. But the whole thing was just ugly, and the loser was the little girl. If you lash out and hurt the ones you love, that's a good indication that grace under pressure isn't your forte.

Here are some big red warning lights that should tell you it's time to take a chill pill before you do some Baldwinesque damage to someone you care about:

• **No one wants to be around you.** This is probably because you're pouring out your sob story to anyone who can fog a mirror and emoting all over the place. That becomes tiresome fast, even to your friends. Yes, it's cathartic to share your pain and have one or two or ten people say, "There there," but have mercy after a while. If people are finding excuses not to come over for a glass of wine and it's been a month since the breakup, you're probably turning into a depressing (and depressive) basket case who brings the room down. Time to think about some therapy, a vacation, or anything that will get your mind on something else.

• **You're thinking desperate thoughts.** I'm not talking about suicide; that's territory for the cops or an emergency help line. But if you're thinking about trashing your boss's BMW because he called you on the carpet in front of everyone . . . if you're thinking that you know exactly where you can score some cocaine at this time of night and a couple of lines would really take the edge off . . . if you're suddenly convinced that because your mother has breast cancer that you need to have an immediate preventive mastectomy . . . if you're thinking about doing anything that would seem totally nuts to you when you weren't in the grip of a raging attack of grief-stricken remorse, stop. Breathe. Tell someone who's not temporarily insane what you're thinking. If their eyes get wide and they start texting your friends to get over here and help, you're desperate and irrational. Accept the coming intervention as an act of love.

• *Part of you is screaming, "What the hell are you doing?"* When you're behaving like an out-of-control jerk, part of you knows it. It's just not as strong as the part that wants to break furniture or yell brainless things at Matt Lauer about prescription drugs. Listen to that voice, if you can. Even if you've let your temper and your desire for retribution swing so far into the red zone that the cops are about to get a call, listen. Deep down, you know that you're terrifying people who care about you or wrecking your apartment and losing your security deposit. If you can, slow down and listen to your inner voice of reason. Imagine the worst thing that could happen if you continue to show zero grace under pressure. Then imagine the worst that could happen if you sucked it up and kept control. Take the option that seems best.

• *Something you own is in pieces.* It could be a piece of furniture. A plate-glass window. An address book. A gift. If you've shattered something in anger or grief, chances are you're not handling it well. I understand the need to vent, to get rid of nervous tension—heck, even to beat the living daylights out of something. But be an adult. Get thee to the health club and take a spinning class until you can't inhale. Go to a boxing gym and whale on a heavy bag for an hour. If you need to express your anger, fear, or pain physically, at least make it productive and spare the furnishings.

• **You've undergone a radical physical change.** Most of the time, this is code for gaining or losing weight. Some people eat when they're stressed or depressed, while others can't muster the appetite for one M&M (I can always do that; I love M&Ms). Whether you're packing on the pounds by soothing your bruised "I didn't win the award" ego with quarts of Chunky Monkey, or you're dropping pants sizes because dinner consists of green tea and a breath mint, it's not a good sign. The same is true if you're subjecting yourself to impulsive body mutilation, aka tattoos, tattoo removal, or piercing (yes, no, yes). I happen to think the phrase "Never get a body part pierced in anger" is one of the great bits of wisdom of our age. I learned that one the hard way.

Grace in the Shallow End

I remember after my first terrible breakup, when I was sure it was the end of the world as we knew it, I got a pierced belly button, thereby violating my own rule from a few sentences ago. Sue me. Then, after my next breakup (with the same guy—he's my soul mate but we're poison for each other at the same time), I got a tattoo on my ankle. So am I a hypocrite? You betcha. Do as I say, not as I do. This worked out okay because I like the ankle art and the navel ring. The point is, the shallow end of grace under pressure is all about two things:

1. Keeping up appearances and never letting them know you're a wreck.

2. Getting yourself through the first seventy-two hours without falling apart.

So you do whatever you need to do, short of self-mutilation. Or, if you're going to get a tattoo or a piercing, at least bring a sane and sober friend with you so you don't end up with something grotesque or ridiculous. Let's go a-shallowing, shall we?

• *Cry in private.* Even if you run into your ex and say bravely, "I guess I didn't need you all that much," you're going to bawl your eyes out later. It's astonishing how we can suppress grief only to have it come calling for us later on. Keep your head high, then cry in your car. I once went to an event sobbing like a baby in a car full of people, then sobbed in the bathroom at the event, then sobbed on the way home. I'm surprised the driver didn't need to make an insurance claim for water damage. But as far as anyone who wasn't in that car knew, I was fine.

• *Say yes to invitations.* Don't become a hermit. Get out of the house and spend time with other people. Remind yourself there's a life after the relationship, the job, or the embarrassment. One condition: *Do not* dump your depression on anyone.

• *Be nice to yourself.* Get a facial, a massage, a manicure. Treat yourself to something special, even a spa weekend if you can afford it. A little pampering goes a long way to remind you that you're worth the best. Remember, something rough is happening *to* you; it isn't who you are. That's an important difference.

• *Get outside.* Go for a walk, swim at the beach, breathe the air, hike in the back country. I find that when I'm feeling down or mad about something in my life, getting outside (in my case, surfing) helps clear my head, brings some beauty into my life, and calms me down.

RED CARPET RULES
Running into Your Ex

- Don't hide. Acknowledge that he's there with his new paramour, especially if he's seen you. Go over and say hello. Let him think the whole affair meant nothing and you're completely fine.

- Avoid places where you know he's likely to be, unless you crave a painful scene. This can take some doing; you wouldn't believe the logistical gymnastics that go on to keep celebrity exes from running into each other on the red carpet. But stars don't always have a choice. You do. Unless you're a glutton for punishment, if you know an ex is going to be at a party, don't go. Surely you have better ways to spend your time than dealing with confrontation, such as being cool, calm, and collected.

- Don't start a fight. You're too over him for that, remember? If he tries to pick an argument, simply walk away and let him stew in his own juices.

- Don't rehash old times. You know as well as I do that after a few weeks apart, exes can forget the terrible things in favor of fond memories and the desire for a booty call. Do not give in to this. You are exes for a reason. Unless both people make real changes, getting back together never, ever works. Don't fall into the trap because you're lonely.

- If you're with a friend or another date and you see your ex, prep them. Let them know who your ex is and how to behave. You're the boss.

- Above all, be sweet and positive and gorgeous. Make him imagine what he's lost and make it hurt. Kill him with kindness, poise, and a cool indifference worthy of Grace Kelly.

- **Don't cut off your hair.** At least you can hide bad-decision tattoos or piercings; it's tough to conceal a full-on Sinéad O'Connor head shaving. I know, your ex-husband cheated on you with a woman who had long, curly hair, but shaving yours down to the nub won't change anything other than making you look like a cast member from *Schindler's List*. Sure, you can get hair extensions, but isn't it better not to need them? If you need to change something dramatically, try your wardrobe. Give everything to Goodwill and go shopping.

- **If you're rebounding, be aware of it.** There's nothing wrong with two consenting adults getting together to shag one's pain away. It's a lot more fun than therapy. But make sure you and your rebound person know that's what's going on. The last thing you need is *mas* drama.

- **Put on your uniform.** Find an ensemble that makes you feel gorgeous and wear it like armor. On rough days, after taking a beating, I'll style my hair and slide into a dress and shoes I know make me look smashing. It's great medicine.

- **It's okay to say, "This sucks"**—just don't say it too much. It gets old, and negativity will bring down your mood.

Grace in the Deep End

If the shallow end was about short-term survival, the deep water here is all about avoiding long-term damage. Instead of talking about quick fixes, I'm talking about attitudes. How do you approach the dark times in your life? You can wallow in them or you can be your own light. Your choice.

- **Let it go.** Rejection hurts like hell, to be sure. But the hurt passes if you let it. Let it go. If you hold on to the pain, you won't get over it. Instead, you'll just become bitter, negative, and self-defeating.

- ***Don't bitch.*** We're all working ourselves to death, and we all have kids and other things we'd rather be doing sometimes. If you want to guarantee that you'll be a pariah at work or school, complain loudly and repeatedly about how rotten your life is. Nobody cares. Everybody has had to hitch up their pants and get the job done when their kids were sick or they just found out they were being laid off. I had to smile and do a Sunday red carpet event while my divorce negotiations were at a nasty, wrenching impasse. I put on my game face, summoned my party-girl enthusiasm, and went out there to make live TV happen. That's called being a professional.

- ***Hold your head up.*** Even if you haven't had a shower all weekend and you've been eating Chinese food out of boxes, come Monday, emerge from your cave with some pride. Smooth on some lip gloss and get out of the car. Put some effort into looking good and you'll feel better. And that's a start.

- ***Remember that this, too, shall pass.*** It's a cliché, but clichés are clichés for a reason. No matter how much it hurts now, remind yourself that it won't always be this way. Unless the bad news was terminal cancer, you will get better. Time really does move on and heal all wounds, and that's the closest thing to magic I think there is.

- ***Do what you do well.*** If you're a great cook, prepare a fantastic meal for the neighbors in your building. If you're a hotshot at your job, throw yourself into it for a while. Excelling is balm for your self-esteem.

- ***Separate yourself from the emotion.*** Learn to see your feelings about what's happening from a distance; they are coming from you, but they aren't you. You can let them slip away

RED CARPET RULES

Losing (a Job, a Promotion, a Competition)

- Don't quit. You're going to lose more often than you're going to win. But you only really fail if you quit. When I got fired from the red carpet, it wasn't the end of the world. It was the beginning of my life as an author and an entrepreneur. Part of me was tempted to retire to my inner sanctum and eat a whole bag of Oreos. But I'm a longtime rider; I got back on the horse.

- Don't play the blame game. You may not have been a hundred percent responsible for losing out on the promotion or not winning the award, but you played an important role. Own up, accept responsibility, and come off looking like a mature leader.

- Don't burn your bridges. Stalking out of the room in a cloud of dust and a hearty "F—you!" is a surefire way to guarantee you'll never hear from those people again. I didn't do that in my meeting with the people producing the stylist reality show, and one of the reasons I didn't was that I know there are always

Continued . . .

without acting on them. This frees you from having to cry, send angry e-mails, or polish off a bottle of Sonoma County cabernet every night.

- *If you're in deep, get help.* If after all this you find yourself six weeks or so after the lost job or lost love still crying yourself to sleep and losing weight, you may need to talk to a therapist. Don't hesitate. Seeking the help of a good shrink is not a sign of weakness, but of strength and self-awareness. A few sessions with someone trained to listen and advise can help you recover your perspective and remember who you are.

more opportunities coming, and you never know from what
direction.

- Don't trash your own work. Deleting files, tearing up Rolodex
cards—that's all juvenile nonsense. Update your résumé and
leave with some dignity. If you must resign, then do it. But move
on and steal all the office supplies that you can.

- Be gracious to the winner. Congratulate the person who beat
you out, even if you think she did it because she slept with the
boss. You can never, ever go wrong by rising above it all and
being ultra-classy.

- Learn. If you didn't get the job, contact the company and ask
them to tell you why. Be honest and tell them you would like to
shore up your professional weaknesses and they'll probably
level with you. Don't take it personally; use the insight to get
better so next time, the prize is yours.

We all suffer from time to time. Nobody ever gets out of this
life unscathed. If you think you're going to be the special one to
escape some kind of trauma, you're going to be unprepared to
deal when the fire starts coming from the sky. But you really can
handle the bad breakup, the loss of a parent, the promotion that
went to someone else, the thing you said in front of a hundred
people that you wish you could take back. You can get through it
all. There were times when I didn't think I could, but I did. So
can you.

Be Prepared

Luck is preparation meeting opportunity.
—OPRAH WINFREY

Somewhere on the Internet is a photo of me wearing an elegant dress and crouching by a trash can. No, I wasn't throwing up after a night of partying. I was actually in a committee room in the United States Senate, where I was going to be giving the members of the Senate a preview of the Prism Awards, which are given for the accurate depiction in entertainment of issues related to mental health, substance use, and addiction. Well, as cool as this was and despite all the entertainment and political luminaries in the room, I was preoccupied with having my picture taken with a Senate refuse receptacle. It was a crazy "See, I was here" impulse to which I surrendered. So there I was, in the room where the Watergate hearings had been held, crouching and pointing at the Senate seal on the trash can, grinning like a fool.

Unfortunately, when the time came for me to accept an award at the *actual* Prism Awards show at the Beverly Hills Hotel, I didn't have a speech prepared. I don't know why; I had known for a while that I would be hosting. I was brought up to believe that preparation was the "magic ingredient" that separated successes from failures. Heck, my mother, the famous comedienne, never goes onstage without virtually every word scripted and planned in advance. But for some reason, I wasn't prepared. Fortunately, years of live television had honed my improv chops to the point where I was able to stand in front of the assembled VIPs and not make a complete fool of myself. I'm sure that most people didn't notice anything amiss, but I felt like I had stepped on my tongue and come across as a total amateur. Such is the fallout when you're used to being exhaustively prepared and you realize that you're not.

Then there's the flip side, when intense and obsessive preparation saves your butt from embarrassment. I have numerous examples from the red carpet, but this one will get us started. We were working the Country Music Awards when I thanked Kris Kristofferson for an interview by calling him Glen Campbell. Kris laughed at me and said, "You don't even know who you're talking to." But I bailed myself out by reciting the lyrics from several of his songs and some details from his bio, showing him that I had done my homework. He was very impressed, but it wasn't just about coming back and showing him that I knew my job or that I could memorize. I wanted to prove to him that I cared who he was. That's what preparation does. It shows people you care enough to put in the time and give your best.

The Boy Scouts Got It Right

Preparation really is the magic bullet in any walk of life—for two reasons. First, it ensures that no matter what happens at the audition, presentation, or sporting event, you'll have the best chance of coming out smelling like a rose. Second, it makes other people love and respect you, because everybody likes the person who comes to the table having worked his or her tail off and prepared thoroughly. It shows that you respect those around you, and that's always a winning strategy.

I learned from the best to be prepared—specifically, to anticipate what could go wrong in a situation and do my best to have some kind of Plan B to get myself out of a tough situation. Preparation is preservation, the advance time and thought you put in to increase the odds of coming out on top in a job interview, a first dinner with your fiancé's parents, or taking the bar exam. After all, you can't control what other people are going to do, and by definition you can't control random events. You can control what you've learned, what you've anticipated, and how you react when things don't go as planned. It's amazing how often a little preparation will let you escape what would otherwise be a catastrophe.

However, when I would walk my friends through my typical preparation regimen for a red carpet event—tape for the possible wardrobe malfunction, spare cash in case my credit card was stolen, a twenty-seventh read-through of my notes on every human being likely to be present—some would say the oddest thing: "You're being so pessimistic." Sorry, but that's wrong. Pessimistic is saying, "This night is going to be a disaster," and going into it with a negative, defeatist attitude before the red light even comes on. Anticipating possible problems before they happen and preparing for them is *realistic*. It's what professionals do, because they know that, like it or not, shit does happen. That's why when you go into a meeting at work, you make notes on a three-by-five card and slide it into your pocket. Most of the time, you won't need your Plan B; you'll cruise through your Red Carpet Moments just fine. But the one time you're asked to address the shareholders' meeting and your mind goes completely blank, you'll be very glad you gave in to Melissa's nagging and kept those notes in your stylish Marc Jacobs jacket.

Another reason being prepared is a critical Red Carpet Life Lesson is that preparation gives you confidence. Some Red Carpet Moments come along only once in a lifetime, so why risk missing the best parts because you're nervous? When you're prepared, you don't worry as much. You know you're on top of your game, you look your best, or you know the right thing to say. Even small preparatory steps can lend you peace of mind when things are otherwise spinning out of control. For example, I had my legs waxed two days before I had my labor induced and gave birth to Cooper. I had my toenails done the day he was born (so I

MEL'S BELLES

Women don't get much more admirable than Oprah Winfrey. It's not just that she came from an abusive background to become the most powerful media mogul in the country, or that she's an inspiration for minority women all over the world. She also uses her immense influence to make the world better. Thanks to Oprah, backlist books become resurrected bestsellers and millions of people discover great literature. Thanks to her, hundreds of thousands of young girls in Africa can attend school for the first time. Thanks to her Angel Network, groups doing incredible work all over the United States get badly needed grant money. She's been amazingly honest about her weight struggles and her demons, and she gets it: When you have so much, you have a responsibility to give something back. Oprah does a lot more than that.

could meditate on them while I had my feet in the air, I suppose). I even had my hair blown out in case I had a C-section. (I still can't figure out why this mattered, but it seemed to make sense at the time.) None of these things helped me push out my son, but at least I knew I looked decent in the photos.

Give Yourself the Edge

The best in any business never wing it, even if they have incredible talent. I would argue that the difference between successful professionals and gifted amateurs is not talent, but preparation and years of hard work and training. Even Michael Jordan spent off-seasons working on his game. That's why he *stayed* great. It takes an unbelievable amount of work and preparation to make something appear effortless. Maybe a genius like Robin Williams can go onstage and perform off-the-cuff and bring the house down, but he's one in a million—and he also prepped for his bravura improvised performances with years of work at Juilliard and still works out his new material in small clubs. The pros know there's no substitute for putting in the time.

One of the beautiful things about really preparing for the Red Carpet Moments in your life is that being prepared frees you to turn your natural abilities loose and be your most creative. When you've stayed up all night making sure your PowerPoint files and printed documents for the big meeting are perfect, you know you have a solid foundation for your presentation. You can wing it and take some risks while knowing that no matter what, your prepared materials will be there to make you look good.

It's the same in entertainment, to be sure. The smartest actors, directors, hosts, and musicians all prepare obsessively for weeks and months before cameras roll or recording begins.

They all know that when you have the structure and readiness that come with preparation, you're really freed to make stuff up, play around, and turn your creative angels loose to invent new things. Jazz is a perfect example. I'm not old enough to have seen the great sax player Charlie Parker back when he used to play bebop at the great Los Angeles jazz clubs along Crenshaw Boulevard back in the 1960s, but his improvisational solos are legendary. But why was the man they called Bird so brilliant at off-the-cuff creation? Because he knew the essentials: chord progressions, song structure, and how the other musicians played. Preparation and study freed him to be wildly creative.

The same is true for the go-to troupe of fantastic comedy actors—Eugene Levy, Harry Shearer, Fred Willard, Catherine O'Hara, Parker Posey, and so on—that Christopher Guest has used to make movies like *Best in Show* and *Waiting for Guffman*. Sure, much of what the characters say is improvised, but the character development is focused by Guest's strict guidelines and happens at the hands of some of the most experienced improv artists in the business. It's planned chaos, a deliberate accident that yields gut-busting comedy as an enjoyable side effect.

You cannot step into a situation like the red carpet unprepared or it will open up, swallow you, and spit out your bones. I went into every red carpet event armed with a ton of information about every nominee and presenter. Weeks before every awards pre-show telecast, I would get a five-inch-thick binder with notes about each celebrity—bios, photos, articles from magazines and newspapers, interview transcripts. I would sometimes even Google a nominee like Frank Langella to find something fresh. I devoured this material in the weeks leading up to the event, committing it all to memory. Then, while I was having my hair and makeup done the day of the event, I would go through all the material again to make sure I was completely prepared. I also had to try to find time to see as many of the nominated films as possible.

The payoff came on awards night when I was able to snag celebs as they walked the carpet and ask them a smart, pertinent question about their film or their personal interests. For instance, at the 2007 Screen Actors Guild Awards, I was able to hit Jamie Foxx with the fact that I knew he was a Ping-Pong fanatic who even holds his own tournament. He looked surprised and delighted that I knew about his hobby and then he opened right up about that and Eddie Murphy's performance in *Dreamgirls*. Questions like that always stop stars in their tracks, because they are used to hearing platitudes from people who haven't done their homework. When something touches them personally or shows that an interviewer has taken the time to learn about the craft, it makes an impression. On the red carpet, everything is fast-paced, and my job is to get stars not only to stop, but to reveal something. My best weapon is study and knowledge, including knowing the pronunciations of the titles of foreign films and the names of their actors, which can be a killer.

Herculean prep work went into every red carpet extravaganza. Mom and I had to know where every camera was placed so we would know where to look depending on where we were along the red carpet, and we had to be prepared with witty segues when we wanted to hand off to each other. Hearing "Back to you, Mom" ten thousand times would have had blood seeping from the audience's ears and put me on the unemployment line. But what people don't get is that for all the unrehearsed look of those live shows, they were scripted extensively. Mom and I would sit down with a team of writers and write our script for the entire two hours—the opening and closing monologues, stories to fill time, those segues, jokes aimed at a certain star.

We'd do a full read-through of the script, replace what

wasn't working, and do another read-through three or four days before the telecast, with a final read-through and most of the changes about 10 A.M. the morning of the show. However, most of the time we used only the first fifteen minutes and the last fifteen minutes of the script and some of the stand-alone jokes and stories—the rest was made up in the moment. That's because you can't prepare for what happens: a shockingly bad outfit, a nipple slip, or a snarky statement by a star. So eventually we had a writer follow the script during the shows and circle unused material so we could use it the next day. And they say only Ed Begley Jr. and Darryl Hannah recycle.

I have no choice but to prep like that. I'm so hard on myself that the few times I wasn't properly prepared for a show, it was debilitating. I felt self-conscious and clumsy. Even though the producer and crew said I did fine, I felt like a cretin. My attitude is that I can demand that other people be prepared only if I'm the most prepared person in the room.

THE GOSPEL ACCORDING TO JOAN

Obsessive preparation means if your project doesn't work, you can never look back and say, "I should have done more." When you're doing something that means a great deal to you, you want to feel that you've done everything humanly possible to make it a success. That's how I work. When I commit to a project, I want to know I've gone every extra mile I can. I don't look at the clock. The only thing you can say to yourself at the end of the day, win or lose, is, "I did my best." That way you can live without regrets.

Life Is Homework

Preparation is second nature to stars. No star, especially a woman, even thinks about stepping onto the red carpet without a campaign that would make Desert Storm pale in comparison. As soon as you have a Red Carpet Moment on your calendar, it's "Avengers assemble!"—time to put together your Dream Team. In Hollywood, it borders on the ridiculous: hair stylist, makeup artist, fashion designer, seamstress, manicurist, eyelash extension lady, spray-tan mister, personal trainer, facialist, body-treatment expert, dentist, dermatologist for Botox and collagen, and even plastic surgeon. I've seen some celebs go into overkill mode with waxers, eyebrow shapers, masseuses, aestheticians, jewelers, lingerie fitters, and, of course, the inevitable personal assistant who has to wrangle all these people and their schedules. That's a lot so you can stand onstage and say, "And the Oscar goes to . . ." Patton had a smaller support staff.

It's both a blessing and a curse for the folks on the Dream Team. For example, at red carpet time every actress wants an appointment with the hot hair stylist, the Ken Paves or Frédéric Fekkai, of the moment. But unless you get an appointment early, you're out of luck. Even the red-hot hairdressers will work with only two or three women in a day. One year, before a big awards show, a hair stylist friend of mine set Portia de Rossi's hair wet the night before. He then visited three hotels the next day to style Calista Flockhart, Kim Cattrall, and Sela Ward. His day didn't end until he twisted Michael Michele's hair into a chignon and set it with a brooch just as her limo was pulling up to take her to her show. Then he collapsed from exhaustion.

If you're a star, looking great is your homework, and it doesn't happen by accident. Life is homework—no matter what you're doing, if you're not prepared, it looks like you don't give a damn, and even if you have the talent to get by sometimes, nobody has the ability to BS their way to the top. There's a reason that the greatest compliment one entertainer can give another is to say he or she is a total professional—it's insider code for "he prepares like an animal" or "she's completely committed to her performance." It means that person not only comes to work completely ready to give the job everything, but makes everyone else better, too. I can't think of higher praise.

There are some actors who are renowned for the extraordinary lengths to which they go to prepare for a role:

• Before they made *The Perfect Storm* for Wolfgang Petersen, George Clooney and Mark Wahlberg went to Gloucester, Massachusetts. They drank in the Crow's Nest, the fisherman's bar where the doomed crew of the *Andrea Gail* hung out. Wahlberg lived in the room above the bar where his character, Bobby Shatford, lived and stayed with Shatford's brother. He got the blessing of Shatford's mother and sisters before filming. That's not just prep; that's respect.

• Daniel Day-Lewis is a Method actor's Method actor. For *Gangs of New York,* in which he played a character called Bill the Butcher, he actually took an apprenticeship as a butcher.

• For his Oscar-winning turn as Idi Amin in *The Last King of Scotland,* Forest Whitaker put on fifty pounds, studied all Amin's speeches, lived with Amin's family in Uganda, learned Swahili, and learned to play the accordion.

It's that kind of incredible commitment that earns people like these the admiration of everyone they work with. Of course, no matter what business you're in you know that the reverse is true: The fastest way to alienate everyone you work with is to be the only one who hasn't done their homework. I see this all the time with radio hosts, and it drives me insane. I've sat down for interviews where the host will open with, "So, what have you been doing?" It's instantly clear that the person has done zero research and that they're wasting my time, and it's hard not to resent them and say something like, "You know, I bet I know more about you than you do about me. Shall we put it to the test?"

How many times have you seen this in your own Red Carpet Moments? You're on a competitive sports team and everybody shows up ready to play the big game except the one girl who's hungover and forgot her gear. You get to the morning of the big sales presentation and all the pieces are in place . . . except for the financials, because the doofus who was responsible for them decided to go clubbing the night before instead of finishing his work. And did you ever do theater in school? Wasn't there always one lead actor who still didn't know his or her lines come opening night? Didn't you hate that person? Didn't the experience make you swear you would never *be* that person?

What really impresses people is when you go out of your way to find something out that's not available in a press kit or on a company's Web site. Like when you're going in for a job interview and you take the time to call the interviewer's secretary, find out his daughter is graduating from high school later that week, and bring him a gift for her. When you take the time to think outside the box and put in extra effort, you will always impress people. For example, it's widely known that Mom and I are crazy for M&Ms. Well, I walked into a meeting once and there was a huge bowl of M&Ms on the table. My host said, "We know how your family feels about M&Ms." They had heard about it on TV and remembered it. It made an impression. Having that kind of information at hand can really set you apart from the pack in a job interview or an audition, and you can only make it happen when you dig deep.

SWEPT UNDER THE CARPET

Until you've done live TV, you don't know all that can go wrong. I've had my earpiece go out, my prompter invaded by aliens, lost all my audio, lost the video feed I use to see what's going on elsewhere—you name it. One time, at the premiere of *Tin Cup*, which E! was covering live, they had paired me with Todd Newton, and it was Todd's first time working live. Wanting to be prepared, bless his heart, he memorized the script. But you don't know what's going to happen, so you have to know the script well enough to know where you're going but still be able to switch gears in a flash. Well, Murphy's Law prevailed that night and Todd's prompter died. Poor Todd, with no live TV background, was so locked in to the script that he couldn't improvise. He never did that again. But he handled the evening like a pro and has become one of the best people to work with in live situations.

Control What You Can, Forget What You Can't

There's no area of life that's exempt from the need for preparation, and the more obsessive you are about the small details, the more successful you'll be, both in performing under pressure and enjoying the big moments of life. The little things matter, like checking the wineglasses for your dinner party before guests arrive to make sure nobody gets a chipped glass. Remember, pressure magnifies everything, good and bad. When you've got college finals coming up, it's easy to be cavalier beforehand, to go clubbing with your girlfriends while your roommate is busy hitting the books. But when you're in class and the clock is ticking, chances are you're going to be sweating if you haven't prepped and made sure you know the information. Trust me, when your heart is pounding and your mind is racing because you know what's at stake, it becomes a lot harder to summon what you know.

I have a good friend who's in ad sales for radio, and she was relocating. She put together a complete dossier of information on each radio station where she was planning to interview, out-lining what each station was doing and how she could meet each company's unique needs. That enabled her to ask intelligent questions and be distinctive when other candidates were pretty generic. That's incredible preparation, and it helped her land a plum job that was just right for her.

Preparation matters so much because most of what hap-pens is going to be out of your control. That's why people sign prenuptial agreements. That's why Michael J. Fox and his beau-tiful wife, Tracy Pollan, have a Plan B for every awards show: If Michael's meds don't kick in before they can get out of the limo, they circle the area until the meds do kick in and his shakes subside. Michael has been public about his Parkinson's disease for years, but he still doesn't want to go on live TV when he's shaking like Kate Hepburn was late in her life.

You never know what might happen that could send you off the deep end emotionally. Encountering your ex-spouse and his new, fifteen-years-younger model fiancée at a social event might send you into a panic attack in private, but if you're pre-pared with something to say because you knew you might run into your ex, you'll be able to keep it together until you can get to the ladies' room for a good cry.

Think about Gwyneth Paltrow breaking down when she won her Oscar for *Shakespeare in Love* when her father had just been diagnosed with cancer and her grandfather was dying. She wasn't smooth, but she showed up and got through her speech. Preparation can't prevent the emotional waves, but it can help you ride them. Hilary Swank didn't have a death in the family as an excuse when she couldn't manage the deed and forgot to thank her husband, Chad Lowe, after she won an Oscar. Now they're divorced.

How You Know You're Prepared

• *You're comfortable.* Okay, you might be slightly nervous. But you're going to be a lot less nervous than if you're winging it at a big company party where you know you're going to be sitting next to the CEO. When I go to a major bash where I know I won't know anyone, I at least read the day's newspaper so I have some way to initiate intelligent conversation. That makes me feel much more at ease than just showing up and hoping I can meet someone to talk with. Preparation gives you peace of mind because you know you're going to be able to deal with ninety-nine percent of what comes up, and that means you won't look foolish. If you see someone making a speech or a presentation who looks like they just drank twenty cups of coffee or they're waiting for the head guard to come and escort them to the lethal-injection booth, odds are they didn't do their homework.

• *You've thought ahead.* Foresight is one of the great gifts of being human. It's also one of the hallmarks of maturity. The brains of young people do not actually develop the ability to look into the future and examine the possible outcomes of their actions until their mid-twenties, which is why nineteen-year-old college guys are capable of such monumentally stupid acts as screwing the dean's underage daughter. We don't get a finely honed sense of what could happen if we do A, B, or C until we're older . . . and some of us never develop it at all.

If you've prepared for something, you've taken the time to sit down and say, "Okay, what's likely to happen if I do this, and how do I deal with that?" That's mature and wise. In entertainment, it's also a survival skill. For instance, when Billy Crudup left Mary-Louise Parker for Claire Danes when Mary-Louise was eight months pregnant, Emmy officials did Cirque du Soleil–style contortions to keep them from running into each other. Of course, Mary-Louise didn't need the help, because she was prepared. Knowing that the press was going to be focusing on her broken relationship, she laughed and talked her way down the red carpet, acting as though everything were fine. It worked; she sailed through the evening. When she won, she even thanked her baby for her new cleavage. Rock on, girlfriend.

• *Your eggs aren't all in one basket.* Nobody with any sense thinks they won't need a backup plan, especially when it comes to their career. No matter how sure you are that you're going to be doing what you're doing until you're ninety, have an alternative, just in case. This does not mean taking a second major so you can have "something to fall back on." That phrase is one of the fastest killers of passion I know; if you love something, you should go for it. But it's not a bad thing to have an alternative in mind.

One night at a dinner party, Sylvester Stallone told me that he knew how to be a house painter, so if everything went down the toilet one day, he could survive. Not that Rocky is likely to be panhandling anytime soon, but you have to admire his humility. Mariska Hargitay of *Law and Order: Special Victims Unit* speaks several languages because she always wanted to be a diplomat. Even my mother got into the act when, at age fifty-four, she was offered the chance to design her own jewelry line for QVC. Millions of dollars in sales later, no one's laughing at her. What's your backup plan? Admitting you have one doesn't mean you're planning to fail; it does mean you're smart enough to know that things don't always work out, sometimes for reasons beyond your control.

• *You can start the conversation.* Whether the situation is a meeting or a social event, I can always tell who's prepared by who begins talking. This is a dead giveaway, because the people who know they didn't do the required reading don't

KNOW-IT-ALL

Judy Schwartz, Veteran Wedding Planner

The most important part of being prepared in my business is being organized. The best events are the most highly orchestrated and come off as though they were just happening spontaneously. With a wedding or other big event, you get only one chance. I can't very well say to a bride, "Sorry, the wine is being delivered after the wedding." There are no do-overs.

You can do a certain amount of preliminary work for an event, like rehearsals and food tasting, and getting a sample from your florist. But for the most part, the best ways to ensure that things go smoothly are to be organized and make things simple and reproducible. I don't work with a computer. I make lists and I work with one list. The more lists you have, the more chances for error. I have one master list for everything.

One thing I'll tell you: Doing the impossible makes the day take a lot longer to be over.

want to expose their ignorance. They would rather have some-one else start and then riff off what the other person said. It's kind of like "drafting," when you get behind an eighteen-wheeler on the highway and let the airstream pull you along.

If you're the first one who talks in a situation where there's something on the line—a business meeting, a sales call, an office party, a negotiation—you can be pretty sure you're the most prepared one at the table. Use this knowledge to your advantage by playing your cards close to the vest. Make the other people jump to your beat or, if you're in a knife-fight negotia-tion, make the other party reveal its weakness.

How You Know You're Not Prepared

- *You're praying no one asks you a question.* Are you in a meeting at your job, sitting low in your chair, taking care to make sure you're breathing softly, praying to all that's holy that your supervisor doesn't ask you to elaborate on last week's big project? Then you're not prepared, and you're hoping you can slide through the meeting without having to utter a word and expose your ignorance. Being fast on your feet won't save you; everyone can spot a tap dance from a mile away. Either you have firm facts and figures at your disposal or you don't. If you don't, being embarrassed might be the least of your worries.

- *You're already inventing excuses.* It's even worse if, on the way to the rehearsal or to meet with your client, you're already figuring out plausible things you can say to get you out of trouble once they find out how unprepared you are. If you're driving through the city weighing the believability of the "my computer crashed" gambit versus the "I came down with food poisoning and couldn't work all weekend" ploy, you're way past the point of no return. Because whether you realize it or not, everybody has heard the classics and nobody believes them. If you really did miss your deadline because you got salmonella from some bad tacos *al carbon,* you'd better have photos of you with your head in the toilet.

- **You're the only one who's shocked.** When the sky falls and the company announces it's gone bankrupt, the only people standing around looking stunned will be the ones who didn't have the sense to look into the future and see that disaster was a possibility. When catastrophe comes, you may not have another job or a new place to live lined up, but you can certainly have your résumé ready or some money saved for a hotel. When I found out Cooper's dad was getting divorced again, I prepared. I didn't wait for the trauma to hit my son, then do something. I circled the wagons so when he got the news he would feel as safe as possible.

Sometimes not preparing isn't a matter of incompetence but being in denial. That robs you of your power to plan for possibilities and to rise above what happens to you. Whatever else you do, please learn to face the facts of the situation honestly and not stick your head in the sand. Otherwise, you're a sitting duck.

- **You're always in crisis.** There's a scene at the beginning of the movie *Jerry Maguire* where Tom Cruise freaks out as he's leaving the sports agency where he's just been fired. For most of the rest of the film, he's clearly running on stress hormones and caffeine, just steps from a breakdown. If you're doing that sort of thing the moment anything in your life goes awry, then you have a problem with mental preparation. Mental preparation means telling yourself, "If what I'm doing doesn't work out, then I'm still going to be okay."

RED CARPET RULES
Making a Speech

- Know who to thank. If you're accepting an award or just thanking your host, be sure you know who's responsible for you being at the podium. Know their names, titles, and how both are pronounced. If you're wearing couture, know who designed your dress.

- Have a beginning, middle, and end to your speech. Don't ramble. Every speech should have an arc, just like a work of fiction. Be sure your audience is able to sense when you're past the middle and sloping down toward the end. That way, they won't sit there thinking, "My God, when is she going to stop talking?"

- Shorter is always better. Unless you're a keynote speaker who's being paid to do sixty minutes, cut your speech short enough so people want more when you're finished.

- Don't spout personal opinions on controversial subjects. Nobody wants you to be Rush Limbaugh. Keep your thoughts on Iraq to yourself unless you're speaking at a political convention.

Continued . . .

Prepared to Go Shallow

Preparedness is really made for the shallow end of the advice pool, because it's such a practical lesson. It's all about pragmatic steps and tools and thinking ahead. Preparation isn't metaphysical; it's very, very physical. But it can be the difference between saying, "Wow, that was really exciting!" at the end of the night

- Everybody likes humor, but don't make it embarrassing or crude unless you're doing something like a roast, where the humor is notoriously bathroom.
- Rehearse in front of a mirror. This lets you see your body language and work on your intonation. There's no such thing as too much rehearsal.
- Know your audience. If they're conservative, slant your material appropriately. If they're under twenty-five, avoid references to things that are better understood by baby boomers.
- Keep it simple. I was at a wedding once where the maid of honor got up to make her speech and pulled out a bag of shoes. Each shoe represented something about the bride or groom. It was as torturous as it sounds.
- Go to the bathroom before your speech. Obviously.

and being hunched over a cup of Starbucks at 3 A.M. wondering how you're going to get out of this mess. To the shallow end:

• Try on your dress and get alterations done before you go to your event. One of my biggest mistakes was going to a big party in a dress I had not test-driven beforehand and finding out that I couldn't sit down without exposing enough flesh to qualify for a pictorial in *Playboy*. There is always time to make adjustments before things get festive; the day of the event it gets tougher and a lot more expensive. Some women have two alternate event dresses lined up just in case the big day comes and they feel bloated or the dream dress just doesn't work.

• Never leave transportation to chance. Always have the business card of a cab company so you can get home, especially if you're going somewhere unfamiliar. I don't have to tell the ladies that this is about safety as much as convenience; you don't want to be stuck in the boonies with an angry guy after a bad date and be dependent on him to get you home. This leads to . . .

• Have an emergency plan. I always go on first dates with the classic "out" prepped and in my hip pocket. If things go sour or the guy turns out to be forty-two and still living in his parents' basement watching old *Star Trek* reruns, I can go to the ladies' room, text "911" to a friend, then head back to the table. In a few minutes she'll call me with a horror story that I can react to and gives me the perfect excuse to dash off to the rescue. Other aspects of the emergency plan include always having a charged cell phone, a credit card, and at least $50 of emergency cash hidden where you can't see it (so it's not a temptation).

• Pack something warmer or cooler. Especially when you're going to a red carpet event like a wedding or fancy party, you're going to be dressed in a way that probably doesn't adapt well to changes in the weather. If you're wearing a slinky backless number to drive your date wild and a cold front sweeps in during the evening, you're not going to be very alluring with your teeth chattering and your arms blue. Bring something—a cashmere wrap, a cooler top—that will allow you to be comfortable should there be a shift in the temperature or humidity. That may not seem like an issue in Los Angeles, but as I said, I've frozen and roasted on the red carpet. These days, I know to prepare.

• Never put your medication in your checked luggage. This is just good common sense, learned the hard way. Airlines lose luggage. While I was writing this book, my flight from New York to L.A. had to make an emergency landing in Las Vegas, and it took me days to get my luggage. If I'd had important pre-scription meds in those bags, it could have been a major inconvenience at the least, a health hazard at the most. Put your meds in your carry-on bag and save yourself a headache.

• Use technology. These days, there is absolutely no excuse not to be organized and prepared because of all the technology we have at our disposal. I have an iPhone and I use its calendar and map functions to help me keep track of my appointments and figure out where in this crazy city I'm going. I'm a MapQuest fanatic. Free tools like Google Calendar and Yahoo! Calendar can track all your appointments, alert you to birthdays, and keep your crazy, chaotic life in something resembling order. That's assuming you can get organized enough to use them in the first place.

Deeply Prepared

The Academy of Achievement, a sort of "living history museum" of greats from the arts, education, sports, politics, and science, considers preparation one of its seven Keys to Success. A member, dance and choreography great Twyla Tharp, has said of her development as an artist, "We thought that there were certain possibilities, in terms of physical movement, in terms of community, and in terms of what dance could address in our society. And those were the issues that we went after. And we worked with a great deal of rigor. Which is to say, we were very, very dedicated. We worked six days a week, we worked at least six hours every day. We did not perform much at all. It was really about the experience of learning and exploring and growing, for five years."

For his Oscar-winning role in *The Pianist,* Adrien Brody got rid of his car and spent weeks locked in a room doing nothing but practicing the piano until his technique was perfect. That intensity paid off not only in his playing, but in the intensity he brought to his role. There are many brands of preparation, but they all require the same qualities: commitment, maturity, foresight, and respect for what you're doing and who you're doing it with. If that's not deep enough for you, check out this advice:

• *Ask for help.* Asking for help is not a sign of weakness but of wisdom. If you're in over your head and need a friend's help to prepare for a Red Carpet Moment, ask for it. Odds are you'll get it. Everybody likes to feel helpful, and nothing's more helpful than a paid professional, like a stylist or a manicurist, working with you. Make it a habit when you're preparing for something really important to say, "Who can help me be as ready as possible?"

• *Respect people's time.* When I'm headed for a meeting I always have the person's phone number programmed into my phone, so all I have to do is hit a button and dial if I know I'm going to be late. In Los Angeles traffic, that's a survival skill, but anywhere it's just respect for other people's time. Preparation shows that respect, because you're making it possible for everyone to make the most of the limited time they have in the day. When you're considering what you should be doing to be ready for a big presentation, project, vacation, or social event, ask yourself, "What would I want other people to do to help me get the most out of my time?" Then do ten percent more.

• *Go easy on people who aren't prepared.* On the red carpet, it was always obvious when somebody on the tech crew or support staff wasn't prepared to do his job, but it wasn't usually necessary to say anything, because any group culture is usually self-correcting. Peer pressure almost always lets the person know he screwed up and ensures he won't do the same thing again. So it's important for you to know how to respond to people who affect what you're doing by not being prepared. Do you tear them a new one? Usually, no. I find that most people are completely aware when they've dropped the ball and are quite embarrassed by it.

I suggest being cool and classy and giving them a chance to self-correct. If they don't get it, or if they drop the ball again, then you're free to drop the hammer. That's my approach; come up with one that works for you and your situation.

• *Prepare for success, too.* As I said earlier, one of the issues some people have with prepping for what can go wrong is that they feel like it's being negative or "jinxing" themselves. My response to that is: Fine, prepare for what can go right, too. What will you do if the first date is a smashing success? What will you say when you win the award? How will you celebrate if your first day leading a wilderness retreat is perfect? It's possible to plan for the best while simultaneously planning for the worst, you know. It's a balancing act, but you can handle it.

• *Make preparation a gift to yourself.* Thorough, foresighted preparation is one of the best things you can do to keep your life running smoothly and give yourself the best chance of enjoying success in your professional and personal worlds. So treat it that way. I find it helpful to think of prep work as a favor, a gift that I give to myself that makes me look better, feel better, and do better.

• *Do your research.* Before anything—and I mean any-thing—hit Google and learn about the people or the organization involved. Before a party, do a little research on some of the people who are likely to be there. Before you go to an interview, learn about the company and its recent history. Before an audi-tion, learn about the director or casting agent and see what their tastes have been in the past. When a red carpet event is

---

RED CARPET RULES

The Audition

- Be honest. If you need a few minutes to work on the part, ask for it.
- If you need clarification, say so. "The role was briefly explained to me, but could you go over it with me so that I understand it?" is perfectly acceptable.
- If you get the material ahead of time, know it! Two or three days is plenty of time to memorize a one-minute scene and work on shadings for your character. Don't waste the advance notice.
- Don't overdress. Young models tend to overdress for interviews. Instead, dress in a way that suggests the character: Give them cleavage or legs for a prostitute (but not both) or a classy suit for a professional woman, and so on. But don't come in character. If the character doesn't fit a type, come clean and simple.
- Know how the people in the room work and what they need. If you know something about the production, let them know.
- Don't apologize. Just ask, "Is that okay? Is that what you were looking for?" Don't bash your own work or make excuses for it.
- Be on time. This is a job interview and no one really thinks creative people can get away with being late.

---

looming, make your first move to the computer, the newspaper, or a personal source who knows the score.

Getting some inside information can be a lifesaver: I know a guy who was invited to a huge charity fund-raiser by a wealthy couple, and before he and his date attended, he Googled the couple's names. At the gala, his date was about to comment to the hostess, whom they had seen two years before, about how much weight she had lost. The guy stopped her in time and whispered what his research had told him: The woman had lost weight because she had terminal cancer. A horrifyingly humiliating moment was avoided.

Once on the red carpet, I asked Nicole Kidman what time she put her kids to bed at night. She furrowed her brow and told me that was the most unusual question she'd ever been asked. But it got her attention, and since she loved talking about her kids, she told me that if she had her way she'd be at home with them and with her feet up, watching the awards on TV. I got a very personal moment that no one else had gotten. Why? Because I'd taken the time to get to know about Nicole and find out that she was a very, very devoted mom who cherished her family time above all else. So preparation made what would have been a foot-in-mouth moment for someone else into a nice interlude of genuine feeling.

You can never prepare too much. And you'll never stop getting benefits from it.

Be Nice on the Way Up

*I have found that among its other benefits, giving
liberates the soul of the giver.* —MAYA ANGELOU

*A*fter the red carpet ride came to an end for me and
Mom in April 2007, Tom O'Neil, who had worked with me during some of the biggest events of the awards season, wrote a
postmortem for the *Los Angeles Times*. Now, Tom, who we saved
from firing multiple times, took some cheap shots to get some
attention, but he got one thing very right: gratitude. Mom and I
asked a great deal of the people who made the red carpet pre-
shows happen, but we always made sure to thank them just as
intensely. As Tom wrote in the *Times*:

> During more quiet times, the gals were always generous
> with compliments, jokes, personal attention and—can
> we talk?—gifts. Joan and Melissa give the best presents.
> They lavish their coworkers with expensive watches,
> Palm Pilots, cell phones and, of course, Joan and Melissa
> Rivers jewelry that sells on QVC. . . . When Joan slips

into her doting Jewish momma mode, she pours it on. At the apartment building where she lives in New York, she doesn't just give building staffers terrific presents and Christmas gifts, but she writes caring, hand-written notes to them all, even the doormen and superintendent. The guy who plays piano at the fancy parties Joan throws at home insists, "She always makes me feel like I'm one of the guests."

Fame, fortune, riches, and trips to the red carpet do not last forever. If you want incontrovertible evidence of that, think Erik Estrada. One minute he's Ponch in *CHiPs*, a *Tiger Beat* stud, and a superstar. The next, he's doing late-night real estate infomercials. It's a tough world, and very few personalities stay hot for long, much less busy, respected, and at the top of their creative game for decades like Steven Spielberg and Helen Mirren. Most people have their red-hot period, then tread water for a while, then experience a slide into hard times before (hopefully) rising from the ashes.

That's happened to me. It's happened to you. It's happened to 99.9 percent of the people in Hollywood. And when the boom times end, one of the few parts of life you can depend on is the relationships you've made along the way. If you've treated people well, with respect and generosity and caring, then guess what? When you're down at the heels and your fortunes aren't looking so great, they're probably still going to be there for you. But if you played the egotistical star when you were in the corner office, no one is going to care when your house goes into foreclosure and the repo men come for your BMW.

Being nice on the way up means being gracious, giving, and generous to the people in your life no matter how important your business card says you are. It means showing respect for the people who got you there and remembering that no matter how smart or talented you might be, *nobody* succeeds alone. We all need people who care about us and will lie down in traffic for us, as well as paid professionals—agents, hairdressers, lawyers—who do what needs to get done. They are all people with feelings who want to be appreciated. Unless you're good on the way up to the people who are good to you, you won't have any real friends on the way down, and that's when you'll need them most.

However, you also have to watch out for the "emotional vampires." These are the fair-weather friends or the significant others who want to be around you only when things are going well and show their love only when you have something to offer. I have a few friends like that; we all do. Beware of them, because they'll suck you dry if you let them. You owe them nothing but basic courtesy; otherwise, delete their e-mails and don't answer their calls. A friend of mine has a saying: "A true friend calls when good things happen, not just bad things."

Memories Are Long

My business is a small one, so it's especially important to be good to everyone, from the names above the title to the "little people" who bring coffee and run errands—because in truth, no one is little. If you're around long enough, you're going to run into people you worked with years before, and that coffee runner could be a producer with the power to hire or fire you. You never know. Of course, that's a superficial reason to be generous, kind, and understanding to the people in your life. The best reason is the Golden Rule: Treat everybody else as you want to be treated. I doubt that you would wish to be abused, screamed at, or have a desk thrown at you (I've actually known some desk throwers).

In any area of human interaction, memories are long, and you're going to give exactly as good as you get. A few months back I was taping a new show, and the producer was someone who's been in the business about 150 years. He shared a story about producing his first local talk show decades before. My mother had become a celebrity by then and she was in town, so he called her and begged her to be a guest. Even though she had given birth to me less than three months earlier, she said yes, and she was the only celebrity to appear on the early days of the show. The producer had never forgotten that kindness, and he was still thankful. In fact, his positive memory of Mom was one of the reasons he had thought of me for his new show.

The opposite is also true: People will always hold a grudge against someone who treats them dismissively or disrespect-fully. I know that's true for me. I remember a few years back when the handsome African-American actor Dennis Haysbert, who played the president on the series 24 for a few years, said to my producer at the Emmys, "I don't talk to her [meaning me], I only talk to Joan." He wasn't being sarcastic; he was being com-pletely serious and saying that I wasn't important enough to talk to him. I can't forgive that kind of deliberate insult, and I won't forget it, either.

The best example I know of why you should be good to everyone you can is the story of Arsenio Hall. Arsenio was a gen-uinely talented comedian who, after paying his dues in stand-up (the hardest gig there is; ask my mom) and doing *Coming to America* with Eddie Murphy in 1988, became a major late-night star when he landed *The Arsenio Hall Show*. Good for him. But then he decided he was the Second Coming. He forgot many of the people who helped him get where he was and treated them like second-class citizens.

The technical and administrative people in Hollywood, the behind-the-scenes professionals who make Hollywood run, are every bit as smart, talented, and hardworking as the people in front of the cameras. Most of them aren't aspiring stars; they're troupers who are great at what they do, but don't get public recognition, nor do they want it. The agents, publicists, and stylists might seem to have more glamorous jobs, but they're around to serve the needs of the star who's in the public eye, so that also makes them easy to minimize and even abuse. But every one of them is important, and without them the careers of many of the biggest stars would grind to a halt—or at least become much, much less enjoyable and fruitful. Those are the people Arsenio Hall turned his back on.

After my father's suicide in 1987, Mom and I were overwhelmed with expressions of sympathy and support from friends and colleagues. The house was filled with flowers, cards, gifts, and heartfelt notes. But which one do I remember most? It was a "buckslip" (a promotional card about the size of a dollar bill) from Arsenio with his picture on it and "Sorry for your loss" scrawled on it. That was it. You know the first producer to give Arsenio his big break on TV? My father, who fought to get him on *The Tonight Show*. So we expected something more personal. What we got said, "I don't care."

Well, Arsenio lost his show in 1994 and guess what? No one he worked with would give him the time of day. They let him free fall and he's never come back. Being good to people matters. At some point in your career, whatever your career is, you're going to need someone to say, "You know, she's a good person. Let's give her a chance." Treat people like dirt when you're on top and that will never happen.

MEL'S BELLES

Some celebrities make the world richer for their presence. One of them is actress Jane Kaczmarek from *Malcolm in the Middle*. She started a charity organization called Clothes Off Our Back that literally takes the clothes off the stars' backs and auctions them for charity. For example, the Dior dress that Jennifer Aniston wore the year she won her Emmy for *Friends* fetched $50,000 for children's immunizations. The year that Teri Hatcher won the Golden Globe for *Desperate Housewives,* her Donna Karan frock raised megabucks at auction for a variety of worthy causes. I have limitless admiration for Jane and her work. She saw a need, realized her position as a celebrity could meet it, and created something out of nothing. That's extraordinary. So is she.

Roots? What Roots?

You don't have to be in entertainment for this lesson to apply to you. When things get going and we're on a roll, we're all tempted to forget how much help we needed when we weren't so flush. Life is a long run through terrain that can get pretty scary at times; there's not one person out there who hasn't needed a friend to lend her a few bucks or give her a lift when her car broke down, or a coworker to cover for her when she dropped the ball. I've lost count of how many times my pals have listened patiently while I told the tearful tale of my latest failed relationship, and I love them for putting up with me.

So when you're in a really great relationship, you're making a lot of money, or you're getting the opportunity you've worked so hard for, it's important to remember that the people who were there for you are still out there, and you owe them a debt. You owe it to them to be there for them. I'm talking about remembering your roots, remembering that just because your life is on the upswing, that doesn't mean you're any different. You still need help. You still need people to listen and care. You're one of the lucky ones and you need to let the people who helped you survive the hard times know that they're partially responsible for your good fortune. That doesn't necessarily mean you have to lend them money or bail them out of jail, though if duty calls and that's what you've gotta do, then do it. No, being good to people when you're on the way up is basically about two things:

- Expressing your gratitude to the people who were there for you. Sometimes all it takes is a card to show that you took the time.
- Being there for them when they need you.

When you've gotten the sweet law job you've slaved for, send flowers to the people who helped you study for the bar exam. When you get a big raise that lets you pay off your bills, celebrate by paying back a debt to a friend with interest and helping him get out of his own financial hole. You don't even have to win the lottery or land your dream job to do this. Take it from me, if you have a strong relationship, a family that loves you, a steady job, a roof over your head, and your health, you're winning at life. Celebrate your lucky spin of fate's wheel by making sure the people in your circle know how much you appreciate whatever they've done to make your life a little easier or better.

If only this were more common in Hollywood. Entitlement

is the opposite of gratitude, and it's a disease in the entertainment business. It's as if some stars, when they get their "big break," undergo some sort of lobotomy that robs them of the memories of the years when they would have killed for a non-speaking part in a toothpaste commercial. I can spot that attitude a mile away but that doesn't mean I understand it. Just because your status in the big world has changed doesn't mean that anyone else's is less important, that their troubles are less horrible, or their joys less transcendent.

Many stars under the age of twenty-five are particularly guilty of a sense of entitlement. Thanks to shows like *American Idol* and the power of the Internet, we're manufacturing our celebrities now in a way that we haven't since the days when Henry Willson was plucking strapping unknowns from small-town America and turning them into superstars with macho names like Rock Hudson and Tab Hunter. So because they don't have to work for years and pay their dues, there's a common attitude among the young things of Hollywood that they somehow *deserve* the money, attention, and adulation. But nobody deserves anything, and nobody owes you anything.

I think not paying your dues is a ticket to an entitled attitude and an ugly trail of broken relationships behind you. I was lucky. My parents went over the top to make sure I didn't grow up a coddled Hollywood brat. I'm grateful to them. If I wanted to ride horses (and I always did), I had to work in the barn. I had to earn my keep. As I've said, I did all the entry-level jobs when my career started, and I wouldn't trade that experience for anything. That's how you learn to appreciate how hard and important all those jobs are—how valuable everybody is. It gives you a level of humility, and while too much humility can harm your career, a healthy amount is *mandatory*.

THE GOSPEL ACCORDING TO JOAN

I ran into a man in New York who had apparently been my body-guard at a show I did on Fire Island twenty years before. He came up to me and asked me if I remembered him, and once he told me who he was I said, "Of course, I thought I knew you!" I didn't know who he was, but I always say that to people when they think I should know them, because it makes them feel good. Where's the harm in it? I'm not going to remember a guy who was my bodyguard from twenty years ago, but I believe in lying to make people feel better.

My husband had a great saying: "You can only yell at your peers." Meaning, only yell at someone who can yell back, not at some-one whose livelihood depends on you. You have to have respect for them and treat them with courtesy. Remember, the people you meet on the way up are the same ones you're going to meet on the way down.

The Reward You Don't Have to Pay For

Mom and I learned our humility lesson during the red carpet tele-casts. With the early shows, Mom and I were buzzing with excite-ment. We knew we were creating something that people would enjoy, and we cherished the illusion that we were part of the Holly-wood scene. But in the first couple of years, stars mostly walked right by us. We didn't get invited to a single Oscar after-party. It was a slap in the face—a reminder that we were just worker bees. We never forgot that feeling, and so we never took it for granted when we became part of the story, not just the storytellers.

After our show became a huge hit, things changed. Stars saw the benefit of talking to us, and we began to make the after-party invitation lists—including the A-list *Vanity Fair* party. It was spectacular. One year when we showed up, it was like the parting of the Red Sea in *The Ten Commandments*. We were the belles of the ball. But we knew the invites were professional, not personal. We were there because stars wanted us to talk about them the next day. So Mom and I didn't make the mistake of believing our own press clippings and acting like goddesses.

Good thing, too. Right when our ratings were at their highest (and the same month my mom was featured in the magazine), our *Vanity Fair* invitation was pulled. To this day we don't know why. We were told it was because we were "press." But it was really a reminder of where we stood in the pecking order. We were hired hands, not peers. We got another reminder a few years later when we were at a Golden Globes after-bash wearing a king's ransom in borrowed Harry Winston jewelry. These rocks were so expensive that we had actually been assigned a bodyguard. At some point in the evening the lights went out, plunging the room into darkness. I felt the bodyguard grab me and my mother and hustle us underneath the staircase for safety. One second we're talking to *The Shield*'s Michael Chiklis, the next I feel like the president. Pretty cool, I thought, until I realized that the guy wasn't guarding our bodies but the expensive sparklies on our necks, ears, and wrists.

After the whole thing ended, our attitude was one of the things I took as a reward. Sure, it was the first time in a dozen years that I wasn't in front of the camera without something else pending or in the works, and I felt adrift for a time. But I was able to reflect upon how I had treated everyone I worked with and feel proud. I knew I had left a trail of people behind me who knew that I was a hard worker, respectful, and appreciative of their work. That's important, because I have to live with myself.

No bull market or boom time lasts forever, but when the good times end there's always a gift you can give yourself that costs nothing: the knowledge that you behaved with class. We all want to believe we're the best people we can be, and it makes the low times easier to take when you can look back and know that you acted with grace and gratitude. Doing so can also help bring your fortunes right back around to a happy place. Take Teri Hatcher, for instance. She was blazing hot during the *Lois & Clark* TV series, but when the show was canceled, she couldn't buy a break. Other than the Bond movie *Tomorrow Never Dies*, you barely heard from Teri for seven years. It seemed like she would be yet another typecast TV star destined for direct-to-DVD movies. Then along came *Desperate Housewives* and suddenly Teri was back at the top of the heap.

It couldn't happen to a nicer person. During those rough years, Teri remained her true, sweet self. She didn't get bitchy or pout. She didn't play the unspeakably obnoxious "Do you know who I am?" card. She knew she had been luckier than most: She'd had her stardom. People wanted to give her a break because they knew they would enjoy working with her. When she came back to the top, Hollywood was happy for one of the good guys.

Take Care of Your Team

People who are successful in business, no matter in what profession, have a team of people around them who help them shine. If you're in entertainment, you have agents and managers, publicists and stylists. If you're an athlete you have coaches and trainers and managers and surgeons. Physicians have nurses and assistants and office managers, attorneys have clerks and paralegals, and so on. Life is like an Everest expedition: Nobody gets to the top alone. We all have Sherpas. That's why it's so incredibly important to remember and acknowledge those people and make sure that when you achieve success, they share in it.

You don't need to be rich or famous to have "people." Who are your people and what do they do for you? They're the people who let you lean on them, who give you advice, who pitch in when you're behind on a deadline, or who tell you the things you don't want to hear but need to hear. They're friends, sure, but they can also be teachers, mentors, parents, spiritual advisors, and even a whole host of paid professionals from tax preparers to dog sitters. It doesn't matter how much you earn or who you are—*they are there for you*. That's your team, and if you want to get very far in this life, take care of the team.

In any part of life, only a fool ignores the people who help her to just get by and live life without too much drama. So no matter how high up the totem pole you climb, you can't forget about your team. If you get elected prom queen, don't stiff the girls who put out your flyers and stumped for votes. If you get a promotion, treat the subordinates who worked to make you look good to a spectacular dinner. Understand that once you have achieved a certain level of success, the people in your past will embrace you as "their" success story. Respect that. Be open and welcoming to people who've meant something to you along the way: school friends, babysitters, your first boss. Remember that you did not get where you are by yourself.

People who take care of their team create a kind of buffer zone between themselves and misfortune. Bad things can still happen, but they don't cause as much damage because the love and support of others soften the blow. The most successful people in the entertainment industry tend to be those who treat their people like gold. Some people have worked for Madonna for more than twenty years. Her closest assistants can practically read her mind, and that makes managing her empire much easier. Madonna works her people hard, but here's the key: She never asks them to work harder than she does. Another celebrity who's benefited from treating people like gold is John Travolta. He's got more lives than a cat. Anybody who could come back after a turkey like *Battlefield Earth* has got to have a secret up his sleeve, and with John it's this: He's a genuinely nice man who is kind and considerate to everyone, even the press. Because he's such a good guy, John has gotten the benefit of the doubt more than once. The press also left his family largely alone during their time of grief.

When your fortunes turn sour, you're eventually going to try to get back to where you were. When you do, yours won't be the only résumé in the stack. You'll have competition. And when people sit around a conference table to talk about who will get the opportunity or whose business proposal they will accept, they won't care that you *used* to be big. What will matter is, how did you treat people? Were you a professional? Did you show up on time? Or were you a diva who showed up hungover and turned your work in late? Your opportunities to climb back up the ladder will be based on how other people feel about you. If they like you, they're far more likely to say, "Yeah, let's try her out and see what happens." If you made nothing but money and enemies, they're going to take great delight in imagining you panhandling on Sunset Boulevard.

In 1992, a comedian and talk-show host who shall remain nameless had his late-night program canceled. He had been a bastard to work for: rude, incredibly condescending, and a just-plain-miserable human being. This is how much everyone on his network despised him: The head of the network flew to the set to tell him face-to-face that his show was being pulled. In front of a crowd of behind-the-scenes personnel, the network chief said, "It gives me great pleasure to announce that you've been canceled." The assembled team, all of whom were now out of a job, broke into spontaneous applause. That's hatred. You can bet that when those people got their next jobs, their former boss wasn't going to get any recommendations.

SWEPT UNDER THE CARPET

In some ways it's the red carpet itself that's the star of the show. But the carpet begins life far from Hollywood. The one for the Oscars is woven in Dalton, Georgia, and dyed a proprietary shade of red (with a touch of purple) that's so secret, if I told you the formula I'd have to find someone bigger than me to kill you.

It's Nice to Share

Earlier I talked about those fancy swag bags that sponsors used to dole out to nominees and presenters before the big awards shows until the IRS decided to pull the plug. Well, even though those bags are no more, their lesson lives on. It's ironic, of course, to give Tom Hanks or Reese Witherspoon, who might pull down $20 million a film, a bag with an iPod, a Dolce &

Gabbana scarf, and an espresso maker when they can afford to buy their own a hundred times over. They don't need them and they may be more trouble than they're worth.

But while those swag bags may have been a taxable pain in the neck to the stars who got them, they were an annual extra Christmas gift to their staffs and support people—their teams. These folks aren't making seven figures a year. They're working folks who put in long hours for zero acclaim, and it's a real treat for them to get free pagers, vacation vouchers, and Kate Spade handbags every few Oscar seasons. That is, assuming their celebrity bosses were classy and smart enough to share their toys. I say smart because that's what it is. When you look at the people who have lasted decades in this business, you can be sure they share their good fortune and take care of the people who make their lives possible.

Another huge aspect of being nice on the way up is being generous and sharing with the people who matter. That doesn't always mean sharing material things, though that certainly doesn't hurt. My friends Melissa Lemer and Lorena Bendinskas run Silver Spoon Entertainment Marketing, a company that sets up lavish gift suites for some of the hottest Hollywood events and birthday parties. Like everyone else who attended their exclusive shindigs, I walked away with a fabulous goodie bag, but I wasn't the only one who got stuff. The Silver Spoon ladies are smart enough to know that the people behind the stars deserve gifts, too. So I took home gifts for my team as well. It was one more way I could thank them for being the greatest and for taking such good care of me. As I tell Cooper, toys are no fun if there's no one to play with.

But there are other, equally meaningful, ways to share with the people who've helped you besides taking a monster gift basket to the office break room or buying the team bottles of wine (not that there's anything wrong with those gestures). I also think it's important to share your finest moments with the people you love. Time is everybody's rarest commodity, so sharing extraordinary times is a gift everyone cherishes.

I've seen many stars share the red carpet spotlight with the ones they love. Jack Nicholson may have three Oscars, but his two youngest kids had never attended the Academy Awards until they came with their famous dad in 2006. His young son Raymond said, "I've only seen this on TV." That year, the Oscars were filled with first-time nominees like Heath Ledger, Terrence Howard, Felicity Huffman, Reese Witherspoon, George Clooney, Jake Gyllenhaal, and Amy Adams. I love first-timers, because they are so genuinely thrilled just to be there. They're also likely to need the support of family and friends, an excellent opportunity to share the experience. Terrence Howard, nominated for his role as a pimp-turned-rapper in *Hustle & Flow,* asked for five tickets from the Academy so he could bring some of the family who have been so important to him. Jeremy Piven, star of *Entourage,* regularly brings his mother with him to red carpet events. She has become such a regular that he now arranges not only for her dress but her hair and makeup.

When she accepted her Golden Globe for *Transamerica,* Felicity Huffman thanked William H. Macy "for believing in her." When she won for *Dreamgirls,* Jennifer Hudson said (unaware of the tragedy to come), "I'm so grateful to have my mother here celebrating with me, my boyfriend, my sisters and brothers . . . thank you all for being with me." Jamie Foxx cried and thanked his grandmother when he won for *Ray;* I was crying with him. Clint Eastwood thanked his ninety-five-year-old mother. Tom Hanks acknowledged his drama teacher when he won in 1994 for *Philadelphia.* When she won for *One Flew Over the Cuckoo's Nest,* Louise Fletcher thanked her deaf parents in sign language. Taking a moment to let everyone know how much this or that person means to you is *everything*.

How have you shared your Red Carpet Moments with the people you care about? That could mean sharing a spotlight dance with your father at your wedding, bringing your support team up to the podium to help you accept a professional award, or just calling your closest friends when you find out you got the lead role in a play to let them share in your excitement. It could mean a thousand things, all with one quality in common: You're taking the time to make someone part of your special moment. That's a gift that no amount of money can ever buy.

The final type of sharing that I think is vital is sharing your good fortune with others who are not as fortunate. I think that when you have achieved a level of wealth or influence, you have a responsibility to try to use it to make others' lives better. This shows that you really have a sense of how lucky you are and that you understand your responsibility. You can always tell the stars who get how blessed they are and how much they owe the world: Angelina Jolie, Russell Simmons, Sting, Rosie O'Donnell, Leonardo DiCaprio, Edward Norton, Sarah McLachlan, Tiger Woods, the late Christopher and Dana Reeve, to name a few. They give with their bank accounts and their hearts, and I don't think it's an accident that they're also wildly successful and have had great career longevity. Sharing the love not only makes you look good, it reflects a personal balance and centeredness that's essential to survival, famous or not.

When you have the power to inspire others or to change lives, how can you *not* use it? A great example is Lance Armstrong. The guy has an incredible story: He beat testicular cancer to become a world-class athlete, and then turned his fame into the Lance Armstrong Foundation, which helps people survive all kinds of cancer. Lance didn't have to do any of this;

he could have sat back after his six consecutive Tour de France wins and said, "I survived metastatic testicular cancer, I did something no other cyclist has done, now I'm going to Disneyland." He didn't. He chose to give back. He knew it was his responsibility. He gets it.

You don't have to be rich or famous to share the love. Most of us aren't, but we can still make a difference. Think about John Walsh, who was building luxury hotels when his son, Adam, was abducted and murdered. He became an advocate and created *America's Most Wanted*. Think about the moms and students who volunteer and give their time to local causes and national organizations without ever thinking about how it will look in the press. They give because it feels good. Making someone else

KNOW-IT-ALL

Lorena Bendinskas, Cofounder, Silver Spoon

Entertainment Marketing

- Give people unexpected gifts that they might never think to buy for themselves.
- Consider giving someone an experience (such as event tickets, a massage, a cooking lesson), rather than material objects.
- Give them a gift that they want, not something that you want.
- Look for unique gifts that have meaning behind them, like something that reminds you both of your relationship with each other.
- Consider a gift that keeps on giving, like a wine of the month club, or a Netflix subscription.

smile or affecting someone's life in a positive way makes us feel alive. What matters is that you have something to give and give it: time, expertise, compassion. If you had the support to make it through school and build your own successful practice as a CPA, why not share the love by volunteering to assist a non-profit with its finances? I know people who live paycheck to paycheck but are great with a toolbox and spend at least six weeks a year helping Habitat for Humanity build houses. It makes them feel like a million dollars and truly changes lives. You don't have to change the world to make it brighter.

How You Know You're Being Nice on the Way Up

• *You respect the people who made what you're doing possible.* Amanda Bynes has said that Lucille Ball, who died before she was even born, is her favorite actress. She even collects things that Lucy used to own. That impresses me. It tells me that this young actress, who specializes in the kind of physical, screwball comedy that made Lucille Ball a star, knows and acknowledges that her career benefited from an earlier generation of pioneers. If you know who made it possible for you to be doing what you're doing and let them know how appreciative you are, be proud of that. That could mean thanking a former professor or the man whose father founded your company, but no matter what the circumstances, being aware of your roots is always a sign that you're on the right track.

• *Old colleagues bring new opportunities.* Every business is like a small town: Word gets around and there are no secrets. If you're a raging prima donna who's impossible to please, everyone in your company or profession will know it in short order. On the other hand, if you are appreciative and under-standing, they'll know that, too. You can tell when your reputation is positive when colleagues you haven't heard from in years con-tact you out of the blue with a project or opportunity. That doesn't happen unless you're treating people the way you should.

• *You're never embarrassed by things people over-hear you saying.* On at least three occasions I've said something that was overheard by someone else and came back to haunt me. We've all done it. You've got to be aware of your surroundings, but more important, don't make a habit of dissing other people or talking trash. I wish I could tell all the actors I've seen on the red carpet what I've heard them say when they thought no one from the media was listening! Catty, ugly, nasty talk that would unravel your dreadlocks. The fact that I won't talk about it doesn't make it okay. If you've never been forced into an apology by an overheard piece of gossip, or wished there were some way to take back a snarky e-mail, that's a good sign you're following this Lesson to a T.

• *People stick around.* Producer Joel Silver has a Midas touch for making incredibly successful films like the *Matrix* series. He, as many people in Hollywood do, also has a reputa-tion for putting his assistants through hell. Supermodel Naomi Campbell is even more notorious; she has a reputation for abus-ing assistants and domestic staff, including alleged assaults and even lawsuits. Come on. If you're so insecure that you have to torture some twenty-four-year-old making eight bucks an hour to make yourself feel important, get some therapy.

But seriously, abusive people don't hold on to staff very long. However, if you've got people like administrative assis-tants who've worked with you since Clinton was president, give yourself a gold star for being respectful, self-aware, and a good boss. I'm lucky enough to have an assistant, Sabrina, who has been a lifesaver for me and my family for more than twenty years. I couldn't tie my shoes without her, and I'm grateful that she puts up with me. Plus, I know that if a woman as gorgeous and together as she is cares about somebody like me, I must be pretty all right. Or my checks don't bounce. Just kidding.

How You Know You're Not Being Nice on the Way Up

- *You pick on waiters.* My father always said, "Never yell at a waiter." Of course, smart aleck that I am, I said, "Does that mean I can yell at everybody else?" What Dad's rule really means, of course, is that you can tell a lot about a person's character by the way he treats someone who can't answer back, like a waiter or a store clerk. It takes a real jerk to abuse someone who has little choice but to stand and take it. It's much nicer to be courteous than to be mean or rude. Apart from the fact that anyone who's working hard deserves your respect, a good attitude also pays off with better service.

- *You shoot from the hip, then apologize.* Sometimes you see a person's true character not in the considered, planned things they do, but in their off-the-cuff actions. Most of us at one time or another have seen a superior repeatedly snap and verbally humiliate a subordinate, only to come back later with a formal apology and a gift. Guess which reflects the boss's true nature? Spontaneous acts are truer, because we don't think about how they'll make us look; we just do them. If your first impulse is always to read someone the riot act, belittle their intelligence, or point the finger, then you might want to consider the face you're showing the world.

- *People come to you for gossip.* For years, my friends would come to me for the latest dish on the stars, especially

RED CARPET RULES
The Big Presentation

- Look appropriate for the venue. You can't redo your first impression. When in doubt, always dress more professionally, neatly, and conservatively than you think you'll need to.

- Keep to your talking points. Don't start ad-libbing and spilling your guts about things you either don't know about or don't want to reveal.

- Listen. People are going to have questions. Be prepared to answer them. If you can't, say, "That's a good question, and I don't have the answer right now but I'll have it to you in twenty-four hours."

- Provide materials in an organized, classy way. Stapled is okay; bound is better. Make sure everything is neat and for God's sake, proofread it.

- If you're presenting out of your element (at another company's office, for instance), try to get some time to do a dry run and at least check out the presentation space ahead of time. This way, you'll know the size of the room, how well the sound carries, and so on.

- Check your technology before you start. The time to troubleshoot your MacBook is before your slide show, not while it's going on.

- Speak slowly. When we're nervous, we tend to speed up. That makes you hard to understand. Take a full, deep breath between each full sentence to slow you down and reduce your stress level.

after a red carpet season was over. They assumed that I had all the juicy stories about who was cheating on whom and so on, and sometimes they were right. But they learned after a few years not to ask, because they found out I wasn't talking. I'm not stupid. Unless you're Perez Hilton, being the source of malicious gossip in Hollywood is a sure guarantee that you won't be working. So if people come to you on the assumption that you'll be their fountain of "who's sleeping with whom" stories, what does that say about you? Is it flattering?

• *Your calls don't get returned.* When you treat people with respect, empathy, and kindness, they want to talk to you. But when you're abusive or call only when you need something, you're going to wind up leaving a lot of voice mails and wondering why nobody "friends" you on Facebook.

Being Shallow on the Way Down

The funny thing about this lesson is that the shallowest gestures can have the deepest impact. Sure, developing an attitude of long-term kindness toward the people in your life is wonderful, but they're going to care a hundred times more about the big-enough-to-live-in candy, fruit, and wine basket that your divorce client sent you and you shared with them. Intention talks, but dark chocolate walks. I do know that a pattern of gift giving and generosity, even if it's small, will earn the love and loyalty of friends, staff, and customers for years to come. Some shallow but oh-so-effective ideas:

• *Don't e-mail your thank-you.* Show some effort. If you can't shop for a gift that's meaningful to the person, keep a supply of thank-you cards on hand. Write one and mail it.

- *Make a donation.* For someone who's generous, making a donation in her name to her favorite charity is a wonderful gift.
- *Bring the extra.* Birthday cake, wine, whatever it is, if you have more than you'll use, share it with your partners in crime.
- *Buy a gift for someone's kid.* You can never, ever go wrong with this one. Even if someone hates accepting gifts for themselves, they will always be grateful for a plush fire engine or a ballerina doll.
- *Send gifts when it's not expected.* Birthdays and anniversaries are mandatory gift days, so there's no buzz of real surprise. But a gift out of the blue, for no reason, is always a delight. For instance, I collect snow globes. I have an entire wall of them. My friends Jay Mohr and Nikki Cox were in Las Vegas and got it in their heads to go to the Liberace Museum. There they found a Liberace snow globe, bought it, and presented it to me. It's still my favorite because it was such a spontaneous, loving gift.

Down Deep

I hope it's clear that sharing the love and being good to others has absolutely nothing to do with how much money you have or whose names you have in your Rolodex. It has everything to do with being mindful of what other people have done for you and how they're trying their best, making sure the good times are special for everyone, and never assuming that other people know you're grateful. When you go to a dinner party, thank the person who held it and compliment them. Thank the person who fixes your car, doormen who greet you, and messengers who bring you flowers. Give gifts to your mailman and the guy who does your dry cleaning. Life is short, and each of these people is the most important person in the drama of their own lives. Treat them that way.

Some tips I have learned from the red carpet:

• *Take the high road.* Being nice on the way up sometimes requires being gracious when you would rather rip someone a new smile from collarbone to collarbone. Yes, there are times to roll around in the gutter, but most of the time you'll come out better if you stay above the fray and be the one who's understanding, magnanimous, and professional. For example, one year at a red carpet event, a woman on the production team said something to me that was deeply unprofessional, rude, and embarrassing. I could have torn into her right then and there, but I didn't. I went off and did my next interview, and after the entire telecast was over, I went to her and said, "I respect you and I respect your work, but I just want to tell you that what you said to me was unprofessional and really hurt my feelings."

I didn't scream. I didn't threaten her job. I think she was expecting me to rant and rave, so when I didn't it threw her off guard. My calm and understanding demeanor embarrassed her, and she apologized. Problem solved. Bottom line, when you're the big cheese, you shouldn't need to raise your voice. Yelling is for amateurs.

• *Show real interest.* This is the interviewer's can't-miss trick. Let people know you care about what they care about by asking questions and listening. People love to tell their stories. Make sure you really listen and pay attention.

• *Acknowledge what's important to others.* When you do this, you validate them and what they do. Everyone craves this kind of validation, no matter how successful they have become.

RED CARPET RULES
Holiday Celebrations

- If it's your birthday, provide small gifts for each person you invite to your party. It's a great touch.
- In the birthday speech (and you will be asked to make one), keep it simple: gratitude, best wishes, more gratitude.
- If it's your anniversary, be sure you don't monopolize your spouse. You'll have plenty of time together later, but at your party, people want to be around at least one of the happy couple.
- For anniversary speeches, don't get cute and rehash old fights or former lovers. Again, keep it simple: how lucky you are, gratitude to everyone present, and so on. Throw in a little humor, as long as it's not too raunchy.
- Whatever the occasion, keep a running list of who got you what gift so you can easily write thank-you notes later on. Assign someone the task of being the list-keeper.
- For family holidays such as Christmas, steer clear of religious and political discussions. I'm amazed by how many people ignore this advice and wonder why everyone's fighting by the time the turkey is served.
- Keep the TV off. *The Twilight Zone* marathon may be cool, but when you're glued to the boob tube, you're not talking.
- Bring games like Scrabble or cards. They're great for getting everyone talking and having a good time, or at least causing a good fight to add to the family lore. We no longer play Monopoly at family gatherings.

- **Say "Well done."** Nothing worth doing is easy. Worthwhile things take time and effort, and that time and effort deserve your recognition. Encourage people by saying things like, "Good job" or "Congratulations." Sometimes that's all it takes to keep someone from quitting.

- **Express your thanks.** This is *huge*. The act of going out of your way to thank someone works wonders. It's natural to expect a reward after hard work, and all the reward most of us need is to be recognized for our effort. Thank your assistant for her work meeting a deadline. Thank your mom for cooking you dinner. Call or send a card. Put effort into your thanks. Send a bottle of wine. You can do more to cement a great relationship with a gracious thank-you than with years of work.

- **Reciprocate.** Return the favor. Pay it forward.

- **Ask for advice.** It's deeply flattering to have someone you respect ask you for advice. Hopefully your friends respect you enough that when you ask them for their counsel, they'll take it as a compliment. When you ask them for their help, they will feel like they're on top of the world, and they'll work hard to make sure they deserve your faith.

- **Offer to help.** Be a role model by offering to lend a hand. People want to know that someone they care about is truly concerned about their interests. I know when Mom or someone else in my life asks me how I'm doing or gives me a simple "Good job," it gives me a lot of fuel to keep going.

I've used a lot of celebrities as examples in this chapter, people with the money to buy expensive gifts for others. But it takes nothing more than thoughtfulness to be good to the people who are good to you. A few years back, a friend of mine and his wife moved hundreds of miles from where all of his wife's friends lived. Who was the only one of her friends who kept in touch and even sent gifts for their kids out of the blue? The one who barely scraped by financially. She didn't have two nickels to rub together, but she cared. She took the time to express her love and let my friend's wife know she was thinking about her. That's all it takes to gain lifelong loyalty.

Your moment in the sun will come. You'll have a bout of good fortune or someone will do something nice for you. Or maybe you'll just wake up healthy and with all your marbles, with some fantastic memories and a great circle of friends and family, and decide you owe them some thanks for your blessings. When that happens, remember their names and make the toast. There's so much to celebrate if we simply remember to do it.

Find the Balance

Beauty is only skin deep. I think what's really important
is finding a balance of mind, body, and spirit.

—JENNIFER LOPEZ

*N*ot long ago, when I was neck-deep in developing a business venture that involved investors and endless meetings, I had a meeting scheduled with some people flying in from New York that coincided with something important going on at Cooper's school. This was what I call a "Where's the balance?" moment. A few years ago, I probably would have assumed that nobody on the business side of the aisle cared about my need to be an active mom, so I would have had to choose Door #1 or Door #2 and feel rotten either way. But I'm a little smarter now. I know that I'm not the only one seeking balance in this life; most people grasp how vital it is, even if they don't have to struggle with it themselves. So rather than force myself to choose between my project and my son, I leveled with the folks from New York. Voilà! Door #3 appeared, we were able to move the meeting up two hours, and I was able to go to Cooper's school on schedule. Balance achieved.

Entertainment is a driven, manic business that chews up and spits out personal time and family life, but in that it's not unique. In fact, the assumption is that if you want to be a success in any competitive field—technology, medicine, law, professional sports—you have to sacrifice your personal life on the altar of commerce. But what does it mean to you to be successful? Does it mean having a ton of money but no time to enjoy it, or does it mean knowing what's most important to you and then building your life and career around that? I think it's the second. For me, nothing is more important than family, especially my boy. I love working and I get a charge out of developing a new TV show or creating a new business. But I make allowances to find time to be with Cooper, my mother, my friends, and alone with myself. If I didn't make that time in my day, the creative energy I need to do my work would quickly dry up.

Every one of us struggles to juggle our work, our relationships, our need for peace and solitude, our spiritual selves, our ambition, and our personal passions. I believe it's the single biggest challenge we all face, especially women. Let's face it, trying to balance home life and work is like herding cats, all of them feral and grouchy and determined to do their own thing. You can't have it all. You can, however, have a *lot*. It all depends on how well you can keep all the moving parts moving (and there are a lot of moving parts)—how well you can balance taking care of yourself with doing things for other people.

Finding the balance in your life boils down to this: What do you say yes to, and what do you say no to? To find the ideal mixture that gives you the life you want, first you've got to be true to yourself and not live according to anyone else's standards. If it's important to you to live without debt, then you might be perfectly content living in a small bungalow that you can pay off in a few years, even if your friends, who all live in huge McMansions and are leveraged to the hilt, think you're crazy. Who cares what anyone else thinks? Balance is about knowing what matters to *you*, setting your priorities accordingly, and filtering out the rest of the junk.

Avoiding the Relationship Grinder

For me, a balanced life centers on relationships. It's so easy to take other people for granted when you're busy with your career; you assume they will always be there, always be available when you want them to be. But that's a fool's game, because they won't be. You have to put people first if you want them to be in your life. More accurately, you have to put the mundane parts of relationships before the most exciting job interview, corporate retreat, or brainstorming session, because healthy relationships thrive on mundane little bits of time: watching *Lost* together or reading the kids *Goodnight Moon* at bedtime. I think a balanced life means taking the daily flotsam of your relationships—the parts of life that bosses might consider unimportant—and making them just as important as anything you do for your career. Something, somewhere has to give or you wind up alone.

I'm not going to lie: This is an endless challenge for me. I'm good at prioritizing time for my son, but it's a challenge to balance that with the other parts of my life. I have been accused more than once of putting relationships on a rung below Cooper and my work, but that's the choice I've made. When the right relationship comes along, I'm sure I'll reorder things once again.

In general, Hollywood is nonpareil at grinding relationships into a fine powder. There are just so many temptations: money, hot costars, media pressure, and the general throwaway air of celebrity culture. Hollywood invented the "starter marriage." If you don't like your marriage after a couple of years, just trade it in for a shiny new divorce decree, and *bang!*—you're back in the dating pool with some great stories to tell and perhaps even some alimony to make ends meet.

But you never hear much about the Hollywood couples who hum along beautifully like Tom Hanks and Rita Wilson or Kurt Russell and Goldie Hawn. That's because those people are well grounded and know what matters most. They've decided that their relationships are the center of their lives; everything else revolves around love, time, and support for each other. My mother and father were the same way: utterly devoted to each other, right up to the time he died. That stability is essential in a business where success is so ephemeral and fortunes can change so fast. Even when one partner is away on set for months at a time, the strongest Hollywood couples find ways to stay strong—travel, video e-mail, sending special gifts, you name it. I really admire that.

Right now, the most important relationship in my life is with my little man, who I know will one day take the world by storm. Cooper is the reason I do everything, and he began making himself a priority early on. If you have kids, you know that balance is a thousand times simpler before they come along. Afterward, the number-one rule of life becomes "Be selfless." You have no choice. Nature trains parents to be selfless through sleep deprivation. It's simple: You're too tired to remember what you need. When you're up at 2:30 in the morning on a day when you've got a meeting at 8:30 A.M., you figure, "While I'm up, I may as well get something done." So you change, feed, or rock the kid, organize your speech, press your suit, squeeze some orange juice, and correct your oldest kid's homework (unless you're in Los Angeles, where you get on the freeway four hours before your meeting because of the traffic). Motherhood is God's version of New York City: If you can make it through the first six weeks, you can make it anywhere.

Because Cooper is what's most important to me, I find ways to mix him in with my work whenever I can. I've been taking him to work with me since he was eight weeks old; he was the unofficial mascot of the red carpet broadcasts. It was a common sight to see the two of us, a couple of hours before the start of the show, me with my makeup and hair half-done, kicking a soccer ball around on the red carpet while the tech guys ran cable and the fans laughed at us. I think it drove my stylist a little batty, but it was so normal, and just so much *fun*.

MEL'S BELLES

It's not enough that Reese Witherspoon is a wonderful, Oscar-winning actress, a superstar, a mogul with her own successful production company, and a mom of two who handled her divorce from Ryan Phillippe with such élan. She's also got the ability to laugh at situations that might turn other hugely successful actresses into tantrum-throwing, hair-pulling divas from hell. In 2006, when she won her Golden Globe for *Walk the Line,* she wore a gorgeous gold metallic vintage dress loaned to her by Chanel. But we found out later that not only was the dress not vintage, but it had first been lent to Kirsten Dunst for the 2003 Golden Globes . . . and there were red carpet photos to prove it. This is like red carpet Watergate—a major fashion scandal. Reese didn't bat an eyelash. She laughed it off. You usually don't see that kind of beauty and talent in a package without a monster ego, but you do in her case.

It's About Choices

On the red carpet, balance is not obvious, but it's always present. The situation seems so fundamentally out of control, with everyone moving at the speed of sound, anyone who's going to be on camera undergoing frantic last-second taping and tucking and hair and makeup touch-ups, with cables and lights all around and fans and photographers screaming. It's really a hang-on-for-dear-life situation. But behind it all, there are people trying desperately to balance, and I'm not just talking about the women's four-inch heels.

I've looked behind the curtain and I know that even the most beautiful, famous women in the world are insecure and have to make hard choices like the rest of us. It's really quite simple: If you have other people in your life and you care about being mentally and physically healthy, you have to choose how you spend your limited time. Time is like having a bank account that gets a fresh deposit each day, but every deposit is only twenty-four hours. With that limited fund, you've got to work and earn a living, take care of your health and your home, spend quality time with the people you love, and carve out a few spare moments to be Woody Allen and play your clarinet at a Manhattan nightclub—or just read a great novel. You can't do it all in one day; the daily deposit of time just isn't enough. So you prioritize. You choose.

In Hollywood, work almost always comes first, out of pure survival instinct. The attitude toward work in the entertainment business is like the attitude toward political power in Russia: If you walk away even temporarily, somebody might step in and take it away. Everyone is terrified of someone else getting the great role, the development deal, the green light to start shooting, the recording contract. So hardly anybody turns down an opportunity, especially early in their careers. One of the goals for any actor or musician is to become like Clint Eastwood or Jay-Z, where you're in control of your opportunities and therefore your time. That's one of the reasons I've become so entrepreneurial since leaving TV Guide Network. It's the only way I know I can get more control over my time.

Balance is all about choices. Based on the things in your life that are most important to you, you have to choose how much time to give to work, relationships, and yourself. And it's not just one choice; you have to keep things liquid from day to day because situations change and new opportunities and challenges arise. There are many types of balance to manage (as if we all didn't have enough to do):

• *Short-term balance*—You've got a master's thesis to write and you just started dating a really cute guy. How do you make time for both? This the essence of short-term balance. It might cover a week or even just twenty-four hours, and during that time, you've got to keep more balls in the air than a Barnum & Bailey clown. Short-term balance requires adjusting on the fly. Some days you do your work while moving a hundred miles an hour with your hair on fire because that's what the situation calls for, while other days you slow down and put work on the back burner. The only thing that's consistent is that no two days are the same.

• *Long-term balance*—You make a bargain with the person in your life that you'll spend so many hours at your new job, so many hours working on the weekend, and so many hours taking care of things at home. This "contract" might last a year or five years, but it's a long-term picture of the balance that you need at this point in your life. As you know, being young usually goes hand in hand with needing to devote more time to work and climbing the ladder. So your long-term balance is going to change as you enter each new life stage—or as you get tired of the way you were living before. Like many things, as you get older, I find you become a lot less tolerant of balance arrangements that truly are not balanced.

• *Small-picture balance*—This means having balance in one area of your life, such as your family relationships. You can be an agent of chaos at your office or your college, procrastinating, doing work in a panic, and constantly in conflict with colleagues or friends. But when you get home, the agreement becomes that you'll allocate time for the kids, for working on the house, for making dinner, and for yourself. This kind of balance lets you create little oases of control while the rest of your life is ricocheting around like a hockey puck in an NHL game.

• *Big-picture balance*—This is the whole enchilada, your approach to balance for your entire life. This is the big leagues of time management, and though most of us never get beyond Little League, it's always worth aspiring to. When you're trying to create big-picture balance, you've got to know what matters most to you, and to ask for help. The reason there are so many personal assistants paddling the waters of Hollywood, picking up prescriptions and dropping off dry cleaning, is not just that big-name actors, directors, and producers don't want to do those things. It's because having help is one of the only ways they can find a spare moment to work out, have a glass of wine with their spouses, or watch a sunset.

Surrounding it all is your vision for the lifestyle you want. It's all well and good to come up with short-term solutions to give you more time for fun and family, but until you really know the kind of life you want to be living, everything else is just a Band-Aid. For instance, a friend of mine decided that he and his family were going to leave Southern California, where he had lived all his life, and move to Washington State. The reason?

After entering his early forties and having kids, he and his wife decided that he was working too much just to keep up their lifestyle. They looked at their priorities and decided what they wanted most was simplicity, peace, free time, and to grow their own food and live green. That's not the life I would choose, but that doesn't matter. I'm happy for them. They have a vision, and that vision will drive the balance they create—short-term, long-term, and all the rest.

KNOW-IT-ALL

Debra Luftman, M.D., Physician, Mom, Author,
Speaker, Owner of Her Own Skincare Line

Family and health are the most important parts of my life. Everything else I do—seeing patients, lecturing at UCLA, doing media appearances for my new book—falls apart if I don't take care of those two things. Knowing what's important helps you prioritize and get things done. Family is important not just for helping you stay focused on what matters, but for actually helping you get things done. That's one of the reasons I moved back to Los Angeles after going to medical school in Boston: to have my family nearby.

Being my own boss and having my own practice has also been helpful because I'm able to schedule my own hours, which a lot of women and mothers struggle with. I think a lot more women should be looking for work at family-friendly businesses, because there are more and more companies that are taking the need for family balance into account. It's a way to find the best people, people who care about balancing work and home life.

Not being able to have everything isn't bad. You don't need everything. People who are described as "having it all" are people who have decided what they care about more than anything else, changed how they live so those things are at the center, and quit worrying about everything else. They don't "have it all"; no one does. They have what makes their lives rich and full.

"Healthy Selfish"

The most difficult time my mother and I ever went through was the aftermath of my father's death. It took years before she and I were able to discuss how each of us reacted. To this day, I will openly say to my mother that I disagreed with her actions. After Dad died, Mom looked me in the eye and basically said, "I can't save you until I save myself." To paraphrase: "You're on your own, kid." I felt horribly abandoned. She went right back to work. She started dating. She talked about his suicide in her standup act. I was horrified. Why wasn't she wallowing in the overwhelming grief? I thought she was being disrespectful to the memory of my father. In a way, I felt like I had lost both my parents.

Now I understand why she did what she did. I know that she was trying to survive her own grief, and her method was to work and move on as best she could. She was being what I call "healthy selfish," taking care of her own needs so she would have something left to give me and help me through my grief. If she hadn't, she would have fallen apart. At the time, I carried a heavy load of resentment and anger toward her; it took a year for us to speak again. But it took me even longer to be able to say, "I don't know if I would have handled it the way you did, but now I understand and accept why you did."

We all hear platitudes about being selfless and giving unconditionally to others, but that's only part of the story. Yes, it's important to give to other people, but it's more important to look after your own needs. Don't let anyone tell you how to grieve. Only you know what you need at the time. If you don't take care of yourself—make sure you're happy and healthy and fulfilled and have your emotional house in order—you're not going to be in shape to help anyone else.

This is why I think it's ridiculous when people say that once you have children, your marriage becomes all about the kids. If you believe that, you're probably divorced. Once you have rug rats crawling around, it becomes more crucial than ever that the marriage be about Mom and Dad. Why? Because they are the fulcrum on which the family moves. If the marriage isn't happy and solid, no amount of attention given to the children is going to make up for the anger and resentment and the sense of being left without anything solid to hold on to. That's deeply frightening for kids. Trust me. I've been there.

This is why when you say, "It's all about me," it should be about sixty-five percent true. If you have friends who are constantly falling apart, an employer that's teetering on the edge of insolvency, or a parent with a health problem, how can you pitch in and make things better when you're always depressed yourself or so disorganized that you never seem to have time to eat, much less help someone else? Part of balance is picking your battles. You make yourself a priority and then decide exactly how much of that time account you'll spend on other people. You become your own person and decide what code you live by. You balance honesty with judgment and compassion and perspective. You discover how to put yourself in someone else's shoes and walk around. When I did that, my mother and I started to heal.

THE GOSPEL ACCORDING TO JOAN

I don't have balance in my life and I don't care. If you have a passion in your life, you go after it. Who needs balance? I think you need balance if you're married and have a family and are trying to have a career. At one time in my life, I was very concerned with this. I had two children: Melissa and my career, and I worked very hard to make sure the wrong one did not get most of the attention. But if you have a passion and you have the freedom to do it, go for it 24/7. You can have balance later.

Finding Time for Passions

A hallmark of balance is that you're willing to create time and space in your life, no matter how busy it may be, for the pursuits that you love, the things you're passionate about. I learned to surf just a few years ago for a reality show, and now it's become one of my favorite things to do. No matter how busy I am with taping or business I always find time to slip on my wet suit, head over to Malibu, and spend a couple hours shredding some waves (if you can call the kind of surfing I do "shredding"). It's not only something that shows that I have balance, it's *part* of my balance, a timeless, peaceful activity that relieves the stress of the day and reminds me what I love about my life. If I don't have time to surf, I get out on the court and beat the daylights out of a few hundred innocent tennis balls—anything to relax and unwind.

I find it astonishing that some of the busiest people in Hollywood also somehow make time for their personal passions. Perhaps the best-known example of this philosophy is Matthew McConaughey, who is as well known for his surf-and-sand lifestyle as for his movies. It's amazing what a little nude beachside bongo playing will do for your press visibility, isn't it? Still, Matt has become something of a symbol of the Southern California beach culture, and he finds time to immerse himself in it even though he's got multiple movies in the pipeline at any time, plus he's now a dad. Other examples of stars who make time for their passions include:

- Clint Eastwood, who composes and plays music when he's not making Oscar-winning films.
- Woody Harrelson, who's a ferocious advocate for environmental responsibility and manages to balance his career with his passion for confrontational activism.
- Mandy Moore, who values being grounded and doing what you love so much that she created www.uPumpItUp.com, a Web site that helps young women discover the things they love and turn them into realities.
- Steve Martin, who besides acting has written novels, films, children's books, and, most recently, a bestselling memoir, *Born Standing Up*.
- Zooey Deschanel, who when she's not appearing in films like *500 Days of Summer* is recording songs and touring as part of the musical duo She & Him.
- Francis Ford Coppola, who years ago leveraged his success as a director to indulge his passion for wine. Today, his Niebaum-Coppola winery produces some of the finest zinfandels and clarets in California.

- Harrison Ford, aside from being one of the most fiercely private superstars in the business, is also an enthusiastic private pilot who owns a collection of small airplanes and helicopters, and has even helped authorities in search-and-rescue operations.

If these people can manage their demanding Hollywood careers and still find the spare hours to engage in the activities that give them joy, then so can you. Add up the hours in each day that you typically spend at work, sleeping, cooking meals, caring for your kids if you have them, and doing anything else that you can't let slide. How much time is left? Great, now how are you using that time? A lot of folks I know spend their

SWEPT UNDER THE CARPET

The seating at the Oscars, Golden Globes, Grammys, or any other award show is always a bone of contention. Everybody wants to sit close to the stage, because it's the ultimate proof of status: If you're hot, you're close so you'll be in some camera shots. Nominees are always close, of course, but it's a crapshoot for many others. My friend John Rich of the country duo Big & Rich told me, "I have gone from being in a successful band and sitting in the third row at award shows to being thrown out of the band, having no tickets, and no one giving a damn. The next thing you know, you are opening the show and sitting in front of your old band." Life's a funny thing, John, and the red carpet is even funnier.

idle time either watching TV or surfing the Internet. If that sounds like you, then I have a suggestion: Turn off the Food Network and use the couch time for something you enjoy, something that's just for you. If you really take a hard look at your schedule, you can find an hour here or there for meditation, gardening, woodworking, writing, or taking a brisk walk in the hills.

Make sure the activity you insert into your already-busy day is something you truly adore—something you'd do for free forever. If it's not, you're likely to feel exhausted and obligated. If it's truly a passion, then you're going to be energized by doing it even for half an hour a day, even when you're tired from work, school, parenting, dating, or whatever else fills up your day. Passion and balance go hand in hand.

How You Know You're in Balance

- *You have energy.* You're not feeling used up and spent because being in balance means having time to recharge your batteries doing something you care about or doing nothing at all. Ever come home from work just dog-tired after a stressful day? How the evening goes depends on whether you have some time after you get home to take care of yourself, drop the worries of the day, and just breathe. If you have that kind of psychological buffer zone, your stress hormones are going to dissipate and you're going to have a lot more vigor for getting together with friends, going out on a date, or doing just about anything else.

- *You're there for others.* I'm able to be available for my friends when there's a broken-down car or a broken-up heart because I always reserve something for myself. Any one of us is like a truck with two gas tanks: main and reserve. The main tank is what we use to give us energy for our own lives, while the reserve tank fuels the things we do for others: pitching in when the babysitter gets sick, providing counsel when a marriage is breaking up, offering shelter during a natural disaster. But when we let our main tank get too low, we start dipping into our reserves just to keep going in our daily lives. Then there's less there for others. So when you're taking the time to keep your main tank filled by meditating, doing tae kwon do, playing the cello, or whatever constitutes your personal, spiritual time, you're ensuring that you'll be ready when others need you most.

• *You're cool under fire.* Panic is an admission that you don't know what to do. That's why in an emergency, cops and firefighters don't panic while civilians do; they've had training so they know what they should be doing when buildings start to shake. If you've got that kind of *Miami Vice* cool going on when everyone around you is freaking out, I'll bet it's because you're not turning the normal episodes of daily living into their own mini-crises. You're not a drama queen. So when a friend gets kicked out by her boyfriend, with her stuff thrown all over the lawn, you're the one who's calm and takes logical, helpful steps.

• *You're able to stop and "be."* Taking time to be in the moment is one of the most pleasurable acts anyone can take. It's such a rare treat to stop everything you're doing, let go of worries about the future or regrets about the past, and just appreciate the few seconds of time that you're floating in *right now*. Whether you're an actor, an administrative assistant, a teacher, a lawyer, or a mom, those quiet heartbeats of time are tough to come by. In fact, they almost never come about by themselves; you have to dig them out of the rush of a day and polish them like gemstones. If you make a habit of such "just be" moments from time to time, then it's safe to say you're balancing quite well.

How You Know You're Not in Balance

• *Life seems like a chore.* It's hard to muster enthusiasm for something when you're always overwhelmed. When you do nothing but work, care for a sick relative, or anything else that drains body, mind, and spirit, picking up your dry cleaning becomes hard. Getting your hair done becomes impossible. Working out at the gym? Unthinkable. Allowing your time to be dominated by one activity, especially if it takes a great deal of mental energy, means you've got little time left for eating well, exercising, or getting enough sleep. All of which makes taking on the mundane tasks of regular life feel like climbing Half Dome.

• *You're always rushing and always behind.* This one probably sounds familiar, because if you're not the one who's always trying to catch up with life, you know someone who is. Your headlong plunge through life leaves you no time to prepare for anything or manage your workload, so you're continually reacting. You're lucky if you can pull all-nighters fueled by massive Dr Pepper infusions just to finish the work that lets you keep your job. Basically, your time management skills are nonexistent.

• *You can't believe how much time has passed.* You had big dreams once upon a time. You wanted to go to dental school. You wanted three kids and a white picket fence. You wanted to be the next Bill Gates and had a plan for making it happen. Whatever your great goal, it would just have to wait until you had a little more time. Only that time never came, did it? There was never enough time, so you always put off those great aspirations and suddenly you woke up and, like Pink Floyd sang, "ten years have got behind you." That's the peril when you're unbalanced in your life and can't control your time. You never make the time to do anything more than dream your dreams. Eventually, maybe it's too late for some of them, and I think if anything qualifies as a tragedy, that does.

• *Everything is a crisis.* You hit a traffic snarl and have a complete emotional meltdown. A bit excessive? Only if you're so tightly wound and scheduled that the slightest deviation becomes a catastrophe. I've known people like this, especially in entertainment: They're trying to cram in every meeting, activity, errand, and occasion out of some ridiculous sense of obligation. I'm tempted to grab them by the shoulders and shout, "Obligated to who?" It makes even less sense in my business, where delays and lots of standing around waiting are the norm, playing havoc with even the most finely tuned schedule. So why turn every reversal into D-Day?

• *Your relationships are unequal.* Balanced people, as I have said, have something in reserve to give to the people they care about. Those for whom balance is something that only gymnasts do find that other people are usually taking care of them—helping them on last-minute projects that should have been done weeks before, saying "There there" after breakups, or lending money yet again. If you step back and take stock of who's reaching out to whom in your circle of family and friends, and you find that you're usually on the receiving end of the assistance, you have a balance deficit.

Shallow but Balanced

Mastering time management and life balance is kind of like getting over a drug addiction: First, you have to admit you have a problem. When you finally do it, the next step is to begin getting

RED CARPET RULES

Reunions

- Take care of personal maintenance the week before the reunion: hair, nails, waxing, you name it. Don't wait until the last minute.

- Make sure you look and feel fabulous in your clothes. Test-drive your dress as if you were going to the Academy Awards, and if it's not perfect, wear something else. You're going to get only one shot at this.

- Preplan your evening. Have a strategy in mind in case the reunion is terribly boring or you hook up with the former quarterback.

- Get over your old grudges before you go. The stuff that happened twenty years ago? You're probably the only one who remembers it. Don't rehash it or you'll end up looking petty.

- Don't take a date you need to babysit. You're there to have a good time, not break social barriers for your awkward friend. Make sure your date makes you look good, not desperate.

- Prepare to be disappointed. Most people won't look as good as you remember them, nor will they be the raging successes you assumed they would be. Take people for what they are.

some control over those hours that are slipping away and robbing you of opportunities to be with the people you love or do what makes life rich. Start with some of my suggestions from the shallow side of the balance beam:

- ***Work out and eat right.*** If you don't care for your health, you're not going to have the energy to get your time under control, much less start playing the guitar again, learn to cook Thai food, or read that Tolstoy novel.

- *Write everything down.* I'm sure that my memory has been damaged by years of inhaling the fumes from whatever they used to clean the red carpet, but whatever the reason, if I don't write something down, I can't remember it. If it's not in my iPhone or on a sticky note, it just doesn't get done.
- *Keep a master calendar* with your entire life on it—birthdays, haircuts, anniversaries, meetings, even favorite movies and the day they open. It doesn't matter whether it's in paper form or software form; having the organization is what matters.
- *Give yourself small kindnesses* like a spa day, some gourmet takeout, or a house-cleaning service. Being kind to yourself when you've been busy can allow you that most wonderful of luxuries: unrequired time.
- *Be realistic about travel time.* If you're in a city, it's always going to take longer to drive somewhere than you hope. Plan for that. You'll be a lot less stressed out when you arrive.
- *Use travel time to get things done.* I get all my phone calls done while I'm in the car on the way somewhere else (always using a headset, of course). That increases my productivity by leaps and bounds and frees up time for relaxation.

Deep but Balanced

Once you've gotten some of the basic time management tricks down and working for you, it's attitude adjustment time. I spoke of having a vision for your life, and there's nothing more critical than that. But there are other philosophies and habits worth learning if you're going to strike the kind of balance that makes other women say, "How does she do it?"

- *Delegate and trust.* Suzanne Somers, who's an author, entrepreneur, and clothing designer, says that she no longer works sixteen-hour days thanks to her support team. She delegates many tasks to people who work for her and trusts them to get the job done. As a result, she's more productive in the time she works and has built a thriving business empire. You may not need a personal assistant, but there are always people who can help you: your kids, your spouse, a secretary, a housekeeper. If you're not sure if they're willing to pitch in, ask them.

- *Learn to say no.* It's a fantastic word, one that I'm just getting the hang of using. Learning to say no *without guilt* lets you set boundaries and retake control of your time. It's one of the most powerful steps you can take in achieving balance. Turning down work or saying "Thanks, but maybe next time" frees you from presumed obligations and opens up blessed empty places on your master calendar—places that you can fill with a whole lot of nothing or healing activities that are personally meaningful.

- *Be honest about what you want.* I'm amazed at the number of people who seem to think they are duty-bound to participate in every work event and social occasion. What's so hard about being honest and saying that you have something else you would rather do? Do you really think you are the only one in the office who is balancing on one leg while holding a stack of china plates? Everyone is juggling the personal and professional, so if you're honest about how you want to spend your time, odds are the powers that be will understand.

- *Know when to multitask and when to focus.* I'm a multitasker's multitasker, and it's enabled me to be incredibly productive at times. But it gets old . . . fast. Multitasking can become overwhelming when it's chronic. There is a time to set your attention on one task. I know a writer who talks about what a luxury it is when he can focus his talents on only one big project, no matter how complicated. Not splitting your attention is a kind of self-generosity that lets you be in the moment a little more. So know when it's perfectly okay to do ten things at once, but also know when the time comes to zero in.

• *Know when to micromanage.* Weddings are times for micromanagement, because what can go wrong, et cetera. Trips to the river, not so much. Micromanagement becomes a habit of control, and sometimes balance means not worrying

RED CARPET RULES
Dirty Laundry Exposed

- Suck it up. It happens to everyone. Don't think you're unique.
- Explain the circumstances, but don't deny your actions. If you cheated with a friend's boyfriend, own up to what you did.
- Deal with the disapproval and don't try to charm people back onto your side. Actions speak a lot louder than words.
- If someone betrayed a confidence, find out who. It's important to confront them so you'll know why they did what they did.
- If potential slander is involved, consult an attorney.
- Destroy the evidence if you can get away with it. Delete incriminating e-mails, burn birthday cards from your friend's ex, and so on.
- If you think you were right, hold your head up. For example, if you had plastic surgery and friends find out and look at you like you're a phony, who cares? You did what was right for you.
- Plan and deliver a formal apology if one is warranted.

about being in control and not trying to attend to every detail. "Let someone else do it" is a phrase that doesn't come easily to people like me or to any driven, perfectionist professional, but it can be a good one to remember. Letting things be means you're trusting that things are going to be all right without your taking charge . . . because they usually are.

Balance isn't ultimately about happiness alone. It's about getting more from every part of your life, including your work. When you're charged up and excited and passionate about how you're living, you're going to do a better job no matter what you do.

Fall Forward

*I honestly think it is better to be a failure at something
you love than to be a success at something you hate.*
—GEORGE BURNS

*E*verybody fails. Not everyone fails with the world watching. That's the downside of being a celebrity. There probably wasn't anyone watching the last time you got turned down for a date or didn't get a job that you knew you were perfect for. But when you're George Clooney, who worked for two years on the movie *Leatherheads* only to watch it tank miserably at the box office, everybody notices. When you're Sharon Stone, and Christian Dior drops you as a spokesperson in China after your comments about the Sichuan earthquake being payback for the Chinese treatment of Tibet, the world smirks. Heck, when you're Kim Basinger and you inexplicably spend $20 million in 1989 to buy the *town* of Braselton, Georgia, only to sell it four years later when you realized it might have been a bad move, everyone remembers. It's tough enough to fall on your face; it's murder to do it in a spotlight.

I was lucky enough to learn about the value of failure early on in my career, before any spotlights were shining on me. Back when I was a researcher at *Rescue 911*, I was working on a typewriter because I didn't know how to use a computer, and I was constantly having story ideas sent back to me because I was turning them in with spelling errors. Spelling is my Achilles' heel, and without knowing how to use a computer, I had no safety net. As a result, I was the only one in my department who had never gotten a story on the air. It wasn't just humiliating; if I didn't get my act together and contribute I could lose my first "real" job. Finally, I realized I'd better learn to use a computer or I was sunk, so I taught myself on one of the few now-antique machines we had in the office. Spell check saved my career; my story ideas started being made into episodes.

In television, people fall backward when they faint. But in real life, they fall forward. That's a great metaphor for learning from failure. That's the Lesson here: Failure can turn out to be the greatest blessing for your career and life—if you approach it the right way. Learn from what went wrong, find the opportunity and growth in it, figure out how to avoid repeating your mistake, own up to it, and then move on. The people who can do that are the ones who rise above past errors to do great things. George Clooney has gone right on to his next two films. Failure doesn't bother him. It doesn't bother the great ones; that's why they're great. Joss Whedon's film version of *Buffy the Vampire Slayer* was a critical and box office flop, but he went on to resurrect the idea on TV and turn it into a sensation. Steven Bochco set our teeth on edge in 1990 with *Cop Rock*, but then just three years later gave us *NYPD Blue*.

I could list Hollywood rags-to-riches stories all day, but the fact remains that in any field, if you're not failing spectacularly from time to time, you're not being daring enough to make a difference. If you're not falling down, you're not reaching for something better. Provided you're smart enough to fall forward, failure is one of the keys to a truly rewarding life.

Nothing Personal

Genius and failure go together like sushi and wasabi. Every great success you read about in school failed miserably many times before he or she got it together to find the success that became legendary. Failure has become such an iconic milestone on the road to ultimate success that our culture is littered with pithy bits of wisdom about it. Here are some of my favorites:

- "Failure is a detour, not a dead-end street."—Zig Ziglar
- "I don't know the key to success, but the key to failure is trying to please everybody."—Bill Cosby
- "We failed, but in the good providence of God apparent failure often proves a blessing."—Robert E. Lee
- "I have not failed. I've just found 10,000 ways that won't work."—Thomas Edison
- "This thing we call failure is not the falling down, but the staying down."—Mary Pickford
- "You always pass failure on your way to success." —Mickey Rooney

The theme that appears over and over again is that failure is an inevitable part of success in any aspect of life. I liken it to skiing: If you're learning to ski and you're doing it so conserva-tively that you never fall down, you're not going to learn to be an adept skier. You've got to get up a good head of steam and have a few good wipeouts before you can really develop decent technique. Otherwise, you're going to be doing that goofball V down the bunny slopes for the rest of your life.

Disaster is really the training field that prepares you for the marathon that is life. Think about what happened the last time you procrastinated and subsequently botched a project or left holes in the wall because you took on a home improvement project that should have been left to a professional. You learned, didn't you? Learned in a way that would never have happened without hard experience. Think about all the ways in which failing and picking up the pieces helps us mature. We learn not to be overconfident. Not to get down on ourselves. To prepare and follow through. To have a backup plan. To see the warning signs before disaster strikes. Most important, we learn not to give up. There's a huge difference between saying, "I am a failure," and saying, "I failed." One is personal and permanent. The other acknowledges that sometimes, crap happens. Sometimes we do our best and the marriage fails or the show gets canceled. It's not about us unless we make it about us.

My major failure so far has been the collapse of my marriage, and that was less about blame than about two people who simply should not have been together, ignored the warning signs, and got sucker-punched for it. But as the saying goes, it's an ill wind that blows nobody any good. Nothing is a total loss if you can learn from it, and my divorce has given me a master class in how I operate. I've learned to listen to my inner voice and trust it. I've learned where my line in the sand is drawn and what kind of treatment I absolutely will not tolerate. And I've learned to demand better for myself, because what affects me now also affects my little boy, and nothing is too good for Cooper.

MEL'S BELLES

Angelina Jolie gets heat from the media, but past her public image is a woman who cares deeply about her fellow residents on this planet. How many A-list actresses hold the position of goodwill ambassador for the UNHCR, the United Nations Refugee Agency, and are also helping to rebuild New Orleans, supporting Fran Drescher's Cancer Schmancer Movement, donating money to help Afghan refugees, and setting up a wildlife preserve in Cambodia, among many other activities? And, of course, she gave birth to the world's most famous twins. Her energy is unbelievable, her commitment incredible. Through it all, she manages to be gorgeous, an Oscar-winning actress, and handle the constant tabloid coverage of her marriage to Brad Pitt with class. Quite a lady.

If You Say "I Can't," Then You're Right

The old saying from Henry Ford is "If you think you can do a thing or think you can't do a thing, you're right." Attitude is everything, whether you're trying to start your own small business working out of your garage or lose fifty pounds and get in the best shape of your life. Nobody's keeping score. It doesn't matter if you try twenty times to quit smoking and finally make it for keeps on attempt number twenty-one; the only thing that matters is that you make it. There aren't points for style or for getting it right the first time. In fact, I think it's safe to say our society distrusts "overnight successes," people whose acclaim or wealth comes too easily.

We know that eventually, without fail, the sky is going to fall. The bottom drops out of the late-1990s tech bubble or the mid-2000s real estate bubble, the pitchers start figuring out that you can't hit a major league curveball, or your boss is going to give you a royal butt-chewing in spite of your Harvard MBA. When that happens, we know that people who haven't developed the thick skin and resilience that failure brings are likely to fall apart. Failure toughens. It strengthens. It can be painful. And the more times you fall down and the more times they tell you, "No, you can't do it," the sweeter victory is.

My business is full of people who bucked the odds and the naysayers to make something out of a dream or an idea no one thought could succeed. It took Barbra Streisand, who was at the height of her career, seven years to get *Yentl* made in 1983. Ben Affleck made a series of dreadful box office bombs before bouncing back as a director with *Gone Baby Gone,* and he still has the cool to laugh about *Gigli*. It took years and a big investment of his own money for Sean Penn, one of the major movers and shakers in Hollywood, to turn Jon Krakauer's book *Into the Wild* into a film. Kevin Costner took years to get a production and distribution deal in 1989 for *Dances with Wolves*. Three near-deals fell through at the last minute because no one believed that a period piece with Lakota subtitles could find an audience; this for a film that ended up taking home seven Oscars.

Everybody in this business has at least one story about being kicked to the curb, having a cherished project dismissed as impossible or noncommercial, or being told they were washed up. It's almost a rite of passage. Nothing fires a person up like being told they can't do something. It's the same impulse that attracts us to stories in which a famous person climbs to the top, gets hooked on drugs, loses everything, goes into rehab, and slowly claws her way back into the limelight, older and wiser for the nightmare. Drew Barrymore is a terrific actress and a doll, but she wouldn't be half as compelling if she hadn't been snorting coke at age thirteen. She failed spectacularly and found her way back. We're suckers for that sort of story, because it reminds us that we can recover from our own failures.

Whether your struggle is with weight, money, or career, the belief that you can get past where you are now is the single biggest factor in whether you will get where you want to be. If you can't see yourself being in shape or free of debts, you won't take action and change the habits that will help you achieve your goals. It doesn't matter if you fail or backslide. That's over. All that matters is getting up and telling yourself you can have what you want if you keep trying. If change were easy, everyone would do it and the self-help-book business would be as dead as the WB Network.

THE GOSPEL ACCORDING TO JOAN

When I was fired from Fox, I learned that nothing lasts forever. You can have everything—cars, houses, servants, fame, everything—and in one split second, on someone else's whim, it can be taken away from you. Nothing lasts forever, everything changes. So you should take nothing for granted. Good doesn't last, but people forget that bad doesn't last, either, and in the end that's what you must remember. This, too, shall pass. That also means when the good times are on you, if you don't appreciate them, you're a fool. You'd better know that the sun is shining and enjoy it before the next storm comes.

Drowning in the Dating Pool

You may never start a business. Odds are you'll never become addicted to meth and have your recovery story appear on Lifetime. But there's one area of life where we've all experienced failure: relationships and dating. The sad fact is, nobody meets her soul mate on the first date. We all know what happens to those fast-and-furious Hollywood couples—like colleagues Robert Rodriguez and Rose McGowan, who got hot and heavy on the set and decided that they should dump their existing commitments because, hey, this is the Real Thing. Said Real Thing lasts about as long as it takes for one of them to go on location again and meet someone else. There's no such thing as overnight success in relationships, just one-night stands. Beyond that, failure is the thread that runs through ninety-five percent of our romantic relationships in the form of breakups, divorce settlements, and custody fights.

Sounds grim, but the lessons we learn from suffering heartache after heartache really do teach us, in the end, what makes us happy. Our hearts are stubborn; we want to believe that the kind of person we've always been attracted to will make us happy, even if every bad boy we ever dated turned out to be a jerk with a roving eye. I know that in the aftermath of my divorce, I've become a much more discerning shopper in the market of love. I'll tolerate a lot less from a guy and I insist on a lot more. While I was writing this book, I met a man who I thought was the One, and I was thrilled. But as time went on his anger began to show and he felt threatened by my work and my celebrity. A few years back I might have tolerated it because I was afraid to be back treading water in the dating pool, but this time I didn't. I called the whole thing off. I'd rather be treading water than drowning. I deserve better, and so do you.

In romance, failure teaches us the warning signs that we're wasting our time, and it also teaches us to see people as they are. I'm not interested in being anyone's mommy and I'm not looking for projects; I'm already the first and I have enough of the second, thank you. We learn not to let things like abusive talk or inconsiderate behavior slide, because if you let it slide once, it's going to happen again. We learn not to give away the store immediately

KNOW-IT-ALL
Kendra Todd, Winner of *The Apprentice*, Season 3,
Host of HGTV's *My House Is Worth What?*

It's important to evaluate how you perceive failure and look at the semantics of failure. Do you see it as the end of the road, something that says, "Stop, you've failed, turn around and go home!" or do you simply see it as an obstacle that you have to get around by whatever means possible? People who realize success in their lives and businesses simply embrace failure as a challenge and an opportunity to grow. Some of the most successful people around actually try risky ventures knowing it's likely they will fail, because they know the lessons they learn will make the second time around an incredible success.

It's through our weaknesses that we grow strengths. It's through our failures that we gain wisdom. Failure is our greatest opportunity to grow and gain.

because we feel chemistry; we're patient and circumspect and give the hormones time to cool down before we start sharing everything. We learn to be clear about what we want and to pull the rip cord if the prospective paramour can't give us what we want. Failure in relationships—feeling like an idiot again because you believed it when he said "I love you" or being stuck at home on a Saturday night crying your eyes out—is the great teacher of wisdom, the Master Po of the heart, for you *Kung Fu* fans.

Give It Your Best

In January 2004, Britney Spears married childhood buddy Jason Alexander at a Las Vegas wedding chapel after a cozy viewing of *The Texas Chainsaw Massacre*. About fifty-five hours later they annulled the marriage. But did Britney learn from this quickie starter marriage? I won't go into all the sordid details, but I think the answer to that question is no. This is the kind of failure that's worthless, the kind you don't learn from. In fact, it's worse than worthless because you won't get those months or years of your life back. They're gone and the time was wasted.

It's important that you don't go into any of the endeavors of your life—a new job, a new relationship, or the first year of graduate school—with the intention of skating along on the ice until you wreck and then seeing what you get from the experience. That's not maturity; it's fatalism. It's saying, "Well, at least if I screw this up I will have learned something." You're already doomed to failure when you say that. That neutralizes the benefits that you can gain from falling down. It's vital that you always give your best and go into everything trying to make it work. Then if it doesn't, you can look back on the honest steps you took to make things happen the way you wanted and figure out what you did right and what you did wrong. You can preserve relationships with people because they'll want to work with you again since you gave it all you had. In the broken pieces of your ideas, you'll find new ideas for trying again and building a better mousetrap.

No one learns anything from a "starter marriage attitude." If you court failure for its "street cred," then you're no better than someone who moves into a drafty loft and fills it with huge canvases even though he can't paint a lick, all so he can look like a starving artist. True failure, the kind of failure that makes us better and shows us new ways to do things right, is earned. It doesn't come cheaply.

Way back in 1983, Diana Rigg, who became famous as the sexy Emma Peel in the 1960s TV series *The Avengers,* wrote a book called *No Turn Unstoned*. It was a collection of some of the worst theatrical reviews of all time, hysterical to read and even more painful to think about receiving as you sat in your dressing room waiting to go on. But who you do think some of the targets of critical slings and arrows were? Try Katharine Hepburn, of whose performance on one occasion a critic said it "ran the whole gamut of emotion from A to B." Rigg even put herself up for some scorn with a review of her (and this just boggles my mind) performing nude in *Abelard and Heloise* by Ronald Millar at Wyndhams Theatre in 1970. John Simon in *New York* magazine wrote: "Diana Rigg is built like a brick mausoleum with insufficient flying buttresses."

That's just cruel, but my point is that every actor in that book worked hard to earn those scathing reviews and the best of them got better because of the criticism. You'll do the same when you go into any venture honestly and give it everything you have. That's the only way to get the most of the failures you'll sometimes suffer through—nude and otherwise.

How You Know You're Falling Forward

You're going to fall. It happens to the best of us. In fact, to the most successful of us it happens a lot. That's okay. The key question is, are you falling forward or are you falling flat? If you're falling forward, then failure isn't an ending but an intermission. You get wiser from what went wrong, come up with new ideas, and start again. For example, when I got fired from *The Celebrity Apprentice,* I walked away with some new friends, great contacts, and most important, good relationships with Mark Burnett and Donald Trump. If you fall flat, then you just surrender, get angry, blame somebody else, and basically turn what could be the most valuable learning experience of your life so far into a complaint-fest. You fall right on your face, in other words.

Which are you more likely to do? You're falling forward when:

• *You expand your contact list of good people.* One of the best parts of any high-risk, innovative venture is that it usually puts you in contact with the kind of people who stimulate you and make you better at what you do. When failure is your teacher and not your master, you preserve your relationships with the best people and find ways to work with them again. How many new Internet companies were built on the bones of failed ones by people who enjoyed working with one another? If your company goes under, you can salvage a lot by keeping good relationships with coworkers and maybe coming away with some friendships or at least a productive network. After all, good people are the most valuable commodity in any line of work.

• *You can't wait to get back on the horse.* You're not discouraged for long. In fact, you're like Christopher Lloyd's Doc Brown in the *Back to the Future* movies, preparing to move on to the next attempt even as it's becoming clear that the current invention isn't going to pan out. You're excited about trying again and seeing what happens. You particularly need this attitude in your romantic life, because without a sense of optimism that *this time* it will be better, you'd give up and join a convent.

• **You never think about quitting.** As John Belushi said in *Animal House*, "Was it over when the Germans bombed Pearl Harbor?" It's never over for you no matter how many times you take the bar exam and fail, or try to quit smoking only to light up again as soon as something stressful happens. You never give up, especially when the cause is something you really believe in: getting in shape, finding a publisher for your book, or that in-house project you know will change the company's future but you can't get the boss to support. It doesn't matter how many times people tell you to forget it. Quitting never enters your mind. You're confident that one day you'll get the job done.

• **You don't take criticism personally.** In my years on the red carpet, I was forced by circumstances to develop a thick skin. My mother and I, because we were all about irreverence toward the holy of American cultural holies, were the targets of some pretty mean-spirited comments, and things got much uglier when the Internet and blogs became a big deal. It's very easy to rip someone apart when you can remain anonymously behind your computer screen. But when I received constructive criticism about how I could do my job better, I always listened. I knew I wasn't perfect and took every opportunity to get pointers or ideas from people who knew what they were talking about or didn't get personal.

This is one of the best ways to turn failure into a win. When your proposal falls flat for a new client, instead of getting defensive, pay attention when the boss explains some of the reasons he thinks you came up short. When your significant other tells you why he or she got angry with you, take the criticism and learn how you can do better rather than getting your armor on and turning a teaching moment into a battle. Think of yourself as an athlete receiving advice from a coach. Most people want you to succeed. Let them help you do it.

• *You're doing something a little better than last time.* Even the most abject failures have some grain of success in them, maybe buried deep but there. Each time you have another Red Carpet Moment, you're improving in some way. Maybe you're becoming a better speaker, a better dresser, or getting smoother at dealing with questions during a job interview. The key is, you're improving slightly and that should encourage you to keep going. If you fail enough, maybe you'll become perfect.

SWEPT UNDER THE CARPET

Pregnancy and the red carpet equal drama. Six weeks after I had Cooper, someone came up to me on the carpet and asked, "When are you due?" It must have been the boobs. But it's amazing how close some women will cut it in order to keep their red carpet date. In 2000, Annette Bening was up for Best Actress for *American Beauty* and literally minutes from her due date, but she stuck around long enough to see husband Warren Beatty accept the Thalberg Memorial Award. In 2003, Catherine Zeta-Jones did a duet with Queen Latifah at nine months pregnant before she won her Best Supporting Actress Award for *Chicago*. But what I love is the attitude of producer Caroline Baron, who in 2006 said, "To be forty-four, pregnant, and up for an Oscar is an embarrassment of riches."

How You Know You're Falling Flat

• *You're easy to discourage.* When you're not approaching failure in a healthy way, it takes only a brief reversal to make you give up your plans forever. I see this more often in young performers who became too big too quickly and never had to endure the rigors of endless auditions and rejection. As a result, they think one small setback equals the end of the world. They don't have any perspective on what it means to fail. They're like the children of rich parents who are given everything, get an automatic invitation to the best university, cruise through to a degree based on their name, then get to the real world and think the purpose of a company is to tell them how wonderful they are for doing their job. One cross word and they fall apart. If that's what happens to you, it's time to reexamine how you handle failure.

• *You're playing the blame game.* Let's be honest: It's you. It's always you. You're the captain of your own ship, and like the situation on a boat, even if the crew makes a mistake, it's your fault. When you don't get the job, don't blame your sister for choosing your clothes, because you had a choice of what to wear. When you botch your speech at the wedding, don't blame your date for distracting you. When a Red Carpet Moment goes awry, it's your fault in some way. Instead of pointing fingers, your first priority should be figuring out what you did wrong and why. That's the only way you're going to learn from it.

• *You take it personally.* Failure happens to you; failure is not who you are. That seems like common sense, but some people take every shortfall as a judgment on their character or abilities. If that happened in Hollywood, every time an actress as good as Joan Cusack (who had her sitcom canceled *during* its premiere episode) wound up out of work, no one would ever step onto a soundstage again. Failure is rarely personal and you can't take it that way. Usually it's a confluence of bad luck, honest misjudgment, poor timing, and competition who act faster or

RED CARPET RULES

Getting Fired

- Don't freak out or make a scene. Don't walk to the center of the office and yell, "Who's coming with me?" No one is. Keep your dignity. People will remember how you act in a stressful time.

- Wait seventy-two hours before you try to contact former coworkers or start salvage operations. And don't contact them at work, where they might feel uncomfortable about talking to you.

- When you do contact people, don't whine. However much you might want them to feel outrage at what happened to you, they have their own jobs and lives to deal with.

- Don't send nasty e-mails to the company after you're gone or from the company server while you're cleaning out your desk. No "Sherman marching through Georgia" acts, please.

- Get the reason you were discharged in writing.

- Don't threaten a lawsuit. If you have grounds for legal action, consult an attorney in a week or so after you cool off.

- Ask for a letter of reference before leaving. Many times companies will gladly give you a positive letter just to ensure that you'll leave quietly.

- Don't sign anything. You might be signing a noncompete agreement or something else that will limit your opportunities.

are smarter than you. That's it. Failure doesn't mean that you're incompetent or doomed to a life of mediocrity. If you tend to think that when things don't go your way, you may want to take a long, hard look at your self-esteem.

• *You repeat the same mistakes.* This is the ultimate embarrassment. What's the point of putting months or years into something, whether it's a TV show, a relationship, or a fitness program, if you're going to blow it, then make the same mistakes all over again the next time? If you get in a relationship with a guy who lives with his parents at age thirty-eight and you find out later that he's an emotionally infantile basket case, stop dating guys who live with their parents! If you take a job with an exciting start-up company only to have it crater a few months later and leave you with worthless stock and rent due, don't take any more jobs with such companies unless you like that sort of thrill ride. Learn and don't repeat. That's the way to make progress.

Shallow Failure

You can always take something from a failed situation, but to do so, you've frequently got to think ahead and not get so caught up in worrying about your job or grieving over the money you invested in a failed Internet dating service that you forget to plan. The shallow end of falling forward is really about hunting and gathering, accumulating valuable information and assets even as the *Titanic* is sinking around you. Just don't wait too long to get into a lifeboat. Remember what happened to Leo DiCaprio.

• *Don't ignore the warning signs.* Don't convince yourself that it's all in your imagination when your boss removes the nameplate on your cubicle for "cleaning." Your gut knows the jig is up long before your brain does. If you admit that something is going on, you can grab a life preserver while the rest of the passengers are still sleeping in their cabins.

• **Update your résumé.** You should be doing this anyway, but nobody ever does.

• **Make sure you have the contact information of people who could be valuable later on.** This doesn't mean stealing Rolodexes; it does mean e-mailing yourself contact lists of influential people, vendors, customers, and even corporate officers. Make sure you can get in touch with anyone who might be able to help you in your next venture—assuming you have a good relationship with that person.

• **Invest in yourself.** Even if things look good, prepare for what might happen later by getting additional training or education. Find a mentor and learn more about what goes on behind the scenes of your job. Even if things don't fall apart, you'll be worth more when you know more.

• **Check out your options.** Find out what's happening. Investigate and do some sleuthing. If the company is about to go belly-up or the relationship is about to crash, there will be signs; there always are. Open your eyes, be as objective as you can, and catalog them. Get a friend, an objective third party, to review the evidence and give you his or her opinion, then be prepared to accept it.

Failing Deeply

At the deepest end of the failure zone, we find the people who turn failure into huge success, people like Albert Einstein, who failed his first college entry exam, and Sir Laurence Olivier, who, upon making his very first entrance in the very first play he ever did, tripped over his feet and fell face-first into the footlights. These are people who have a "there is no failure" mind-set. For them, there are only chances to learn and grow and become stronger. Some of the core principles of that attitude:

• *Reward risk taking.* Don't punish people for failure that comes from trying too hard or taking a smart risk. Laziness is one thing, but you don't chew out a stagehand who just went and got lunch for twenty people because he forgot one person's extra mustard. When you do that, you don't assert authority, you just prove to people that you're an asshole and convince them never to take a risk again.

• *Walk around the car.* Look at the problem from all sides like somebody kicking the tires on a used BMW. Get everybody's perspective before you judge. That way you get a clearer idea of what went wrong so you can avoid repeats of the same errors.

• *Communicate.* Talk to people, especially if your failure hurt them or you were hurt by them. Silence solves nothing. Phrases like "I understand that when I said . . . you may have felt . . ." and "I could have handled that better" work wonders. Reach out and discover what other people are feeling about you and themselves. Things may not be as bad as you fear, but you'll never know until you open your mouth.

• *Take notes.* Think about the failures you've experienced in your life. When you got past the hurt, you were probably more open to new ideas and new opportunities. Write down the things you can remember that you did right and wrong so you can learn from them. Some people keep "failure journals" in which they write down their most audacious mistakes.

• *Be gracious in losing.* Walk across the room to congratulate the person who won what you wanted, even if you're digging your nails into your palms while you're doing it. Graciousness speaks volumes about you and helps preserve both your positive frame of mind and the relationships that can be so important to recovery from failure.

RED CARPET RULES

Failing Publicly

- Fess up. Here's what not to say: "I did not have sexual relations with that woman."
- Don't blame. Take the heat if the heat is deserved.
- Count on the truth coming out. If someone else is responsible for the failure that's being pinned on you, people will find out.
- Be honest with your emotions. It's okay to say that you feel disappointed about what's happened.
- Don't throw others under the bus. This doesn't mean you have to cover for people who genuinely screwed up, but don't try to cover your butt by sacrificing the innocent.
- Save your files. If you didn't do anything wrong, you might need them later to clear your good name.
- Don't tolerate gossip. If you learn that people are talking about your failure behind your back, call them on it. Unanswered gossip becomes truth.

None of us is exactly where we want to be. We've all fallen short in some way. We all look at stars on the red carpet and think, "God, why can't I look like that?" or "Why aren't I driving that kind of car?" Or we look at a family walking together on a summer night and feel a pang in the pit of our stomach that we

don't have what they have. But that envy, that pain, is a motiva-
tor to get back up and keep trying. There's an old saying that
goes, "Happiness isn't having what you want but wanting what
you have." It's great to aspire to something bigger, to grow, and
to learn. But don't lose perspective on who you are today. Don't
spend so much of yourself chasing rainbows that you forget to
appreciate the rain.

Take a Risk

Life, like poker, has an element of risk. It shouldn't be
avoided. It should be faced. —EDWARD NORTON

*I*n the wonderful documentary *Man on Wire*, we see Philippe Petit in 1974 walking back and forth between the World Trade Center towers on a cable three quarters of an inch thick. He stops, talks to birds, kneels, and even sits down and looks at the ground like he's having an Americano at the neighborhood Starbucks. He's completely at ease in an environment of risk so sheer that it would leave 99.9 percent of us completely paralyzed with terror and vertigo. He's incredible to watch.

Yet the most wondrous thing about this Frenchman, now fifty-nine but looking not much different from the day he and a team of coconspirators pulled off their feat of guerrilla aerialism, is that he talks about his wire walk not as risk but as artistry. He said in an interview with Salon.com: "If it's a question about risk and danger and death, I would say that surely this was a life-affirming moment; it was solid in its fragility.

The wire walker's life is framed by losing your life, but I don't have any death wish. I have a life wish, so I work in that direction, and I am extremely steady on the wire. So there is no danger, no fear, and certainly there is no risk."

That's a perspective that's hard to imagine, since I for one get queasy just looking at the guy sitting up there laughing at the police gathered more than 1,200 feet below on the New York streets. But that's the thing about risk: One man's wire walk is another man's cakewalk. We all have things in our lives that scare us and they're different for everyone. Some people find what I do, getting up in front of a live audience or a television audience of millions, terrifying. To me, it's second nature, as automatic as breathing. For me, risk was learning to surf at age thirty-three or getting up in front of a Silicon Valley venture capital firm and asking them for millions of dollars to fund my idea. That had my heart pounding, but I did it. I'm a calculated risk taker as long as it's something I believe in, because I know the power of risk: When you get outside your comfort zone and put it all on the line, great things happen.

A Cousin to Failure

The final Lesson in our journey together is that doing a Keanu Reeves in *The Matrix* and jumping off a building—taking smart risks that carry a chance of failure—can lead to a brighter and more fulfilling future. You could say that if you're not failing enough, you're not risking enough. If each failure is another doorway on the way to success, then risk is the key to the door (how's that for a pretentious literary metaphor?). Your failures aren't meaningful unless they open your eyes to something new about yourself or to a possibility you haven't explored yet, and you don't get into that revealing new territory until you get out of your comfort zone and take some risks.

I'm not necessarily talking about walking on high wires; in fact, if I hear about you doing that, I'm personally calling the men in the white coats. But in all seriousness, risk doesn't have to mean defying death, though it can if that's what gives you a charge. There are all kinds of risk:

- Physical risks such as skydiving, bungee jumping, and free climbing
- Creative risks such as karaoke singing and public speaking
- Business risks such as starting companies
- Financial risks such as day trading
- Emotional risks such as getting married or sending your kids off to college
- Identity risks such as changing your personal style or going back to school to study a different field

The essential truth to remember is that risk has nothing to do with danger; in fact, some people would say that when you're so poorly prepared for something that it becomes dangerous it crosses the line of risk and become recklessness. So with risk, there's an element of implied control. You're hanging your behind out there, trying something you've never tried before, but you're not being stupid about it. You pack your parachute with the help of a professional. You invest money that you can afford to lose, not the mortgage money. Risk is getting outside of the small pool of light where you feel safe and comfortable and checking out what's in the shadows, not diving into the dark without any idea of what might be there.

What might be spine-freezing for one individual is going to

be a yawner for another. That's something else to keep in mind as you're looking around at the risks you've taken. Don't judge according to what others have done, because they're wired differently. I know two guys, one the singer and front man for a great blues band here in Southern California and the other a deepwater recreational scuba diver who goes down 120 feet to harvest clams and mussels off the legs of old oil drilling platforms off the coast of Santa Barbara. Each is very comfortable doing what he does and gets a thrill from it, but considers the other's activity far outside his comfort zone: The singer has no interest in such dangerous deep diving, while the diver can't imagine singing in front of a live audience. For each, the other's act is unacceptable risk. So when you're thinking about risks that might get you into new territory, nothing matters except what makes you feel alive and awakens you to new possibilities in your life.

MEL'S BELLES

Jennifer Aniston is one of the few actresses I know of who is universally beloved. That's why it was so heartbreaking to see her in so much pain when she walked the red carpet after breaking up with Brad Pitt; we all knew her pain wasn't feigned for the cameras. But to her credit, she showed up. Jen is a healthy enough woman to know that she didn't need to see her therapist or pop some Valium to deal with the situation—she needed to get out and shake her groove thing. She's a beautiful, talented lady who is wonderfully normal and genuine. And in a business of pretenders, that makes her one in a million.

Risk and the Red Carpet

I'm a calculated risk taker, and I was even before I became a mom. Joining with my mother back in 1996 to do the red carpet shows was certainly a venture into unfamiliar country, but it was also very, very worthwhile. What did I have to lose? I wasn't risking a huge Hollywood career. I had very little to lose by getting out of my small comfort zone, slipping on something from Valentino or Carolina Herrera, and stepping into the lights to ask Julianne Moore about her cleavage. In fact, the riskiest part of the whole red carpet scene was the edgy tone my mother and I took toward the celebrities and their fashion choices. Everything was done under the umbrella of excitement and celebration, but we knew we were bringing a heavy dose of candor and biting humor to an event that Americans tend to regard as sacrosanct. We didn't mock anyone in anything other than fun, but we certainly weren't taking the whole scene as seriously as many viewers expected. There was outrage on the part of some viewers, but, as they say, if you're not offending someone, you're not trying.

We were also pushing against a glass ceiling that existed at the time for women in comedy. Mom had shattered the previous one decades ago when she played the Catskills "Borscht Belt" and the Greenwich Village cabarets at a time when women simply didn't do that, and she opened the way for every female standup to come along since. But a new ceiling had been installed by the time we slinked onto the red carpet, and we gave it a good crack with a hammer by the time we were done. So there were multiple levels of risk involved aside from the down-to-earth one of putting together a live program and possibly risking humiliation in front of millions.

Red Carpet Moments are about risk. When you stage your wedding, walk into a conference room to interview for a job, or step onto a stage with your band, you're putting yourself in the spotlight and also risking failure. But it's precisely the risk that offers you the chance to shine—to perform with grace and skill—when you're the center of attention. That is what makes these moments special—or is it? After all this time, I wonder if it's not the risk itself that makes a moment a Red Carpet Moment. Maybe it's the very act of putting yourself out there and walking across that wire between safety and abject humiliation that makes the time special, whether you're attired as a princess at your engagement party or sitting alone in your office putting the first words of your memoir to paper.

I think it's both. The moments themselves are exceptional, but it's also the act of taking a risk and living bravely—something many people are never able to do—that creates a special zone in the flow of time that's forever yours.

THE GOSPEL ACCORDING TO JOAN

I take risks all the time. We mortgaged our house to do my film *Rabbit Test* back in 1978. What I'm doing now is a risk: I've stopped my income completely and I'm working for union scale to make this play based on my life work, at an age when most people are terrified of risk. You don't know what's going to happen, so if you're in the position to take a risk, take it. I've never taken anything for the security that it offered. I've always taken risks. If you love what you're taking a risk to do, it will come out good in the end.

Over the Edge with Their Eyes Open

Hollywood is a town of risk takers, but the major film distribu-
tors—Paramount, Universal, etc.—are not among them. They're
owned by huge corporate entities now, so their major concern
is profit and shareholder value, not artistic originality. Movies
like *Little Miss Sunshine* scare the hell out of mainstream
executives; they would rather have *Harry Potter 15: Harry Gets
a Hip Replacement*. But once you get away from the big players, you can't swing a dead cat without hitting a creative risk
taker.

Consider Peter Jackson (yes, he's from New Zealand, but
we're using Hollywood in a nongeographical sense). Here's a
director who had previously made small horror films who somehow convinced New Line to give him $300 million and three
years to make three films out of one of the most impossible-to-
film books ever published, *The Lord of the Rings*. Talk about hanging your butt out there in the wind! But Jackson and his team not
only did it, they created a work of brilliance that swept the 2004
Oscars and will probably end up earning billions. That's taking a
risk and making it pay off.

Al Gore with *An Inconvenient Truth*, Guillermo del Toro with
Pan's Labyrinth, Frank Darabont with *The Shawshank Redemption*
(a title everyone said would doom the movie)—the entertainment business is overflowing with people who put themselves
on the line to bring a personal vision to life and have reaped
great rewards. I would argue that greatness isn't possible without great risk of failure. When you play it safe, you make *Maid in
Manhattan*.

When you risk, you're Stephen Colbert at the 2006 White

House Correspondents' Dinner, speaking truth to power in an incredible, blistering, and hysterically funny keynote. You're Carrie Fisher leaving Princess Leia behind, not just by becoming a bestselling author but coming clean about your depression. You're Penny Marshall going from *Laverne & Shirley* to huge acclaim in a male-dominated field with films like *A League of Their Own*. You're Diane Keaton doing a full-frontal nude scene at age fifty-nine in *Something's Gotta Give,* something I wouldn't even do today, and I'm nearly twenty years younger. The creative world thrives on people who jump over the edge of the ordinary with their eyes wide open, hoping for something soft to cushion their landing but jumping anyway.

Of course, any business is littered with risk takers who weren't as fortunate, sometimes because of bad luck or bad timing, not because their work wasn't as good or their ideas as fresh. Silicon Valley is bursting with the unmarked graves of dot-com companies based on great ideas but that were before their time or just beyond the abilities of their founders to run. But you know what happened as a result of that late '90s Internet boom and crash, an orgy of inspired and insane risk taking? The software, hardware, and infrastructure that today gives us broadband, YouTube, Twitter, and iTunes was created and refined. From that risk came improvement and progress, better business models, and smarter young entrepreneurs.

Think about the times in your life you've taken a big risk. Going to college is a huge one; it's a new world where you're no longer the best student in your high school. Suddenly, you've got a new mountain to climb. What about getting married? Not only is a wedding a classic Red Carpet Moment, but the act of committing to another person for life is a wire walk unto itself. You're risking so much—from financial security to emotional health—in the hope that you and this other person can grow closer, not further apart, as the years pass. I can attest from personal experience that it doesn't always work out, but it's most certainly a risk worth taking.

Have you traveled to a country where you didn't speak the language? Started a new job? Sung karaoke? Those are all risks, and for some people they are no big deal while for others they represent the pinnacle of courage. You're already a risk taker, and if you didn't know it, those risks enriched you. They made you a different person. Just because you don't skydive doesn't mean you're not a daredevil. Skydiving is dangerous, but it's a hobby. Real risk means taking your life into new and unknown terrain on a regular basis.

KNOW-IT-ALL

Jesse Billauer, Paraplegic Surfer, Founder of Life Rolls On

I take risks like cage diving with sharks and skydiving because I'm just trying to live my life as normally as I could before my injury. Now I just need a little more help. It makes me feel like I'm alive to be doing the kinds of things I would have done before my injury. Of course, it all takes more planning. The risk is still there, except I don't think about it. I've gotten the hurts, I've broken my leg surfing, but I just let it heal for nine months, then went back to Hawaii and surfed the same wave. You just figure out how to get it done. You don't worry about the possibility of injury. You live your life and do the things that matter to you.

Never Jump Unless You're Wearing Wings

When it comes to risk, the watershed moment for me was when I pushed Cooper out of the birth canal. That changed everything, and if you have kids, you know what I mean. When you're childless, very little sticks to you. You can careen through relationships and dash off to base jumping class or whitewater rafting school at a moment's notice, because you're just responsible for you. When another life is depending on you for everything, that changes. Recklessness becomes a dress that never leaves your closet. Instead, life is about *calculated risk*. You don't jump off a building unless you're wearing wings.

All of my ventures since leaving the red carpet have involved risk, but it's been carefully calculated risk that I've mitigated by having more than one thing going on. I don't put all my career eggs in one basket anymore; I am a woman of many baskets. You don't have to risk disaster or death with everything you do in order to push the envelope and make great things happen in your life. You can mitigate your risks: Ask for a promotion instead of quitting outright, date a guy for a while instead of saying yes to his marriage proposal, get a new haircut instead of having plastic surgery.

Courage and smart risk taking are not the same thing. Yes, it takes courage to venture outside your carefully cultivated comfort zone and speak in front of an audience or wear a bikini at the beach for the first time in years. But having the courage to get yourself into a hazardous situation and dare disaster doesn't make you a smart risk taker. Leave that to the Navy Seals. You're not a wacky iconoclast if you drive drunk because you "know you can"; you're just a fool. When you're older and people depend on you, I think risk becomes more important than ever so you don't end up stuck in a rut. But it has to be wise risk, where the odds of disaster are small and the chance for a thrilling payoff is great.

The Allure of the Makeover Show

From *What Not to Wear* to *Queer Eye for the Straight Guy,* makeover shows have always been a big deal on television. *Extreme Makeover: Home Edition* is particularly addictive. I love them for the inherent drama: Some person or family agrees to risk changing everything about how they look or how they live in order to get a fresh start in the eyes of others and themselves. It's a great story line, and the popularity of such programs reveals the true value in risk taking: It makes us feel alive and renewed.

Think about it: When was the last time you did something that took you outside your comfort zone and scared the daylights out of you? Learning to drive stick? Taking the lead in a big presentation at work? Posting your first blog entry for the world to read? How did you feel after you survived? Great, I'll bet. Really alive. Getting outside your comfort zone—which I define as the circle of experience where you know the people and know you have the skills to be okay—feels fabulous and opens you up to so much that's new and exciting. It can be a small thing that pulls you out of that complacent zone: Being one of the few divorced parents at Cooper's fairly conservative school, I was terrified of the other moms in his class. I was afraid they would look at me as "that divorced woman" and that we would have nothing in common. I was one of three single moms and the only one working full-time. I kept to myself for the first year. I felt sheer terror that I would be left out or looked at as a bad parent. But I fought through my trepidation and got to know them, and you know what? I really liked them, and now, because I stepped out of my comfort zone as a mom, I have some new friends.

You have lots of comfort zones: physical, relationship, creative, financial, sexual. They all confine and define what you can do and how you can live, and they limit you in many ways, making you feel safe. But there's a fine line between safe and stifled, and if you begin to feel that your life has become too predictable, I have one piece of advice for you—*play against type*. Change your wardrobe. Change your hair. Date someone unlike anyone you've ever dated before. Go on vacation where you know nobody and don't speak the language. If you're normally glamorous, be plain for a while. If you're used to driving to work, walk or take the bus. If you typically listen to jazz, download some Sex Pistols, throw it

SWEPT UNDER THE CARPET

The assumption is that Oscar night is one big party and the ultimate date night for the stars. But that's not really true. The stars know that at the Academy Awards, the last thing you want to do is babysit. That's why so many of them don't even bring dates at all. They bring family, their manager, or come alone so they can focus all their attention on the event. George Clooney always brings his mother, publicist, and agent to the Oscars, or he comes alone. He doesn't need some arm candy who's going to be gushing about all the stars and whipping out her digital camera, God forbid. At the end of the night, when you're exhausted, you just want to be with someone who "gets it."

on your iPod, and listen while you work. Do something to change your pattern, mess with your routine.

This may not seem like much, but getting out of your safe space doesn't have to be a big gesture. If you do something that changes your perspective and gives you a different view of your own life, that's a risk in itself. For some people who have spent years peacefully incarcerated in their comfort zone, just getting up on the roof of life and looking around can be unnerving but exhilarating. Try it, and you'll see that it's not so hard to begin giving yourself a makeover from the inside out.

Risk and Reward

Investors know that if you want a big potential return on your money, your risk of losing it all will also be higher. In Hollywood, big rewards come with big risks. Halle Berry took a massive risk when she took on a decidedly unglamorous role in *Monster's Ball,* including a raunchy sex scene with Billy Bob Thornton. But it paid off with her winning the Academy Award for Best Actress. The awards season is a kind of payoff window for a previous year of gambling at the high-stakes table of creative risk taking. Make the right bet and you might walk away with a statue and immortality. Make the wrong bet and you're watching at home with the dog.

My final lesson when it comes to the art of risk taking is that the greater your risk, the more profound your reward will be. Think of the familiar as a shield that you can hide behind all the time if you choose to. It protects you from just about everything that life might throw at you—which not only means you're tucked away safely from most of the bad things that can happen, but there's also little chance for something new and wonderful to come into your life. You're insulated.

The more you stick your head up above that shield by taking a risk, the more you're exposed to the potential good stuff. Sure, the bad can come along and smack you right in the face, I'm not going to deny that. You could date a new type of guy and just get your heart stepped on in a new kind of way. But there's no way to know until you get out from behind your shield and see what comes your way. The more you stick your head out, the more surprising and great things that can happen to you. For example, let's say you're not happy in the area you're living. You want more restaurants, more of a sense of community, and not to have to drive so much. You want an adventure. Which option do you choose?

- Risky—Moving to a new neighborhood
- Riskier—Moving to a new city in a different part of the country
- Riskiest—Moving to a new country

If you take the least risky option and move to a new area, you'll have less chance of wasting your money, not knowing anyone, or uprooting your life for nothing. But you'll also run the risk of having the same problems you have where you live now, because you haven't made a radical enough change. There is risk in not taking great enough risks. If you move to Paris from Los Angeles, you'll certainly be risking not knowing a soul, being isolated by a language barrier, and wasting a lot of money and time if things don't work out. But you'll also create the possibility of finding a whole new life that's far more fulfilling and joyful than the one you have now. Small risk equals small payoff, maybe happiness of a slightly higher degree than you have now. If that's all you need, great. But if you want to change your life—really change it—you can't get there without daring to do something audacious and borderline crazy.

How You Know You're Taking Enough Risk

• *You're always finding opportunities.* Risk is like the seed of opportunity. Plant it and you never know what will grow: maybe weeds, but maybe something valuable and beautiful. People who regularly throw caution to the wind and leave their comfort zones are constantly running across new people and new ways to test their talents, make money, and be creative.

• *You're rarely bored.* When you make a habit of trying new things, you're never sitting at home wondering what's on TV. Why would you? There's always a new sport to try, someplace new to visit, a new store or technology or cuisine that you haven't experienced yet that you're dying to check out. So you do. Risk is an attitude above all else, and when you have the attitude that you're in this world to discover it and taste it in all its variations, boredom becomes an impossibility.

• *You're appreciative of what you have.* That feeling of exhilaration that you feel when you master a risky situation gives you a genuine feeling of being grateful to be alive and well. I'm not just talking about shooting a Class V rapid, though getting through that in one piece will make you kiss the ground for sure. I'm talking about something as seemingly ordinary as driving down a road you've never been on before into country you've never seen. In our lives, we become accustomed to the things and people we see every day and they lose their transcendent qualities. When we surprise our senses with something completely new and out of our experience, we reawaken. Everything seems and feels more precious . . . though it's always been precious.

- **_You fail regularly._** If you're not failing, you're not

RED CARPET RULES
Changing Your Look

- Don't go radical. Going from prep to Goth in one step will scare children. When you change your look, you're asking for attention. Making it too radical will get you the wrong kind. Don't go from wearing Abercrombie to Doc Martens. Find a middle step.
- Be clear on why you're making the change. Don't do it just for shock value or because of a breakup.
- Don't be afraid to make little changes instead of harsh ones. Try some new jewelry or tinted contacts.
- Consult a professional. A pro makeup artist or clothing stylist will have some great new ideas that are worth a little cash.
- Be age-appropriate. Nothing is more pathetic than a forty-year-old woman trying to look twenty-five.
- Buy quality. If you want to shop for thrift store chic, fine. But if you're going for a more grown-up, polished look, be prepared to spend some money on some classic pieces from quality manufacturers. They will look great on you for years.
- Either accept your body type or change it by getting in shape. Don't defy your body type by wearing clothes that are too small or fit in completely the wrong way. You don't want to look like a high-school girl with a "muffin top."

trying. When you risk you will fall flat on your face from time to time. Embrace it. Some people enrich their lives with their failures because they're hooked on trying new things and pushing against the edge of convention and normality. If you're failing on a regular basis, chances are you're getting some successes, too, and those wins make the rest worthwhile. Like they say, when you're learning to ski, if you're not falling, you're not getting any better.

How You Know You're Not Taking Enough Risk (or Too Much)

• *You feel "stuck" (too little).* Feeling like your life runs in a rut that's just as wide as a grave is a horrible state to be in. That's what a rut does: becomes just big enough to hold your casket. If you feel like this year is the same as the last and you're on a big treadmill to nowhere, then you've got a risk deficiency.

• *Your life is all drama, all the time (too much).* You're taking over-the-top risks if you're always being rescued, getting bailed out of jail, borrowing money, or recovering from injuries. Remember, there's a difference between risk and recklessness, and the ability to risk wisely is not the same as having the guts to do something stupid. Know the difference.

• *You're ashamed of yourself (too little).* Regret is a cancer that eats away at peace of mind and there's not one person who doesn't know when she is approaching life from the point of fear. You will never regret the risks you take, because we were born to dare and grow and try. But you will regret the risks you did not take, because when you look back you'll see only that you lacked the courage and self-belief to try. You won't like what your refusal to risk says about you and how you're living. If you take risks, you have pride even if you occasionally have sprained limbs.

- **You're constantly regrouping (too much).** Do you commonly find yourself looking for a new job or a new place to live? Do you constantly recycle relationships after doing something silly? Do you always feel like you're taking one step forward then leaping back about a hundred yards? You may be overdoing your risky behavior. Again, go back to calculated risk. Taking smart risks that you're prepared for doesn't make you a wimp, it makes you an adult. Leave the crazy stunts to the kids at the X Games.

At the Risk of Sounding Shallow . . .

For my final dive into the shallow end, I would like to do a half twist in the pike position—that is, something difficult. That's what risky behavior is about, challenging yourself but not being dumb. Don't dive into a pool before you see if there's water in it. These tips are about basic preparedness for stepping outside your comfort zone:

- **Have a buddy.** Have someone in your life who can be your safety net in case things don't go as planned. I might also say, have an accomplice so someone else can take the blame with you. This can be handy when you have to get to an emergency room, need someone to bail you out of jail, or just need a pal to commiserate over drinks.

- **Train.** Don't jump into something with zero preparation. Even if you love the idea of getting on a plane and getting off in Mumbai with a backpack and nothing else, at least learn a few phrases in Hindi, buy a map, and get your vaccinations. In other words, do a little basic education so you're not flying blind. Not being prepared at all can turn a reasonable risk into something very unpleasant.

• **Remind yourself why you're doing it.** There must be a reason you're free-climbing Half Dome—what is it? To test your physical limits? To feel more at one with nature? Everything has a valid purpose behind it, so find out what the purpose of your risk is. That will help keep you on track.

• **Keep it to yourself.** If you tell someone what you're planning before you do it, someone will try to talk you out of it. There are people in this world who can't tolerate the idea that there might be someone who has the guts to try what they won't. That or they're just worriers. Either way, keep mum until whatever you have in mind is a fait accompli. Then brag.

You're So Deep . . .

At the other end of the pool, we're getting into the mind-set of habitual risk takers. I'm not talking about adrenaline junkies—you're not one of those. Your risks are smart, life-affirming, and targeted toward discovery and growth. Or at least, they should be. If you're looking to fall in love with leaping out of your comfort zone on a regular basis, then I have some advice for you:

• **Don't listen to the naysayers.** My mother's father was completely against her career in comedy, because it was a time when the woman's place was in the home. She paid no attention, and after she hit it big, he became her biggest fan. If you choose to tell people what you have planned, you're going to hear a lot of negative talk. Unless the person has actually done what you're thinking of doing and has real war stories to share, tune them out. Stick to your plans. Then again . . .

- *Listen to people who have been there.* Someone who has hiked the Appalachian Trail and knows the potential pitfalls is worth talking to before you set out to walk 2,175 miles with a pack on your back. If somebody you know has already walked the walk, ask them for advice. Don't let them talk you out of your plans necessarily, but certainly take their guidance seriously. There's no voice like experience.

- *Don't make it about your ego.* Don't take risks just for the sake of proving someone else wrong. Shedding your comfort zone should be about your becoming the best you can be, not sticking an "I'll show you" finger in the eye of your critics. I didn't start my Internet company and develop new TV shows to prove something. I did it because I wanted to prove something to myself. That's the only valid reason for risk.

- *Protect your ideas.* If you're starting a business or doing something else in the public arena, one area where risk never pays off is with your ideas. Protect your intellectual property or invention with legal documentation. Hire a lawyer and do it right.

- *Know who you're in bed with.* You want to make sure that the hang gliding instructor with whom you're about to take a tandem flight actually has two hundred hours of hang gliding under his belt. People lie, mislead, and exaggerate, but if you're going to put your job, health, or finances on the line, you've got to know the character and background of the people you're involved with. Get résumés, references, and even background checks.

- *Don't be discouraged by someone else's failure.* Just because someone else drinks poison doesn't mean you're going to die. It doesn't work that way. Someone else's failure at the same risk you're about to take isn't an omen that you're destined for failure. It means nothing, other than that it might be a great lesson in what not to do. Take it for what it is, then move on.

RED CARPET RULES

Buying Your First Home

- Enjoy the process. This is one of life's great milestones. Savor it.
- Read everything before you sign it. Have your Realtor or attorney go over anything you don't understand.
- Have the place inspected before you commit. No house is structurally perfect.
- Get in writing what stays and what goes.
- If you love a house but it's just too expensive, let it go. Never make the mistake of thinking any house is the One. There will always be others—just like boyfriends.
- If the seller tries to change things after the papers are signed, refuse or walk away. That's a warning sign.
- Tell your friends and plan a work party so you'll have help moving, painting, or whatever.

Risk separates ordinary lives from extraordinary lives—the people who live lives of quiet desperation from those who become living legends. You don't have to become a legend, but you owe it to yourself to live as fully as you can. That's possible only when you're approaching risk with wisdom but no fear.

Take the Red Carpet Quiz

*A*ttention, class. You've made it. Congratulations. You've weathered the paper cuts and the thousand natural shocks that flesh is heir to and gotten to the end of Melissa's Red Carpet Life Lessons. I sincerely hope you've picked up a few ideas along the way that will be useful to you in life's Red Carpet Moments. I also hope you've discovered that you, me, and the superstars who walk down the red carpet are not all that different from one another. We all work hard, we all have insecurities, and we all want the same things: the respect of the people we care about, to spend our days doing what we love, and to learn a little something from life as we meander along. If you found some pearl of wisdom that helps you make the most of your own trip down the carpet—and you had some laughs and a few tears along the way—I'm pretty damned happy with that.

But we're not done yet. Oh no. Not by a long shot. You don't graduate from a class until you pass a test. Didn't your mother ever tell you that? Consider this your Red Carpet SAT—proof that you've done your homework and didn't just sit at the back of the lecture hall and watch YouTube movies on your iPhone. I can see it now: one of those study montages from movies like *Gross Anatomy* or *Back to School*, you cramming for your final at all hours of the day and night, mainlining coffee and reading in the shower while "Eye of the Tiger" plays in the background. Then test day, with everyone trying not to look at their neighbor's paper, sharpened number-two pencils lined up on the desk, and the smell of nervous anxiety thick in the air . . . or, as Kathy Griffin once expressed it so eloquently to my mother, "I have butt crack sweat."

The Red Carpet Quiz is a kind of summation of my case so far, or at least it would be if I were an attorney doing my best Sam Waterston impression before a jury. The question before the court: Can the misadventures of celebrities (and those of us who've made a career out of talking to them) really teach you something about squeezing the greatest joy out of your wedding day, keeping your head above water after a terrible breakup, and dealing with all of life's other Red Carpet Moments? It's up to you to supply the verdict with your answers to the quiz. Shall we get this party started?

The Red Carpet Quiz

The quiz aims to answer one simple question: *Are you red carpet ready?* Have you picked up enough insight and tips to face the Red Carpet Moments of your life—planned and spontaneous—and come out smelling like a rose? Here's how it works: nine Lessons, five questions per Lesson, four possible answers to each question. You pick one, you move on, and at the end of the chapter, you learn how you scored. Based on the number of questions you got right, I'll rate your red carpet readiness according to the following scale:

>*Oscar*—Wow. You're smart, prepared, self-aware, and ready to come out on top in any situation. Will you be my best friend?
>
>*Golden Globe*—Still a few rough edges, but you're pretty together.
>
>*Directors Guild*—You're a work in progress, but there's hope. Rome wasn't built in a day.
>
>*People's Choice*—The mental toolbox is looking a little empty; just a few paper clips and a stray Tic Tac.
>
>*Razzie*—Your more in-tune, self-aware friends are thinking of staging an intervention. I'm right there with them.

All sarcasm aside, while some of the questions and some of the answers are meant to be funny, the quiz really is designed to see how prepped you are to stand in the spotlight with your head held high, your dress securely on, and nothing green in your teeth. Life is serious business; it should not be left to amateurs. If I've done nothing else in this book, I hope I've passed along some survival skills developed in the TV trenches where the lights are hot and the tux-clad men are hotter. You can do this; I did. It took some hard knocks, but I'm better and smarter than I was just a few years back. Let's see how smart you've become.

Are You Red Carpet Ready?

LESSON 1 Be Comfortable in Your Own Skin

1. Trying on the dress of your dreams before the big event, you realize it's a nightmare that will have you bleeding by the end of the evening. You . . .

    a. Declare "Donna Karan wouldn't want me to give up," grit your teeth, and wear it anyway.

    b. Wear something less fashion-forward but more you.

    c. Beg a seamstress friend to reconstruct the gown to make it more wearable . . . in forty-five minutes.

    d. Stay home with HBO and go on a frantic hunt for the receipt so you can take the demon-dress back.

2. At your school reunion, you discover that many former pals are doctors, lawyers, Internet millionaires, etc. You . . .

    a. Fake a loose contact lens so you can get to the bathroom, then escape through the window.

    b. Make up a convincing story about your own meteoric career. After all, you'll never see these people again.

    c. Remind each of the high achievers of their worst flaw or most embarrassing high-school moment, just to even the playing field.

    d. Tell them what you're currently doing, no matter how humble, and take pride in it.

3. Friends invite you to a Botox party. You . . .

    a. Go only so you can discreetly inform other guests how dangerous it can be.

b. Go. What's a few forehead injections among friends?

c. Absolutely do not go. Fatal allergic reactions are not your idea of a wild and wacky Friday night.

d. Decline but start planning your own "gluteal implants" party.

4. You declare your allegiance to a certain candidate or political party, and right away someone starts telling you why you're wrong. You . . .

a. Ignore them. Opinions are like assholes: Everyone has one and they all think theirs doesn't stink.

b. Immediately repent and switch views.

c. Stick your fingers in your ears and go "La-la-la" to suppress the cognitive dissonance.

d. Listen, ask respectful questions, and defend your views.

5. You look in the mirror after a shower. You . . .

a. Decide on the spot to lose twenty pounds and throw away every cookie in your house.

b. Scream "Damn you, Heidi Klum!" over and over until a neighbor calls the police.

c. Realize that you're not just your reflection. People also see your wit, personality, kindness, and courage. That's your real beauty.

d. Ask your doctor about weight loss surgery and a boob job.

LESSON 2 Get Some Perspective

6. You find out a friend's mother has died the same day you get laid off. You . . .

a. Call the friend and say, "What can I do?" then do it, even if "it" is just being there and listening.

b. Turn off your phone and put on your flannel "bad mood pants."

c. Go to the friend's house and start the conversation with "Boy, I know how you feel . . ."

d. Leave the friend alone. Nobody wants to feel like compassion is being forced on them.

7. You find yourself looking out over the most beautiful sunrise, sunset, or landscape you've ever seen. You . . .

a. Grab your phone so you can take pictures.

b. Breathe and appreciate the incredible moment that will never come again.

c. Find someone to share it with you.

d. Think of how smog is what makes sunsets so gorgeous.

8. You see a television documentary about starving children in Darfur. You . . .

a. Turn the channel to *Keeping Up with the Kardashians* and make some microwave popcorn.

b. Stop for a second and appreciate that you have enough to eat and a roof over your head.

c. Think about that time you were ravenous and had only cottage cheese and celery in the fridge.

d. Get online and find a Darfur charity you can donate to.

9. You hit thirty-five and you've still never been married or had kids. You . . .

a. Throw yourself a monster birthday party and invite every eligible bachelor you know.

b. Join Match.com with the user name "smokingovaries."

c. Remember how much freedom you have, how fantastic you look and feel, and how much wiser you are than when you were twenty-five.

d. Watch every episode of *Sex and the City*.

10. You receive an award for excellence at work. You . . .

a. Get drunk at the awards dinner and tell your boss you're in love with him.

b. Address your main competitors for the honor while making an *L* on your forehead with your fingers.

c. Buy flowers for the folks on the selection committee.

d. Thank the people whose contributions helped you achieve what you've achieved.

LESSON 3 Trust Your Gut

11. You're three hours from your wedding ceremony and you can't stop throwing up. You . . .

a. Call the whole thing off until you can figure out why you're a wreck.

b. Chug a bottle of Pepto-Bismol and go through with it.

c. Publicly accuse the groom of sleeping with your maid of honor (because he probably is anyway).

d. Do deep breathing to calm yourself down and share your anxiety with your intended.

12. Someone comes to you with an investment opportunity that's exciting but seems insanely risky. You . . .

a. Ask for everything in writing, then send it to your lawyer.

b. Empty your 401(k) account and hand the prospective CEO a check.

c. Begin planning your theft of office supplies as you leave your job.

d. Wish them luck but pass.

13. A guy asks you out. You get a creepy vibe from him. You . . .

    a. Pepper-spray him.

    b. Decline until you can check him out first.

    c. Accept but go only to a public place where you know cops hang out.

    d. Thank him for liking you, since you haven't had a date in six months.

14. You're shopping and a friend tries on a swimsuit that she loves but that you know isn't working for her. She asks what you think. You . . .

    a. Lie like a tobacco company CEO in front of Congress and tell her she looks marvelous.

    b. Fake a migraine.

    c. Be honest and tell her she'd look better in a different cut of suit.

    d. Say, "Sure, if you lost about fifty pounds!"

15. You're asked to make a speech in front of hundreds of people, something that scares you witless. You . . .

    a. Agree, then create a killer PowerPoint presentation to help you get through it.

    b. Agree, then pay someone to show up and pretend they're you.

    c. Acknowledge that this is outside your comfort zone, decide that's healthy, agree, and prepare like a pro.

    d. Pretend you don't speak English.

LESSON 4 **Show Grace Under Pressure**

16. You've procrastinated on a big work project, and it's due tomorrow. You . . .

   a. Begin "Operation Scapegoat."
   b. Accept the blame for your failure and take the consequences.
   c. Hire an IT worker in Mumbai to pull an all-nighter for $2.49.
   d. Put on the coffee, stay up all night, and get it done.

17. You lose out on the big promotion and have to go to work the next day knowing everyone knows it. You . . .

   a. Come to work drunk wearing a "Work sucks but I need the bucks" T-shirt.
   b. Put together a presentation for your boss detailing why you really are the best person for the position.
   c. Come to work and do your job better than ever, just to show 'em.
   d. Immediately take all seventeen weeks of vacation time you've saved up.

18. You ask an acquaintance's wife when her baby is due, but she's not pregnant. You . . .

   a. Keep your cool and sincerely apologize.
   b. Ask the man, "What are you, sterile or something?"
   c. Start waxing poetic about how wonderful she would look if she *were* pregnant.
   d. Get a paper bag. Breathe into it.

19. You're asked to fill in for your superior for a day. You . . .

   a. Vow to outwork everyone else in the company on that day.

b. Walk around with a riding crop conducting "surprise inspections."

c. Meet with all your managers to let them know you'll be a benevolent leader.

d. Replace the nameplate on the boss's door with your own.

20. Your recent ex calls you a few weeks after the breakup about a late-night get-together. You . . .

a. Laugh in his face and remind him the sex was never that good to begin with.

b. Politely say no, then remind yourself of all the reasons you broke up.

c. Politely say no, then sob yourself to sleep because you're so lonely.

d. Ask if he has condoms, or if you need to buy some.

LESSON 5 Be Prepared

21. You have a major job interview. You . . .

a. Update your résumé.

b. "Forget" to wear underwear.

c. Learn something about each person who's likely to be in the interview.

d. Rehearse your funky "I got the job and you didn't" dance.

22. You're going to be wearing a very slinky dress and no bra to a special event. You . . .

a. Ask yourself, "What would Tara Reid do?"

b. Make sure you're in fantastic shape and don't have an extra ounce of fat on you.

c. Come up with a catchy line to toss off in case your boobs tumble out.

d. Bring tape to cover poking nipples or keep you in your dress.

23. You're planning your best friend's fortieth-birthday bash. You . . .

    a. Immediately find someone else to do the hard work.

    b. Create a master to-do list and set firm deadlines for each major part of the party (entertainment, catering, etc.).

    c. Start a notebook containing every name, phone number, and scrap of paper.

    d. Stay up all night, angry that she's never thrown you a big party.

24. Your philosophy of dealing with the unexpected is . . .

    a. "Hope for the best, but prepare for the worst."

    b. "Every day, in every way, things are getting better."

    c. "Cry until someone else volunteers to take over."

    d. "Things are always darkest before they really go to hell."

25. You live in earthquake country. The trunk of your car contains . . .

    a. A flat spare tire and rancid workout clothes.

    b. Your girlfriend who was too drunk to drive home.

    c. A toolbox containing one socket wrench, no sockets, a ball of twine, a razor blade, and a mechanical pencil.

    d. A complete, FEMA-approved survival kit.

LESSON 6 Be Nice on the Way Up

26. You receive a huge gift basket during the holidays, but you live alone. You . . .

    a. Bring it to work and plop it on the break room table with a sign that reads, "Help yourself."

b. You do the same thing as in **a.**, but make sure everyone in the office knows it was you who brought the basket.

c. Turn off the phone and settle in for a weekend of gluttony.

d. Take out the best treats for yourself and leave the mini dill pickles, sardines, and jalapeño jelly for everybody else.

27. You get a sought-after promotion at work. You . . .

a. Invite everyone out after work for drinks on you.

b. Do a touchdown dance worthy of an NFL receiver in the company lobby.

c. Send small but meaningful tokens of esteem to the people whose work helped you achieve your new position.

d. Start plotting to take your boss's job.

28. You receive a sincere request for help from someone who hasn't been nice to you in the past. You . . .

a. Offer to help, but then cruelly back out at the last second.

b. Be the grown-up by offering your help without attaching conditions to it.

c. Offer to help but explain to the person how he or she has hurt you in the past so it's clear how magnanimous you're being right now.

d. Cackle with evil glee and slam down the phone.

29. A frazzled waiter in a very busy restaurant can't seem to get your table's orders right. You . . .

a. Talk to the manager and ask for a different server.

b. Scream, throw plates, and leave a nickel tip in an upside-down water glass.

c. Tell the server you understand things are crazy and that you will be as patient as possible.

d. Stalk out in the middle of the crème brûlée.

30. During the holidays, you give your cleaning lady or gardener . . .

    a. A hearty handshake.

    b. A frisking and a walk through a metal detector.

    c. Zilch.

    d. A nice thank-you card containing a check for at least triple their normal fee.

LESSON 7 Find the Balance

31. The office expects you to take your cell phone and laptop with you on vacation in case they need to get in touch. You . . .

    a. Find someone to cover for you while you're away so you don't have to accept calls or e-mails.

    b. Tell your boss if you can call him whenever you like, he can do the same.

    c. Back over both devices with your car.

    d. Take them, but conveniently turn them off and insist there was no cell coverage and no Internet access.

32. Your parents come to town and offer to watch your kids for the weekend. You . . .

    a. Crawl into bed and sleep for thirty-six hours.

    b. Book just one night at a snazzy hotel and spa in case you miss your kids; you can always extend your stay.

    c. Turn them down and instead offer to make *them* dinner.

    d. Go to a movie and text-message your mom every fifteen minutes to see if Tommy has choked on a piece of microwave popcorn yet.

33. Your significant other insists that he needs time to do "his own thing" once in a while. You . . .

a. Irrationally accuse him of cheating on you and ask if she's prettier than you are.

b. Ask if you can come along.

c. Agree, then follow him in your car one night, sitting outside his buddy's house until 3 A.M. watching "the guys" play poker through a sliding glass door.

d. Suggest that you designate one night every week that you both get to do your own thing.

34. You deal with stressful times in your life by . . .

a. Meditating, doing yoga, working out, or getting outdoors.

b. Screaming obscenities at passing cars and slamming your fists on the dashboard, yelling, "How dare you do this to me?"

c. Two words: *dark chocolate.*

d. Unloading your woes on your friends into the wee hours of the morning.

35. Your company picnic and your son's soccer game fall at the same time. You . . .

a. Hire a body double to send to the game.

b. Leave the picnic halfway through and get to the game for the second half.

c. Get to the game, because there won't be many more seven-year-old soccer games.

d. Neither; go shopping instead.

LESSON 8 Fall Forward

36. You're two weeks into your diet and cheat. You . . .

a. Forgive yourself, note the mental state that made you eat, and start again.

b. Figure "in for a penny, in for a pound," and eat everything in the kitchen.

c. Do an extra workout to burn up the additional calories you consumed on your binge.

d. Put on your "fat pants" and sulk.

37. You compete fiercely for a customer but eventually lose out. You . . .

a. Thank the team for its hard work and send everyone home for the day.

b. Ask the customer for a frank analysis of why they chose your competitor over you.

c. Fire everyone and then rehire them in a fit of remorse the next morning.

d. Apply for a job with your competitor.

38. You don't get into any of your first choices for college and have to attend your safety school. You . . .

a. Throw a tantrum, forget about college, and get a night job at a local convenience store.

b. Attend but decide that you're going to spend all your time getting high and being the dorm slut.

c. Attend and try to make the best of it.

d. Decide to go to community college to see if you can improve your qualifications, then reapply.

39. Your Internet business goes belly-up. You . . .

a. Don't know, because you're in a coma from too many Doritos and Diet Cokes.

b. Thank everyone who helped you get this far and thus preserve the valuable relationships you've built.

c. Immediately turn around and launch another business based on the same flawed business plan.

d. E-mail your customers with the bad news.

40. Your failures have given you a treasure trove of experience that would be valuable to others. You . . .

a. Decide to write a self-help book.

b. Decide your screwups are nobody else's business and begin a life of bitterness and regret.

c. Become a mentor to someone in your field, or even a student who's thinking about getting into your line of work.

d. Run for president of the United States.

LESSON 9 Take a Risk

41. You're offered an opportunity that you think might be beyond your abilities. You . . .

a. Understand that the only way to improve your skills is to stretch them, so you give it a shot.

b. Cower in that small closet underneath the stairs.

c. Ask people who've done it how they were successful.

d. Run away, then reconsider, then run away again, so they get a clear idea of just how resolute you are.

42. You've never traveled overseas, and a group invites you to a country where you don't know the language. You . . .

a. Go on the trip, language barrier or not. Shop where the locals shop, even have dinner with a local family.

b. Go on the trip, but attach yourself to another member of the group so you're never alone.

c. Say yes, buy a phrase book, and master *yes, no, and please.*

d. Say no and Magic Marker over that country on your map.

43. You have a chance to take a job that has little security but the potential for great financial and personal reward. You . . .

a. Head in the opposite direction, going after complete security even in the face of bureaucratic incompetence: the U.S. Postal Service.

b. Demand a signing bonus and a Nintendo Wii.

c. Forget what you owe or how you'll pay the mortgage and join the team.

d. Weigh your financial responsibilities to others, and if you can go for it, you go for it.

44. You have to choose between the college major you're passionate about and the one that gives you "something to fall back on." You . . .

a. Take the fallback major, because Depressing Russian Poetry really isn't paying very well these days.

b. Take a double major just in case.

c. Throw caution to the wind and go for your "calling," knowing that you'll make the best of it.

d. Spend the next seven years undeclared.

45. You have friends who don't have safe sex anymore because "HIV is under control." You . . .

a. Sell your Trojan stock immediately.

b. Ignore them and continue to have safe sex until you're in a long-term monogamous relationship.

c. Think "Hot damn!" and start walking around in a shirt that reads, "Sometimes I feel like a slut, sometimes I don't."

d. Vow never, ever to sleep with those friends or anyone they have slept with.

ANSWERS

1. **b**	10. **d**	19. **a**	28. **b**	37. **b**
2. **d**	11. **a**	20. **b**	29. **c**	38. **d**
3. **a**	12. **d**	21. **c**	30. **d**	39. **b**
4. **d**	13. **b**	22. **d**	31. **a**	40. **c**
5. **c**	14. **c**	23. **b**	32. **b**	41. **a**
6. **a**	15. **c**	24. **a**	33. **d**	42. **a**
7. **b**	16. **d**	25. **d**	34. **a**	43. **d**
8. **b**	17. **c**	26. **a**	35. **c**	44. **c**
9. **c**	18. **a**	27. **c**	36. **a**	45. **b**

So how did you do? You may not have agreed with a few of my correct answers and that's fine. The quiz was designed to have one right answer, one possibly right answer, and two absurd answers for your amusement. Now that you're done, total up your right answers and see how red carpet ready you are:

Oscar (40 or more correct)

You're conscious, wise, and brave, capable of the foresight and planning that anyone needs to make the most of life's Red Carpet Moments.

Golden Globe (31–39)

You've got a few areas to work on, but you're doing very well. You probably have one or two glaring areas of weakness that you already know about, so get working on them.

Directors Guild (21–30)

You're taking one step forward, one step back. That's the personal development cha-cha, and we don't want that. Time to take a good look at some of the ways you may be sabotaging your life.

People's Choice (11–20)

Does your life feel like a neighborhood in Baghdad a lot of the time? This is why: You haven't mastered many of the strategies for dealing with the Red Carpet Moments. You're ready for some serious introspection and some tough work.

Razzie (10 or fewer)

One step forward, three steps back, then you fall on your ass. You're flailing in virtually every area this book talks about. You can't do this alone. Talk to friends. See a therapist.

The Best Worst Thing
That Ever Happened

The future will be better tomorrow. —DAN QUAYLE

*T*V Guide Channel is very appreciative of Joan and Melissa Rivers' contributions to the success of our red-carpet programming over the past three years. We wish them the best in their future endeavors." That was the official statement from Ryan O'Hara, president of TV Guide Network, after our contract wasn't renewed in April 2007, ending our most recent foray onto the red carpet, a genre of television that Mom and I essentially created.

Why? According to competing rumors, we weren't drawing big enough ratings, our "entourage" was causing problems, or we were difficult to work with, none of which was true. We felt that more resources were needed to make the broadcasts better and up to the standards to which we wanted the Rivers name attached. We wanted to do something new and different, bringing fresh ideas to a genre that was being replicated by everyone, and the prevailing feeling at the network was to cut back as much as possible. It was beyond frustrating. However, we were brought in to put the network on the map, and we did that. We were then unceremoniously dumped, and I'm truly sorry to say that TV Guide has yet to recapture the ratings that we gave them.

In the media postmortems some praised us, and Mom especially, rightly calling her a comedy pioneer and a showbiz survivor, while others took the opportunity to kick us viciously when we were down. Well, as my mother says, "Thirty-five years ago a smart man in this business told me that audiences will either watch somebody because they adore them or because they hate their guts. If everybody thinks you're just okay, you won't have a career."

All I knew was that my dream job was over, and it was devastating at first. But here's the funny thing: It wasn't as devastating as I thought it would be. Sure, I wasn't doing the old Mary Tyler Moore throw-the-hat-in-the-air move, but the most depressing thing about the whole affair quickly became all the people who wanted to commiserate with me about how shattered my life must be. I thanked them and hugged them for their kindness, but let's face it, I survived my father's suicide when I was barely a legal grown-up. Compared to that, TV Guide Network and the red carpet were blips on my radar screen.

My Red Carpet Moment

So why am I looking back on the end of my red carpet run? Because it's only in that context that you can understand how I've come to look forward. What I've realized is that while each red carpet event from 1996 to 2007 was its own Red Carpet Moment, my real, personal Red Carpet Moment started the day Mom and I were let go. That's when the pressure was on. That's when I was in a pretty intense and occasionally embarrassing spotlight, wondering which path I should take next. I had to see what I was made of. I could choose to sink into a depression or wage a war of criticism in the media against my former bosses. Or I could take my own advice and fall forward.

I've always been an entrepreneurial girl. I've created shows and produced shows. I know my way around the business. So I kept a bank of "someday I'll get to this" ideas in the back of my mind, projects I knew I would bring to light when I had the time. Of course, I rarely had the time. The red carpet ate up the first and last quarter of each year and other commitments ate the rest. There was little time left to work on my pet projects or get anything major off the ground. The lesson for me was that what appears to be "success" can sometimes turn into its own kind of prison. You end up bound by a sense of obligation and by the fact that you're employed and getting paid and feeling comfortable, and before you know it, twelve years have gone by; you're married, divorced, and a mom; and those special projects are still sitting in your head waiting to get out.

So, in a weird way, leaving the red carpet has been a huge blessing in disguise. Finally, I was free to let all those ideas out of their cages, and two years later I'm busier than I've ever been. I've written this book, the first of many, New York publishers willing. I've developed new TV shows, hosted numerous others, and had a blast doing *The Celebrity Apprentice* with my mother. Just watching her and Donald Trump go toe-to-toe was something I'll never forget. I'm busier than I've ever been before, and not only am I looking forward these days, I'm also most definitely not looking back. Maybe that's my last Red Carpet Life Lesson: No matter what happens, keep walking down the carpet. If you fall, get back up, stick your broken heel back on your shoe, make sure everything is tucked into your Vera Wang dress, and keep right on moving ahead. Above all, learn why you fell and don't make the same mistake again.

The Lessons, Clearly

What have I learned? For one thing, I realized that it was only after the red carpet was in my past that I truly saw the Lessons in clear focus. Before, I was too close to the celebrities and the whole chaotic scene. It was only when I stepped back and looked at it from a distance that I saw that many of the pearls of wisdom I had found during those years of creating red carpet magic—be prepared, suck it up when things get dodgy, take care of the people who take care of me—had seen me through my own rough times in my career, marriage, and life. In a way, the end of the red carpet roller coaster was the best thing that could have happened to this book.

Only after it was all over could I see how much I grew during those years. Only after I graduated from that real-life school of entertainment hard knocks did it become clear how completely the skills and attitudes I picked up influenced the way I handled events, good and bad, away from the red carpet and bright lights. I preach having perspective, and I couldn't have asked for a stronger dose of it. Leaving the red carpet behind has been the best "worst thing" that's ever happened to me. It opened my eyes and tested me in more ways than I can count, and I'm proud to say I think I've done pretty well.

But enough about me. This is about you. This is about having all nine Lessons in the back of your mind as you move into your future so you can ride out the storms with minimal damage, bounce back from the heartaches, and make the utmost of those shimmering, amazing times that we all live for. Anybody can shine when times are great; all you have to do is remember to thank your agent and your mother and smile for the camera. It's the times when you don't win, don't get the client, find out your ex is engaged, or do something incredibly stupid in public that you find out what kind of heart beats beneath the couture.

When you absorb the Lessons and make them a part of who you are, you'll always come out on top in any Red Carpet Moment. That doesn't mean you'll always be the best or the brightest or the richest. That's not what this is about. This is not "she who dies with the most shoes wins." Boil it down and a triumphant Red Carpet Moment emerges from having three qualities:

1. Loving yourself and everyone else around you.
2. Knowing who you are and what you want.
3. Appreciating every precious second of being alive.

When you've got that calm, confident, balanced place at your center, you can tumble like Jennifer Garner at the 2008 Oscars and bounce right back up without missing a step. You'll be delightfully surprised by your resilience and your ability to find blessings in the most painful events—and the deepest blessing will be the knowledge that you are wise and you are strong. I'll elaborate, but first a story.

The Worst Dating Experience of My Life

I met a guy (let's call him Daniel) at a friend's party and we hit it off immediately. He flew down from San Francisco to have dinner with me and we got along fabulously. Before long, we were talking on the phone every day for six weeks straight. It was very high school, dizzy, and a lot of fun. However, the night before he was supposed to fly down to spend the weekend, he got cold feet, tried to cancel, then changed his mind and came down anyway.

Oh boy. The Rivers radar was on and in overdrive by this point. You don't get burned by as many relationships as I have without being able to smell the lighter fluid. But I took a "let's wait and see" attitude. Turns out that my independence and strength had given Daniel terminal cancer of the confidence. "I think you're just too independent for me," he said. Okay, whatever. I decided since he was already here to try to make the best of things. My instincts screamed not to waste my time, that he was a wrong number, but I hit the override button.

We went out Friday night and had a good time. Then came another party Saturday night, and Daniel was making the rounds and unabashedly chatting up every woman in the room but me. My friends were appalled, but I didn't want to make a scene at someone else's party, so I calmly took him aside and said, "Look, I don't care if you get numbers, just be discreet about it." This wasn't about dating anymore; this was about respect. I took lots of "hold your head up" breaks to regroup and made it through the evening with my cool intact.

Afterward, the guy had the gall to beg me to go to another party with him. I refused, called him a cab, and went home. Lo and behold, he called at 5:00 A.M. telling me he was on the way back to my house and wanted to go to brunch later that morning. I told him I would be going back to bed and he should catch a cab to the airport. Security system and locked gate, I love you. The aftermath was a nasty e-mail from him on how validated he felt in not wanting to date me, and my own discovery that at age thirty-eight, he'd had only one serious relationship but had been in seventeen weddings. Once again, my gut spoke up and said, "See? You should listen to me more often!"

The blessing in this mini-drama was that I kept my composure in a potentially humiliating situation. A few years back I might have made a screaming scene, but I chose not to. I had *perspective:* This was not about me, but about his immaturity. I showed *grace under pressure:* I decided not to poison a small birthday party by making it about my ego. I was *comfortable in my own skin:* I didn't feel like I had to prove I was hotter or more interesting than the women Daniel was talking to, because I didn't need his attention to validate me. I was strong and classy and smart, and that was its own reward. Of course, my pals and I brutally trashed him in private later on, and I won't say that wasn't fun, too.

The Sweetest Lesson

A few years back, when I was younger and a lot more foolish, I might have behaved differently. I'm sure it would have felt great in the moment and I would have regretted it later. That's the wonderful thing about the Red Carpet Life Lessons: You get better at them as time goes by. However you scored on the quiz, every day that you live bravely and with your eyes open to what you and other people need, you get better at the Lessons, more able to . . .

1. *Be comfortable in your own skin*—Be who and what you are without apology and have the courage of your convictions.
2. *Get some perspective*—Realize how lucky you are no matter what your life is like today.
3. *Trust your gut*—Follow your instincts and have faith in your inner voice to guide you to what's best for you.

4. *Show grace under pressure*—Do what needs to be done when the chips are down and all eyes are on you.
5. *Be prepared*—Think ahead and outwork everybody else.
6. *Be nice on the way up*—Be generous with everyone in your life who has brought you blessings, kindness, or wisdom.
7. *Find the balance*—Make time for what matters to you, not just for your obligations.
8. *Fall forward*—Learn to see the incredible opportunity often hidden within failure.
9. *Take a risk*—Get out of your comfort zone, so you know you're alive.

In October 2007, wildfires were raging across Southern California, driven by inferno winds. Smoke was making the midafternoon as dark as twilight. Hundreds of homes were being consumed in the back country despite the best efforts of overtaxed firefighters. Not far from where I live, the hills of Malibu were going up like a torch, as they would again just a month later. During that frightening time, I was called upon to prepare to evacuate my home. What did I take? Other than my computer, my cell phone, important papers, and a few paintings that I grew up with, I took mostly pictures of dead people. They were the only things that couldn't be replaced.

Fortunately, the fire stopped two traffic lights away from my neighborhood, but the lesson was as obvious as the clouds of black smoke that still columned into the sky: Nothing's forever. Appreciate what you have because you may not always have it. Every day when I drive up my winding hillside street to my house and look out over the ocean view, I always pause for a second before I use my clicker to open the driveway gates and park. I take that moment to remember that one day, when things aren't the same as they are now, I'll be able to say that I lived in a house with pretty gates.

The point is, I'm lucky. You're lucky. We're all blessed to be here and alive with the opportunity to grow and live wondrous lives. When all is said and done, the best Lesson is that you can do this. You can grow and learn and be strong and evolve. Whatever you're doing today, whoever you see yourself as today—they don't have to be the same tomorrow.

Take it from someone who every day battles preconceived notions about who she is and what she can do. Even I don't know what I'm capable of. As my agent says to clients who are reluctant to meet with me, "Take the meeting. You'll be surprised."

ACKNOWLEDGMENTS

Thanks to Tim Vandehey first and foremost. I could not have asked for a better coauthor. He helped me find my voice, thought I was funny, and dealt with my crazy schedule. Who could ask for more?

Thanks also to Jillian Manus for believing in me and this idea, Julia Pastore for hand-holding me through the process, and Shaye Areheart, who saw the possibilities of this book and took a chance.

There are so many people who have helped me, not just with this book, but also with so much more: Steven Jensen, Michael Karlin, Ken Browning, Jocelyn Pickett, Vera Vanatko, Betty Corpeno, Kevin and Debbie Brennan, Elizabeth Much, Amy Rosenblum, the *Apprentice* team, Nancy Collins, Robert Higdon, Tommy Corcoran, Mark Bone, Sue Solomon, Henry Edwards, Marilyn Lee, Melanie Smith, Kari Hill, Adele Fass, Cary Fetman, Dr. David May, Conrad Hitchcock, Max Osswald, Peter, Tommi and Robert Tilden, Charlie Cook, Mike & Lola, and my amazing friends who refused to take my calls until the day's work was done. Without you guys, I would still be sitting at the kitchen counter staring at a blank screen.

INDEX

Adams, Amy, 159
Adaptability, 88
Advice from others, 88, 170, 235
Affleck, Ben, 6, 19, 93, 200
Alba, Jessica, 1, 64
Alda, Alan, 66
Alexander, Jason, 204
Allen, Woody, 177
Angelou, Maya, 144
Aniston, Jennifer, 7, 149, 219
Anniversary celebrations, 169
Apologizing, 35, 86, 164
Arkin, Alan, 21
Armstrong, Lance, 160–161
Attitude, 199–201
Auditions, 142

Bad situations turned into good,
    107–108
Balance in your life, 264
    choices and, 177–178
    conflict between work and family,
        172–173
    deep approach to, 191–194
    Gospel According to Joan,
        183
    "healthy selfish" attitude and,
        181–182
    how you know you're in balance,
        186–187

how you know you're not in
    balance, 188–189
passionate pursuits and, 183–186
Red Carpet Quiz questions,
    249–250
relationships and, 174–176, 189
self-knowledge as key to, 173–174
shallow approach to, 189–191
types of balance to be managed,
    178–180
Baldwin, Alec, 109
Ball, Lucille, 162
Barkin, Ellen, 90–91
Baron, Caroline, 208
Barrymore, Drew, 201
Basinger, Kim, 109, 195
Beatles, the, 77
Beatty, Warren, 6, 208
Begley, Ed, Jr., 125
Being comfortable in your own skin,
    263
    deep approach to, 35–37
    Gospel According to Joan, 20
    how you know you're comfortable,
        18–19, 21–22
    how you know you're not
        comfortable, 23–25, 27, 29
    loving who you are and who you're
        becoming, 14–16
    Manheim's story, 13–14

Being comfortable (*cont.*)
    Red Carpet Moments and, 17–18
    Red Carpet Quiz questions,
      240–241
    Rivers's worst dating experience
      and, 263
    shallow approach to, 30–33, 35
Being in the moment, 55–58, 63–64,
    187
Being nice on the way up, 264
    deep approach to, 167–168,
      170–171
    Golden Rule of, 146–147
    Gospel According to Joan, 152
    gratitude and, 144–145, 150
    how you know you're being nice,
      162–164
    how you know you're not being
      nice, 164, 166
    knowledge that you behaved with
      class as reward for, 152–154
    meaning of, 145–146
    people's attitudes toward you later
      on and, 146–148
    Red Carpet Quiz questions,
      247–249
    remembering your roots,
      149–151
    shallow approach to, 166–167
    sharing, 157–162
    taking care of your team,
      154–157
Belushi, John, 207
Bendinskas, Lorena, 158, 161
Bening, Annette, 208
Berry, Halle, 13, 14, 228
Bertrand, Marcheline, 104
Betrayals, 102–103
Bezos, Jeff, 74
Billauer, Jesse, 224
Binoche, Juliette, 2
Birthday celebrations, 169
Birthing tips, 60–61
Björk, 36

Blame game, 209
Blanchett, Cate, 33
Bochco, Steven, 196
Bono, 27
Boredom, 230
Boyle, Susan, 44
Breakups, 56–57, 100
Breslin, Abigail, 62–63
Brody, Adrien, 139–140
Bruckheimer, Jerry, 74
Burnett, Mark, 206
Burns, George, 195
Busey, Gary, 42
Bynes, Amanda, 78, 162
Byrne, Gabriel, 51

Campbell, Naomi, 60, 163
Canfield, Jack, 81
Career collapses, 102
Cattrall, Kim, 126
Chiklis, Michael, 153
Cho, Margaret, 18
Clinton, Hillary, 101
Clooney, George, 6, 19, 37, 127, 159,
    195, 196, 227
Clothes Off Our Back charity, 149
Coblenz, Walter, 48
Colbert, Stephen, 222–223
Confidence, 121–122
Control, illusion of, 42–43
Conversation starting, 133–134
Coppola, Francis Ford, 184
Cosby, Bill, 197
Costner, Kevin, 200
Courage, 225
Cowell, Simon, 44
Creativity, 122–123
Criticism, responding to, 207–208
Crowe, Russell, 77, 91
Crudup, Billy, 132
Cruise, Tom, 2, 135
Cusack, Joan, 209–210
Cynicism, 53–54
Cyrus, Miley, 44

Damon, Matt, 6, 19, 93
Danes, Claire, 132
Dangerfield, Rodney, 47
Daniels, Samantha, 79
Darabont, Frank, 222
Dates, bad, 87, 261–263
Day-Lewis, Daniel, 127
Death and dying, 102
De la Renta, Oscar, 9
Delegation, 192
Del Toro, Guillermo, 222
Denial, 135
De Rossi, Portia, 126
Deschanel, Zooey, 184
Desperation, 24, 109–110
DiCaprio, Leonardo, 160, 211
"Dirty laundry exposed" situations,
    193
Discouragement, 209
Disney, Walt, 73
Divine Right of Bling, 45
Divorce, 101, 198
Douglas, Michael, 7, 95
Drescher, Fran, 199
Dress selection, 30–32
Driver, Minnie, 93, 99
Dunst, Kirsten, 176

Earnhardt, Dale, Jr., 104
Eastwood, Clint, 159, 178, 184
Edge, The, 27
Edison, Thomas, 197
Edwards, Elizabeth, 101
Efron, Zac, 78
Egotism, 54–55
Einstein, Albert, 212
Emergency plans, 138
Emotional control, 106
Emotional vampires, 146
Empathy for the masses, 46–48
Energy, 186
Entitlement, sense of, 150–151
Epstein, Brian, 77
Estrada, Erik, 145

Excuses, 134–135
Exes, running into, 113

Failure, dealing with. See Falling
    forward
Falling forward, 264
    attitude and, 199–201
    deep approach to, 212–215
    failure as learning opportunity,
        195–197, 198
    giving your best and, 204–205
    Gospel According to Joan, 201
    grace under pressure and,
        213–214
    how you know you're falling flat,
        209–211
    how you know you're falling
        forward, 206–208
    perspective and, 214–215
    public failure, handling of, 214
    Red Carpet Quiz questions,
        250–252
    relationships and, 202–204
    risk taking and, 213, 217–218,
        231–232
    shallow approach to, 211–212
    success-failure relationship,
        197–198, 203
Fame, 44–45
Fatalism, 204–205
Fearlessness, 36–37
Fekkai, Frédéric, 126
Fetman, Cary, 26
Fiennes, Ralph, 4
Firing from a job, 210
Fisher, Carrie, 223
Fisher, Derek, 105–106
Flaunting what you've got, 33, 35
Fletcher, Louise, 159–160
Flockhart, Calista, 126
Ford, Harrison, 185
Ford, Henry, 199
Foresight, 131–132
Fox, Michael J., 130

Foxx, Jamie, 124, 159
Fun in life, 37

Garner, Jennifer, 33, 42, 261
Garofalo, Janeane, 38, 65
Gates, Bill, 188
Gellar, Sarah Michelle, 88
Generosity of spirit, 22, 51–52
Gere, Richard, 77
Gershwin, Ira, 43
Gibson, Mel, 77
Gift giving, 167
Giving up, 84, 207
Gladwell, Malcolm, 73
Goldberg, Whoopi, 1, 99
Gooding, Cuba, Jr., 83
Gore, Al, 222
Gossip, 164, 166
Grace under pressure, 264
    awards season and, 97–98
    Barkin's story, 90–91
    deep approach to, 114–117
    exes, running into, 113
    falling forward and, 213–214
    Gospel According to Joan, 103
    grace displayed by others,
        sensitivity to, 103–105
    how you know you're not showing
        grace, 109–111
    how you know you're showing
        grace, 105–108
    instant gratification and, 96–97
    losing and, 116–117
    meaning and lessons of, 91–95
    911 Moments and, 98–99,
        100–103
    Oops! Moments and, 98–100
    perspective and, 98
    Red Carpet Quiz questions,
        245–246
    Rivers's worst dating experience
        and, 263
    shallow approach to, 111–112, 114
Gratitude, 144–145, 150

Grazer, Brian, 74–75
Griffin, Kathy, 238
Grudges, 147
Gruss, Shoshanna Lonstein, 45
Guest, Christopher, 123
Gyllenhaal, Jake, 159

Haircuts, 33, 86–87, 114
Hall, Arsenio, 147–148
Hall, Monty, 43
Hanks, Tom, 7, 75, 157, 159, 175
Hannah, Darryl, 125
Hansen, Mark Victor, 81
Happiness for others, 64
Hargitay, Mariska, 132
Harrelson, Woody, 184
Hatcher, Teri, 149, 154
Hathaway, Anne, 14
Hawn, Goldie, 37, 175
Hayek, Salma, 37
Haysbert, Dennis, 147
Health catastrophes, 101–102
"Healthy selfish" attitude,
    181–182
Help, asking for, 140
Hemingway, Ernest, 90
Hepburn, Katharine, 130, 205
Hilton, Perez, 166
Holiday celebrations, 169
Home buying, 236
Hopkins, Sir Anthony, 99–100
Hot Hollywood Party, 77–79
Howard, Ron, 74–75
Howard, Terrence, 159
Hudgens, Vanessa Anne, 78
Hudson, Jennifer, 36, 159
Hudson, Rock, 151
Huffman, Felicity, 159
Humility, 151, 152
Hunter, Tab, 151

Impulsiveness, 80
Infidelity, 100–101
Instant gratification, 96–97

Instincts. *See* Trusting your gut
  instincts
Ivins, Molly, 54

Jackson, Michael, 102
Jackson, Peter, 222
Jackson, Phil, 49
Jay-Z, 178
Job interviews, 34
Johnson, Magic, 101–102
Jolie, Angelina, 64, 103–104, 160,
  199
Jordan, Michael, 122

Kaczmarek, Jane, 149
Karan, Donna, 9
Keaton, Diane, 36, 223
Kelley, David E., 14
Kelly, Grace, 113
Kidman, Nicole, 29, 33, 69, 143
Kimmel, Jimmy, 100
Krakauer, Jon, 200
Kristofferson, Kris, 119
Kutcher, Ashton, 16

Langella, Frank, 123
Latifah, Queen, 36–37, 208
Lauer, Matt, 110
Ledger, Heath, 159
Lee, Robert E., 197
Lemer, Melissa, 158
Levy, Eugene, 123
Limbaugh, Rush, 136
Linney, Laura, 42
Liu, Lucy, 55
Lloyd, Christopher, 206
Lohan, Lindsay, 53
Longoria, Eva, 98
"Look at me!" attitude, 24–25
Lopez, Jennifer, 172
Losing, 116–117
Lowe, Chad, 131
Lucci, Susan, 97, 98
Luftman, Debra, 180

Macy, William H., 159
Madonna, 156
Madsen, Virginia, 21–22
Makeovers, 226, 231
Making an entrance, 76
Manheim, Camryn, 13–14, 18, 37
Marshall, Penny, 223
Martin, Steve, 184
Matchmaking, 79
May, David Scott, 53
McCarthy, Jenny, 99
McConaughey, Matthew, 184
McCormack, Eric, 98
McGowan, Rose, 202
McLachlan, Sarah, 160
Medication in luggage, 138–139
Mendes, Sam, 15
Mental preparation, 135
Messing, Debra, 5, 98
Michele, Michael, 126
Micromanagement, 193–194
Millar, Ronald, 205
Miller, Dennis, 46–47
Min, Janice, 29
Minutoli, Michael, 108
Mirren, Helen, 145
Mistakes, learning from, 81
Moore, Demi, 15, 16
Moore, Julianne, 220
Moore, Mandy, 184
Multitasking, 192–193
Murphy, Eddie, 21, 124, 147

Newton, Todd, 129
Nicholson, Jack, 6, 106, 159
911 Moments, 98–99, 100–103
Norton, Edward, 160, 216
Notoriety, 45

O'Connor, Sinéad, 114
O'Donnell, Rosie, 160
O'Hara, Catherine, 123
O'Hara, Ryan, 257
Olivier, Sir Laurence, 212–213

Olsen, Eric, 5
O'Neil, Tom, 144–145
Oops! Moments, 98–100
Organization, 139
OutKast, 108

Pacino, Al, 48–49
Pain of wearing beautiful clothes and
    shoes, 61–62
Paltrow, Gwyneth, 130–131
Pampering yourself, 112
Panettiere, Hayden, 18
Paralysis by analysis, 84
Parenthood, 175–176
Parents of a boyfriend, first meeting
    with, 82
Parker, Charlie, 123
Parker, Mary-Louise, 132
Party crashing, 108
Passionate pursuits, 36, 68, 75–76
    balance in your life and, 183–186
Paves, Ken, 126
Penn, Sean, 51, 54, 200
Perelman, Ron, 90–91
Perspective, 263
    deep approach to, 62–65
    dropping the illusion of control,
        42–43
    empathy for the masses, 46–48
    falling forward and, 214–215
    Gospel According to Joan, 46
    grace under pressure and, 98
    how you know you have
        perspective, 48–53
    how you know you lack
        perspective, 53–56
    moment of blinding perspective,
        38–40
    preparation and, 58–59
    pseudo-celebrity and, 43–46
    Red Carpet Quiz questions,
        241–243
    Rivers's worst dating experience
        and, 263

savoring the moment but seeing
    the big picture, 39–41
shallow approach to, 57–62
Pessimism, 120
Petersen, Wolfgang, 127
Petit, Philippe, 216–217
Phillippe, Ryan, 176
Phoenix, Joaquin, 54
Pickford, Mary, 197
Pink Floyd, 188
Pitt, Brad, 7, 19, 104, 199, 219
Piven, Jeremy, 159
Pollan, Tracy, 130
Posey, Parker, 123
Pregnancy, 208
Preparation, 264
    by actors, 126–127
    anticipating possible problems,
        120–121, 132–133
    for auditions, 142
    confidence and, 121–122
    controlling what you can,
        forgetting what you can't,
        129–131
    creativity and, 122–123
    deep approach to, 139–143
    Dream Team for, 126
    failures at, 118–119, 127–128
    Gospel According to Joan,
        125
    how you know you're not
        prepared, 134–135
    how you know you're prepared,
        131–134
    impressing others with, 128
    mental preparation, 135
    perspective and, 58–59
    Red Carpet Quiz questions,
        246–247
    risk taking and, 233–234
    Rivers's experiences with,
        118–119, 123–125
    shallow approach to, 136–139
    for speech making, 136–137

success and, 122
value of, 119–120
Presentations, 165
Prism Awards, 118–119
Pseudo-celebrity, 43–46
Psychotherapy, 116–117

Quality, spending on, 32
Quayle, Dan, 257

Recklessness, 218
Record keeping, 65
Red Carpet Moments, 6–7
Red carpet pre-shows, 1–6, 42,
        123–125, 144–145, 152–153,
        220, 257–258
Red Carpet Quiz, 9, 237–239
    answers and scoring, 239,
        254–255
    the questions, 240–253
Red carpets, making of, 157
Redford, Robert, 43
Redgrave, Vanessa, 64
Reeve, Christopher, 101, 160
Reeve, Dana, 160
Reeves, Keanu, 217
Reginald, Rex, 108
Regret, 232–233
Relationships
    balance in your life and, 174–176,
        189
    falling forward and, 202–204
Research, 141–143
Respect, 107
Reunions, 190
Rich, John, 185
Richards, Denise, 100
Rigg, Diana, 205
Ringwald, Molly, 77
Rinna, Lisa, 64
Risk taking, 264
    calculated risk, 225–226
    comfort zone and, 218–219,
        226–228

control and, 218
courage and, 225
deep approach to, 234–236
falling forward and, 213, 217–218,
        231–232
in film industry, 222–223
Gospel According to Joan, 221
how you know you're not taking
        enough risk (or too much),
        232–233
how you know you're taking
        enough risk, 230–232
Petit's story, 216–217
preparation and, 233–234
Red Carpet Moments and,
        220–221
Red Carpet Quiz questions,
        252–253
rewards and, 228–230
shallow approach to, 233–234
in tech industry, 223
types of risk, 218
Rivers, Joan
    on balance in your life, 183
    on being comfortable in your own
        skin, 20
    on being nice on the way up, 152
    on falling forward, 201
    gaffes by, 99–100
    glass ceiling in comedy, breaking
        of, 220
    on grace under pressure, 103
    husband's suicide, reaction to, 181
    jewelry line for QVC, 132–133
    on perspective, 46
    on preparation, 125
    red carpet pre-shows, 1–6, 42,
        124–125, 144–145, 152–153,
        257–258
    on risk taking, 221
    on trusting your gut instincts, 72
Rivers, Melissa
    birthing experience, 121–122
    divorce of, 101, 198

Rivers, Melissa (*cont.*)
    falling forward experiences, 196,
      198
    father's suicide, reaction to, 102
    Hot Hollywood Party experience,
      77–79
    moment of blinding perspective,
      38–40
    "next great stylist" reality show,
      96–97
    post-red carpet life, 258–260
    preparation experiences, 118–119,
      123–125
    red carpet pre-shows, 1–6, 42,
      123–125, 144–145, 152–153,
      220, 257–258
    virtual world project, 71
    wedding and marriage of,
      70–71
    who she really is, 9–12
    worst dating experience,
      261–263
Robbins, Tim, 16
Roberts, Julia, 7, 41, 77
Rodriguez, Robert, 202
Rooney, Mickey, 197
Rosenberg, Edgar, 10, 102, 148, 164,
    181
Ross, Katharine, 70
Russell, Kurt, 175
Ryan, Meg, 43

Sarandon, Susan, 2, 16
Schwartz, Judy, 133
Scorsese, Martin, 63
Seacrest, Ryan, 64
Seating at awards ceremonies, 185
Second-guessing yourself, 87–88
Seinfeld, Jerry, 45
Self-criticism, 25, 27
Self-esteem. *See* Being comfortable
    in your own skin
Selfishness, 181–182
Settling, 27, 29

Seymour, Jane, 94
Shallowness, 30
Sharing, 157–162
Shearer, Harry, 123
Sheen, Charlie, 1, 100
Shepherd, Cybill, 71–73
Shoe care, 32, 59–61
Shue, Elisabeth, 1
Silver, Joel, 163
Silverman, Sarah, 100
Silver Spoon Entertainment
    Marketing, 158, 161
Simmons, Russell, 160
Simon, John, 205
Simpson, Jessica, 47–48
Smith, Will, 52–53
Somers, Suzanne, 192
Sorvino, Mira, 1
Spears, Britney, 3, 48, 204
Speech making, 136–137
Spielberg, Steven, 145
Spitzer, Silda Wall, 101
Spoiling yourself, 58
Stallone, Sylvester, 132
Stanton, Harry Dean, 51
Sting, 160
Stone, Sharon, 1, 76, 195
Streep, Meryl, 7
Streisand, Barbra, 200
Stylists, 23, 26, 126
Swag bags, 51, 157–158
Swank, Hilary, 33, 131

Tartikoff, Brandon, 101
Thank-yous, 166, 170
Tharp, Twyla, 139
Theron, Charlize, 33
Thomas, Kristin Scott, 4
Thoreau, Henry David, 27
Thornton, Billy Bob, 228
Todd, Kendra, 203
Travel time, use of, 191
Travolta, John, 4, 156
Trump, Donald, 74, 206, 259

Trusting your gut instincts, 263
    deep approach to, 87–89
    difficulty of, 70–73
    Gospel According to Joan, 72
    great moments in trusting one's
        gut, 73–75
    how you know you can trust your
        gut, 80–81, 83
    how you know you can't trust your
        gut, 83–84
    matchmaking and, 79
    Red Carpet Quiz questions,
        243–244
    shallow approach to, 84–87
    Ward's story, 66–67
    when *not* to trust your gut, 75–78
    your instincts are (almost) always
        right, 67–69

U2, 25, 27

Valentino, 66–67, 99
Vila, Bob, 60

Wahlberg, Mark, 63, 127
Walsh, John, 161
Walsh, Kate, 14
Ward, Sela, 66–67, 126

Wardrobe malfunctions, 99
Washington, Denzel, 29
Waterston, Sam, 238
Weather in L.A., 49
Weaver, Sigourney, 96
Weddings, 28, 43, 133
Weight loss or gain, 111
West, Kanye, 78
Whedon, Joss, 196
Whitaker, Forest, 127
Willard, Fred, 123
Williams, Robin, 122
Williams, Vanessa, 37
Willson, Henry, 151
Wilson, Rita, 175
Winfrey, Oprah, 26, 118, 121
Winslet, Kate, 15
Witherspoon, Reese, 157, 159,
    176
Wonder, sense of, 62–63
Woods, Tiger, 160

"You're Out of Your %$#@& Mind"
    Law, 71–72

Zeta-Jones, Catherine, 5–6, 33, 95,
    208
Ziglar, Zig, 197

ABOUT THE AUTHOR

MELISSA RIVERS is a writer, television producer, and live event host best known as cocreator of the groundbreaking *Live with Joan and Melissa* series of red carpet fashion/interview specials, which ran on E! Entertainment Television and the TV Guide Channel from 1996 to 2007 as a top-rated lead-in to the Oscars, Emmys, Grammys, and Golden Globes. Her recent adventures include developing several new television projects and appearing as a contestant on the hit show *The Celebrity Apprentice*.

Melissa graduated with distinction from the University of Pennsylvania in 1989. In "the business" practically since birth, she has been a features reporter for *CBS This Morning*, a regular contributor to MTV's *Hanging with MTV*, a voice-over artist, and a spokesperson for PETA. She is involved with such organizations as Suicide Survivors, Heal the Bay, the Make-a-Wish Foundation, and the Cystic Fibrosis Foundation. Melissa lives in Los Angeles with her son, Cooper.

MelissaRivers.com

BOCA RATON PUBLIC LIBRARY, FLORIDA

3 3656 0510612 8

158 Riv
Rivers, Melissa, 1969-
Red carpet ready

MAY   2010